Motor Fleet
Safety Manual

Motor Fleet Safety Manual

Fourth Edition

Edited by John E. Brodbeck, CSP

National Safety Council

Project Leader: Patricia M. Laing
Technical Advisor: Daniel E. Jones

First Edition ©1966
Second Edition ©1972
Third Edition ©1986
Fourth Edition Copyright ©1996 by the National Safety Council
All Rights Reserved
Printed in the United States of America
01 00   8 7 6 5 4

Library of Congress Cataloging-in-Publication Data

Motor fleet safety manual / edited by John E. Brodbeck.—4th ed.
    p. cm.
    Includes bibliographical references and index.
    ISBN 0-87912-188-2
    1. Motor vehicle fleets—Safety measures.   I. Brodbeck, John E.
(John Edward), 1948- . II. National Safety Council.
TL165.M68   1995
388.3'2'0683—dc20   95-33267

5C698   Product No. 22133-0000

Contents

Appendixes

Foreword

The mission of the National Safety Council is to educate and influence society to adopt safety, health, and environmental policies, practices, and procedures that prevent and mitigate human suffering and economic losses arising from preventable causes.

Each year thousands of drivers are killed or injured in motor fleet crashes. These accidents don't just affect fleet operators; they affect each of us. Whether we're driving a truck that's part of a fleet, driving a company car on a business trip, or sending children to school on school busses, we are all involved in motor fleet safety. The National Safety Council believes that most of these losses can be prevented with the proper training and safety programs.

One of the Council's best training aides for fleet safety directors has been the *Motor Fleet Safety Manual*. The primary purpose of the *Motor Fleet Safety Manual,* fourth edition, is to help fleet safety directors develop and/or revise the safety and health programs in their organizations that will reduce or eliminate these preventable accidents.

This revised and updated fourth edition focuses on the major issues relevant to the late 1990s and the new century:

- compliance with Occupational Safety and Health Administration and other federal and state regulations
- awareness and use of the latest technology and safety equipment
- ongoing driver training relevant to the type of vehicle operated.

This manual provides detailed instructions, references, and resources that will help the individual with minimal background in fleet safety to become better equipped to recognize hazards and to develop programs that will safeguard personnel. Many of the most knowledgeable fleet safety professionals have included their expertise in revising this manual, making it an excellent cornerstone to a successful safety program.

However, safety goes far beyond books and training—it is a lifestyle, a commitment to preventing accidental deaths and injuries. To enhance the training and educational methods found in the *Motor Fleet Safety Manual,* I encourage fleet safety directors to participate in the National Safety Council's Motor Transportation Division meetings, conferences, and training programs. Your participation will expand your opportunities to learn from other fleet professionals. Such professional development will increase your ability to eliminate preventable accidents from your fleet operations.

JERRY SCANNELL
President, National Safety Council

Preface

The fourth edition of the *Motor Fleet Safety Manual* has been updated and expanded to provide the technical resources needed to build and maintain an effective accident control system for all fleets, from automobiles to large commercial vehicles. Where applicable, the latest technology, such as video cams and on-board computers, has been recommended to support safety and record-keeping efforts.

Motor fleets, through their safety directors, are, more than ever, concentrating their efforts toward controlling the direct and indirect costs of accidents and injuries. The reduction of these errosive drains on profits is recognized as an urgent goal:

- the costs of disabilities, injuries, and wage loss, hiring and training temporary help, and delays and inconveniences.

- higher insurance premiums.

- uninsured costs (deductibles) of repairing vehicles, replacement values of damaged materials and merchandise, payroll hours spent in investigating and cleaning up after an accident, losses due to the interruption of normal business, and, sometimes, the loss of customer loyalty and good will.

Accident cost is a controllable business expense. Motor vehicle accidents can be prevented. Collision causes are as identifiable as any other business or production mistakes, wastes, and errors. The safety program can do for fleet operations what a preventive maintenance program does for the vehicle: stop potential problems before they can cause damage and require costly reparative actions.

The Motor Transportation Division of the National Safety Council is internationally recognized for the development of motor fleet safety programs that do work. Members of this group, through field work and professional experience, have formulated and refined methods that effectively reduce vehicle accidents and resulting personal injuries. This manual distills and presents their collective knowledge. Their continuing support and contributions are greatly appreciated.

Reader comments and suggestions are welcome.

JOHN E. BRODBECK, CSP

Motor Fleet
Safety Manual

Benefits of Accident Prevention

People generally agree that it is pretty much a waste of time to worry about events over which they have no control. When the risk of an event affecting them adversely is small enough, they accept it as "a part of life." For example, tornados and earthquakes are events that cannot yet be prevented; nevertheless, millions of people continue to live in areas where these natural disasters frequently occur.

Unlike tornados or earthquakes, motor vehicle accidents—which killed an average of 40,000 people each year in the mid 1990s—*can* be prevented. Safety analysis shows that accidents always have a cause; and where there is a cause, there is also a cure. The excellent results achieved by motor fleets who participate in safety efforts—over the billions of miles they drive—prove that accident prevention is not only possible and necessary; it is also financially rewarding for companies that work to make it a success. Accident prevention saves lives and pain and money. Any program with these important goals should be implemented by every motor fleet company.

Over the past few decades, occupational accident and illness control has become an issue of national proportions. This is due largely to tighter regulations, the possibilities of costly litigation, pressures from the general public and labor unions, and increased attention by members of the medical profession. Thus, the future is wide open for individuals entering the field of safety specialization. Likewise, companies in the forefront of the safety movement are certain to reap economic and other benefits because of their participation.

A strong accident prevention program gives an organization a valuable competitive edge. Almost all businesses that operate motor vehicles compete with other fleet operators and with alternative means of transportation. Reducing operating costs by reducing accident and injury costs enables a company to pass the savings on to its customers. The firm will be able to charge less while providing more efficient service and to capture a larger market share. Also, because a financially stable company can afford to offer and maintain satisfactory wage rates and benefit programs for its workforce, it will attract and retain higher skilled, more experienced employees.

Finally, and perhaps most importantly, every motor fleet has a duty to provide safe transportation to its customers—whether carrying passengers or transporting cargo. Both passengers and suppliers entrust a carrier to deliver them or their goods quickly and safely to a given destination. Any company that doesn't fulfill this trust can be driven out of business by its safety-conscious competitors.

This book will show *how* and *why* such a program can work to reduce losses in the three main areas of incidence—motor vehicle accidents, employee injury accidents, and off-the-job accidents.

EMPLOYEE INJURY STATISTICS

According to the annual survey conducted by the U.S. Bureau of Labor Statistics (BLS), the incidence rates of occupational injuries and illnesses for most transportation industries are greater than the private industry average. Those with higher-than-average rates include:

- local and suburban passenger transportation
- intercity and rural bus transportation
- school buses
- trucking and courier services, except air
- public warehousing and storage

Transportation industries with occupational injury and illness incidence rates below the private sector average include:

- taxicabs
- bus charter services

Workers in these seven industries are also at greater-than-average risk of dying on the job. In 1993, there were about 23 deaths per 100,000 workers in the seven industries listed above, compared to an average of 5 deaths per 100,000 workers for all industries, according to BLS data.

COSTS OF ACCIDENTS

As mentioned earlier, the three main types of fleet accidents are those arising from (a) vehicle accidents, (b) employee injury accidents, and (c) off-the-job accidents. In the case of passenger carriers, there is a fourth area, namely passenger accidents that do not result directly from vehicle accidents.

Vehicle Accident Costs

In a typical fleet, vehicle accidents (especially those involving injury) usually represent one of the largest areas of financial loss. Every time a company vehicle moves on or off the premises, there is a risk it will become involved in an accident. The risk has little to do with whether the vehicle comes from a large or small fleet or from a common or private carrier, whether the vehicle is a passenger car or a semi-trailer truck, or who is driving it. If the vehicle becomes involved in an accident, the company may be held liable. The actual cost involved will depend on many variables over which the company has little control.

Although a fleet owner may buy insurance to cover such contingencies, the fact is that in the long run every fleet pays for its own accidents. When an insurance company

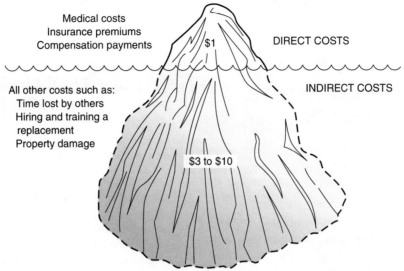

Medical costs
Insurance premiums
Compensation payments

$1

DIRECT COSTS

INDIRECT COSTS

All other costs such as:
Time lost by others
Hiring and training a
replacement
Property damage

$3 to $10

Figure 1–1. Accident costs can be compared to an iceberg—the hidden (indirect) costs usually add up to much more than the obvious (direct) costs.

pays for a vehicle accident, it does so with fleet money (from premiums paid). In addition, the insurance company gets paid for its overhead costs, its taxes, and its profit. Depending upon the accident rates of the fleet, the insurance premium can be modified. More accident costs mean higher premiums to pay. Therefore, the best way to reduce insurance premiums is to reduce accidents.

Insurance, however, is not only a method that allows a firm to distribute accident costs over a period of years (in other words, budgeting to meet them). It is also a means of obtaining expert claims and legal service, which serves as a valuable buffer between the fleet owner and claimants. Although infrequent, some injury claims can exceed the limits of the insurance policy. In today's litigious society, it is possible that such a claim could result in a firm's bankruptcy. For instance, a jury in Mississippi awarded a claimant more than $20 million for a single injury case. In Texas, the settlement for a multiple fatality collision exceeded $100 million.

In addition to the insurance premium and other direct costs of vehicle accidents, there are many indirect costs to the company. These costs arise from disruption of service to customers, cargo loss, downtime of damaged vehicles, supervisory time and expense involved in cleaning up after the accident, overtime, and many other expenses. Total indirect costs are often many times higher than direct costs (Figure 1–1).

Employee Accident Costs

Injuries incurred on the job by the company's employees also represent a significant accident cost. Companies contribute to another form of insurance—known as workers'

compensation—which compensates an injured worker for (a) loss of wages while recovering from an injury or (b) any permanent bodily impairment resulting from the injury.

Regardless of the type of insurance carried, the premiums a firm pays over the years are about equal to its employee injury costs. In addition, the company must pay the indirect costs associated with accidents. Although these costs often are difficult to assess in dollars and cents, they can drain an organization's resources and efficiency.

Examples of indirect accident costs include:

- working time lost by other employees leaving their regular jobs to assist the injured employee

- cost of equipment repairs

- extra labor and supervisory costs to restore operations or clean up after the accident

- cost of supervisory and management investigations and reporting

- cost of training temporary replacement workers

Off-the-Job Accident Costs

Injuries to employees while off the job represent another fleet expense that is seldom included in budget calculations. The principal cost to the fleet of such accidents is absenteeism, which results in lower productivity through the loss of skilled, experienced workers. Another cost is wages paid for nonproductive time or for less-efficient work done by a person returning from an injury. If replacement workers are hired, then the company must add personnel department costs, medical fees, and training costs into the equation. In every case, experience-rated health care plans will show a rate increase.

One fact is certain: when accidents are prevented, accident costs are also prevented.

HUMAN AND SOCIAL COSTS OF ACCIDENTS

Although cost saving motivates management to strive for maximum accident prevention effectiveness, there are higher motivations: management's moral obligations to their employees and to the public.

- A disabling injury sustained by an employee, or by a member of the employee's family, inevitably involves losses to the worker in terms of reduced income while away from the job as well as pain and suffering from the injury. If the injury results in a permanent physical or other type of disability, the worker must live with it for the rest of his or her life. No amount of financial compensation will offset such a loss.

- Deaths and disabling injuries due to accidents also have a social cost that affects the worker's family and the entire community. When a family loses a parent and wage-earner, it loses many intangible things as well, including emotional security and, in some cases, future plans.

- Management also has a civic obligation to prevent accidents because company vehicles travel on the public streets and highways. Not only should such vehicles be operated so as to safeguard the lives of other highway users and pedestrians, but, in fact, carrier drivers should set an example of exemplary traffic safety.

- Personal involvement helps people at all levels of the organization appreciate the human cost of accidents. One method is to have management personnel adopt the injured worker and family. Such an assignment would begin with visits to the worker in the hospital and then to the worker's home during recuperation. The managers' responsibility is to help the injured employee's family through the difficult times that always accompany serious injuries. If they do no more than ensure that workers' compensation payments are begun on time and relieve the family's anxiety about medical bills, the company objective will be met. Both managers and workers benefit from such involvement. Managers see the results of safety program failures up close. Workers and families know the company hasn't forgotten them.

Some additional benefits also come out of this approach. Workers may recuperate faster, the overall cost of claims may be reduced, and there is less chance of protracted litigation. Everyone wins—and the outcome will probably be a better safety program.

CONTROLLING VEHICLE ACCIDENTS

To what extent, then, do companies consider accidents controllable? A few facts may tell the story.

- Some fleets control accidents only when economic factors force them to do so. Their insurance rates may have become several times higher than those of their competitors, or they may be unable to obtain insurance through normal channels. To survive, such fleets are forced to institute accident prevention programs to reduce their accident rates and their premiums.

- Others control accidents only when their operating rights are threatened. The Office of Motor Carriers reports many fleets allow their compliance with regulations to fall so low that they jeopardize their operating rights. To forestall this eventuality, carriers must institute effective safety programs and give safety the priority required. Most fleets admit that if they had started a safety program earlier, they could have saved considerable sums of money. Some single-fleet savings have totaled millions of dollars.

- The National Safety Council's National Fleet Safety Contest records tell the story of many individual fleet improvements. Accident frequency rates over the past decade have shown substantial reductions. In 1932, the all-contest rate was over 30 reportable accidents per million vehicle miles. Today, this accident frequency rate has been reduced to less than 10.

CONTROLLING EMPLOYEE INJURIES

Even though vehicle accidents are numerous, more employee injuries occur outside the truck cab or driver's seat. These include injuries resulting from slips and falls, overexertion, cargo handling, or accidents incurred while transporting passengers.

Studies have shown that work injuries, like vehicle accidents, can be controlled. Even rudimentary accident prevention efforts can prove successful. For instance, the construction superintendent of a large building project became alarmed at the rise in accidents on the site. The superintendent called the foremen and supervisors together and told them in no uncertain terms that the organization wanted no more accidents on the job. The order was repeated several times, placing responsibility on key workers and ordering accident records to be kept. These actions alone resulted in a 30% reduction in the number of accidents during the rest of the project.

CONTROLLING OFF-THE-JOB INJURIES

Another dimension of accident prevention, off-the-job accident losses, can be controlled as well. See Chapter 15, Off-the-Job Safety Programs, for detailed information on setting up an off-the-job safety program.

SAFETY AND ITS RESULTS

Managers will find that even though they must spend time learning accident prevention techniques, such knowledge—and the ability to apply it—can provide personal satisfaction as well as contribute to the welfare and profits of the company. Accident prevention training offers several rewards.

- Most important is management's pride in their executive skills. Managerial skill has many components; the ability to make accident prevention work and work well is one of them. Stockholders often regard a company's accident rate as an index to the overall efficiency and skill of the firm's managers. A good executive should be able to control vehicle accident and personal injury loss. As one fleet manager put it, "You can't separate management effectiveness into good and bad. If the top man is good at marketing, but loses money through a poor accident record, he's still a poor manager. A good manager is good all the way around: he includes accident prevention as one of his top responsibilities."
- One of management's basic functions is to provide leadership. Through the safety program, employees see the chief executive in the role of inspirer and persuader, balancing the interests of employees with those of the organization in the area of safety—where it is easy to see how those interests are mutual. By accepting management leadership in this role, the average worker is more likely to follow that same

leadership in working to achieve other goals of the fleet.

- Improved supervision is another fringe benefit of the safety program. Enforcement of safety rules by the supervisor is merely a reflection of the company's interest in the personal welfare of its employees. This fact provides the basis for improved communications between supervisor and subordinates whether they be drivers, mechanics, dock workers, or other employees.
- Finally, the company committed to a strong safety program is a better place to work than the company that pays little attention to safety. Workers not only have less chance of being injured, they are more motivated to work because there is evidence of concern for their dignity and worth. The safety program thus contributes to good morale, company loyalty, and improved job performance.

SAFETY AND PUBLIC RELATIONS

Safety is not limited to the operations function of the fleet; it also can contribute to the marketing function. A reputation for safety is a definite asset in the marketplace for several reasons.

Because the motor vehicle fleet operates in the public eye, people expect the fleet to be operated by highly trained, professional drivers. This expectation is so universal that when a company vehicle has an accident, it's news. But it can also be news when the fleet wins an award for safety or when its drivers earn safety awards. (See Appendix A, Getting Publicity from Safe Driver Awards.) A well-maintained vehicle driven by a courteous, skilled driver is as effective an advertisement for a company as an attractive billboard placed in the high-traffic area of a city. (See Chapter 12, Fleet Purchase and Maintenance.)

The fleet manager is justified in actively seeking a reputation for excellence in traffic safety. Such a reputation is without doubt a strong public relations asset for the company and for the industry. Companies should remember, however, that ultimately the public judges a firm for what it is rather than for what it pretends to be. Any bid for public recognition of safe vehicle operation should be based on sincere effort and on solid achievements by all members of the motor fleet.

CHAPTER 2

Elements of a Fleet Safety Program

What is a fleet safety program? What are its main elements? What and whom does it involve?

The fleet safety program encompasses all that the fleet owner does systematically to prevent accidents—vehicle accidents, work injury accidents, and off-the-job accidents. This chapter discusses the four main elements of a fleet safety program:

1. setting management standards and policies
2. recording accidents, injuries, and fleet safety program results
3. selecting, training, and supervising employees
4. encouraging and rewarding improved performance through awards, recognition, and other interest-sustaining activities.

Later chapters will discuss in greater detail the parts of the program and its application to fleets.

SAFETY PROGRAM STANDARDS AND POLICIES

The cornerstone of any company activity—and especially of a safety program—is management. The success of the fleet safety program depends largely upon what the top manager knows about safety, expects from the safety program, and is willing to invest in it.

To begin with, the fleet manager must be convinced that accident prevention is a good investment. A good manager also should know the basics of accident prevention and be able to tell when the fleet is doing well and when it is falling short. He or she should be willing to provide leadership through face-to-face talks with other top managers, supervisors, and employees, and through policy statements and a written safety policy. The top manager should convey enthusiasm for safety, set a good example, and work well with the safety director.

The manager's interest in accident prevention should be sincere because insincerity can damage the entire program. A former chief of staff of the United States Army once said,

The leader must be everything that he desires his subordinates to become. Men think as their leaders think, and know unerringly how their leaders think.

In some cases, the fleet manager may not place sufficient emphasis on accident and injury prevention because accident problems in the firm are not clearly understood. To help remedy this situation, the manager must take the following steps when starting a program:

- Arrange for accident summary reports that truly reflect the total costs of accidents and reveal the entire scope of the problem. Such reports should indicate not only the direct costs of accidents—such as workers' compensation, fleet insurance, and medical costs—but also provide estimates, or actual figures, of the indirect costs. (Studies have shown indirect costs average three to ten times the amount of the direct costs—Figure 1–1.)

- Publish a clear, easily understood company safety policy. One of the classic policy statements is that of the former Bell Telephone System:

No job is so important and no service is so urgent that we cannot take time to perform our work safely.

- Owners of a large fleet should seriously consider hiring a trained, experienced safety specialist to set up and administer the program. In other cases, a current employee can be designated to take responsibility for the safety program. If the person is not a professional safety specialist, he or she can be trained to administer the safety program. Some opportunities for accident prevention training are discussed later in this chapter. If possible, the safety director position should be full-time.

- Make it clear to all levels of supervisory management that
  (a) they have responsibility for preventing vehicle accidents and employee injuries, and
  (b) the safety specialist works with and through them.

- Budget sufficient funds to provide all necessary safety equipment for employees, vehicles, garages, and terminals. Supplies such as eye, face, head, and body protective equipment and all necessary respiratory equipment should be included in the budget.

- Budget sufficient funds for training foremen, supervisors, superintendents, and nonsupervisory employees in safety practices.

- Budget sufficient funds to cover the cost of holding safety committee meetings and at least one or two general employee safety meetings annually. The latter meetings can be used for the presentation of safety record awards, such as safety cards or certificates or plaques.

- Budget sufficient resources to permit a reasonable investigation of each accident. Investigating nondisabling injuries may require only a little extra time of a foreman or supervisor. Serious injuries will require more time to do an investigation. This task is not a responsibility that can be shifted to an insurance company.

- Budget sufficient funds to permit periodic safety inspections of the facility, tools, and equipment. The hours spent on such activities are usually regarded as "nonproductive time," when they should be considered "productive time." If the total of all injury prevention costs are compared realistically to uncontrolled injury costs, the value of safety programs will be clear.

- The most important budget consideration is ensuring that the true cost of all accidents is charged to the correct organization, division, or department. Any unit that permits unsafe practices and conditions to continue should feel the economic consequences of their failures. The budget may be the most powerful management tool available to enforce safety policies and practices. Management should use it as one means of measuring and rewarding success in this area.

- Provide personal leadership for the program. As often as possible, managers should plan to attend safety meetings and safety committee meetings to show personal interest in these activities. This approach also gives them an opportunity to highlight outstanding safety records achieved by departments, divisions, sections, or the company as a whole. They should underscore management's sincere concern for the personal safety of each and every employee. They can express personal concern over accidents and injuries by requesting information on causes and corrective actions taken. Managers should encourage group pride in what has been accomplished and establish more challenging safety goals.

This list of activities can be adjusted to fit the size and accident experience of each fleet.

THE SAFETY POLICY

Management's attitude toward safety should be carefully phrased in a written safety policy communicated to all employees, supervisors, and top management. A written policy can serve as a reference to settle issues of safety versus expediency and to help supervisors enforce safety rules. The precise form of the written policy will vary, but it should be a clear, forceful statement of management's desires.

One of the first policy statements on safety was issued in 1906 by Judge Elbert Gary, President of the United States Steel Corporation. It has now become an historic safety document.

> The United States Steel Corporation expects its subsidiary companies to make every effort practicable to prevent injury to its employees. Expenditures necessary for such purposes will be authorized. Nothing which will add to the protection of the workmen should be neglected.

Sometimes a company's safety policy can be expressed in a very brief form, almost in the nature of a motto. An example is the policy of the former Bell Telephone System, cited earlier: "No job is so important and no service is so urgent that we cannot take time to perform our work safely." This policy was printed on dashboard decals, desk mottos, and posters, and displayed in so many other places throughout the company that any former Bell employee could probably repeat it verbatim if asked.

Assigning Safety Responsibility

Top management has ultimate responsibility for the safety performance of the fleet. However, as authority for safety tasks is delegated to managers and supervisors, this responsibility must extend in a direct line through the operating departments down to the drivers and other employees. Management must ensure that this responsibility is fully accepted by all employees and hold supervisors and foremen accountable for the safety performance of their respective departments.

All managers and supervisors must believe that accountability for safety is as important as all other elements of the management function. If they consider the safety effort less important than on-time delivery, safety practices will be pushed aside. This attitude will ripple throughout the organization and affect drivers and other workers. However, top management can weigh safety records equally with other management measures when making merit raises and promotion decisions. That message will also spread quickly throughout the organization.

Designating a Safety Director

It is true that every supervisor in the organization has a responsibility to help prevent accidents. Nevertheless, a specific person should be assigned responsibility for directing the accident prevention effort through line management. The job title of this person may be "safety director," "safety manager," or "safety supervisor." Whatever the title, the position should be given significant responsibility, authority, and respect.

In larger fleets, safety direction will be a full-time assignment. Often, additional personnel are needed to carry on departmental and specialized functions. In smaller fleets, safety direction may be a part-time responsibility, added to an employee's other duties. Where such an arrangement is necessary, the safety duty portion of the job should be defined carefully to ensure that sufficient time is allotted for accident prevention work. The press of other duties should not interfere with this necessary work. In a very small fleet, the owner or manager can direct the safety activity. The important point is that no matter what the size of the firm, one person in the organization should assume this special responsibility.

Defining the Safety Director's Duties

The safety director's duties shall be to organize and administer an effective safety program through line management, as described in this manual. The director must study all hazards existing in any part of the fleet operation and formulate practical plans to eliminate or control them or to protect employees and others against harm. The director's recommendations in this regard are submitted to management for approval, after which they become the official directives of the company. (This fact is why management interest is essential to success.) The safety director should keep records of the fleet's safety performance (see Chapter 4, Motor Fleet Accident Data, for details) and keep management informed as to the degree of the program's success.

Considerable money can be saved by developing and implementing a carefully planned and administered safety program. As a result, the selection of a qualified person to direct the program is as important as the selection of a good sales manager or of a superintendent of transportation or maintenance. The person chosen should be knowledgeable, sincerely interested in safety, a good administrator, a sound technician, and one who can sell ideas equally well to the newest driver or to the boss.

More details are given in Chapter 3, Fleet Safety Director Function.

Assigning a Part-Time Safety Director

Anyone who is assigned the job of part-time safety director must be capable of learning basic accident prevention techniques. Unfortunately, few schools or colleges provide complete courses in fleet safety engineering. The National Committee for Fleet Supervisor Training and Certification, part of the American Trucking Associations, Inc., is accredited through Indiana University of Pennsylvania. The National Committee conducts training programs at locations throughout the country. Their address is 2200 Mill Road, Alexandria, VA 22314. State trucking associations and private truck groups sometimes conduct their own courses.

More information on these courses may be obtained by writing to:

Motor Transportation Department
National Safety Council
1121 Spring Lake Drive
Itasca, IL 60143-3201

These courses can provide a new safety director with the fundamentals of the job. He or she will have to increase his or her knowledge of accident prevention by reading manuals such as this one, by participating in regional and national motor vehicle safety conferences, and by keeping posted on current information from safety periodicals and trade magazines.

ACCIDENT REPORTS

Every accident prevention program must include (a) carefully gathering information about the fleet's accidents and

(b) applying this information to prevent future accidents. The accident reporting system also plays an important role in handling claims. A good system with sound accident reporting discipline is absolutely necessary for a company to develop and maintain an effective accident prevention program. More details on reporting systems are given in Chapter 4, Motor Fleet Accident Data, and Chapter 5, Accident Investigation.

SELECTING, TRAINING, AND SUPERVISING PERSONNEL

The purpose of a fleet safety program is to protect employees, to prevent and control accidents, and to increase the effectiveness and reduce the costs of operations. Elements vital to a successful fleet safety program are described in the following sections.

Selecting Drivers

When hiring new employees, management should ensure that the selection procedure properly evaluates the employee's past safety and loss prevention experience and potential.

Safety experts generally agree that proper driver selection is so important to the success of a fleet safety program that it can account for at least half of the program's good results. New drivers, who generally are experienced when hired, may have ingrained (and possibly unsafe) driving habits. If an unsafe driver is hired, the person's actions may haunt the company for a long time to come. The safety director is responsible for helping employment personnel determine, as far as possible, the ability of each new driver to work and drive safely. The high-risk driver normally can be detected by reviewing the person's driving record. Failure to deal with a driver's unsafe behavior means that management is inviting accidents to happen. More details about screening new employees are given in Chapter 8, Driver Selection and Hiring.

Training Drivers

Every organization conducts a certain amount of orientation and training for new employees regarding company policies, work rules and conditions, and job essentials. In some cases, this task is accomplished by assigning the worker to an experienced employee; in other cases, the supervisor does the training. In larger fleets, training the new employee may involve formal instruction. One of the primary functions of the fleet safety program is to ensure that the training program teaches the new employee not only what to do, but how to do it safely.

This topic is covered in more detail in Chapter 9, Driver Training.

Ensuring Vehicle Safety

The safety director should be consulted in the specification, selection, painting, purchase, and maintenance of vehicles. Color or color combinations should be selected with safety in mind. Managers and drivers must keep vehicles in safe working condition and make sure all needed safety and emergency equipment is on board. Management should establish adequate pre-trip inspections, procedures for reporting problems enroute, and procedures for reporting and correcting mechanical defects in vehicles. See the Purchasing and Maintenance Programs section in Chapter 12, Fleet Purchase and Maintenance.

Ensuring Employee Safety

The fleet safety program must include policies and practices for preventing work injuries to all employees. Drivers, clerical staff, dock help, maintenance employees, outside sales force, and all others should be included in the overall safety programming.

Buildings, grounds, and all other physical facilities should be planned to control accidents. Interiors should be well lighted, heated, and ventilated. The selection of attractive color schemes for interiors not only makes the workplace more pleasant, but enhances safety measures. Poor housekeeping, especially at garages and terminals, should not be tolerated. Safety thrives in a well-planned, orderly environment that says "management cares about safety." Not surprisingly, efficiency thrives in such an environment as well.

The employee safety program should include thorough injury reporting with corrective follow-up to ensure that an accident will not be repeated. Hazardous job operations should be carefully studied and safe practices devised to safeguard against all hazards. Machine guards and protective clothing should be provided and used wherever needed. All workers must then be trained to follow safe practices and procedures.

When workers are injured, management should establish good supportive communication with them and their families. This policy can encourage workers to make a quick recovery and return to the job as soon as possible.

Ensuring Off-the-Job Safety

The safety program also should include activities designed to encourage workers to practice safety while off the job. In this area, management can take a number of effective steps. A safety program animated with the spirit of "Safety Everywhere—All the Time" reinforces all safety work in the three areas: safe driving, safe work practices, safety off the job. See Chapter 15, Off-the-Job Safety Programs, for details.

Supervising Safety Activities

The most important person in any safety program is the *worker's immediate supervisor.* Only this person can truly motivate the employee and carry out an effective program. If the supervisor is not motivated or, worse still, belittles the program in front of the workers, the company's safety program will fail.

Supervision has two aspects: supportive and corrective. The first aspect is concerned with motivating employees to provide high quality and quantity of work; the corrective aspect is concerned with finding and correcting substandard performance.

The safety responsibilities of supervision contain the same two aspects. Safety standards must be met in every job. The supervisor's supportive task is to inspire total compliance with safety rules (policies) and encourage a strong safety performance among drivers. On the other hand, unsafe procedures and conditions must be identified and corrected. The high-risk driver can normally be detected by reviewing the driving record. Failure to deal with the unsafe procedures will ultimately result in accidents.

Good safety supervision depends on top management support and on the quality of safety training supervisors receive. They must be taught that safety is a part of every job, not apart from any job. See Chapter 10, Driver Supervision, for details.

AWARDS AND RECOGNITION FOR SAFETY ACTIVITIES

Every successful safety program includes activities aimed at arousing employee interest in safety and keeping it at a fairly high pitch. The inexperienced safety director is likely to think that a safety program is solely concerned with this objective. The truth is that awards and recognition, while important, have no significant impact unless they are actively coordinated with the other elements of a sound safety program.

Awards and recognition, known as interest-sustaining activities, can be classified as three main types.

• **Informative activities.** These cover such items as safety meetings, special campaigns, posters, dash cards, driver letters, bulletins, and magazines. Their function is to provide information as well as to remind and inspire. Their effect is cumulative.

• **Competitive activities.** These include various contests and awards based on group and individual safety performance. They appeal mainly to workers' competitive spirit.

"Safe driver" and "safe worker" awards recognize continuing accident- and injury-free performance. These appeal to the pride of a driver or worker.

• **Expressions of management interest.** These activities include award presentation ceremonies, safety banquets, rallies, carnivals, and special events attended by management to express their personal appreciation for group and individual safety efforts. Workers generally regard the scale of such events, the care with which they are planned, and the sincerity of management's participation as measures of the company's true attitudes toward safety.

The objective of all three interest-sustaining activities is to keep alive the employee's interest in safety, maintain the desire to achieve a good safety performance record, and instill an element of fun in the program. See the section on maintaining interest in accident prevention in Chapter 7, Employee Safety Program.

INTEGRATING SAFETY WITH THE JOB

Every company should ask these questions: Are safety activities merely superimposed over the daily functions of the fleet? Or are they an integral part of the job?

Certainly, every job has an objective, whether it be grinding a valve or driving a vehicle to deliver goods. Think of safety as those necessary precautions, integral to the job, that make sure workers achieve the job objective without accident or harm.

During training there may be some justification for separating the safety and functional aspects of a job. But in actual performance, any distinction between the two should be eliminated. Safety practices and job functions should blend because the safe way is usually the most efficient way to perform a task.

This integration of safety and function should apply to the whole safety program. Over time, the safety program will become less and less intrusive. It will be accepted as part of the normal, daily activities of the fleet.

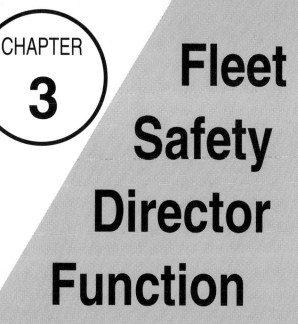

CHAPTER 3

Fleet Safety Director Function

The safety director provides the expertise and leadership to develop and maintain a successful safety program in a company. This chapter discusses the qualifications, training, and duties of a fleet safety director. It also outlines the procedures involved in establishing a fleet safety program.

BACKGROUND REQUIRED

It has often been said that a safety director must be a "jack-of-all-trades." In many respects this is true. Fleet safety directors often come to the job with varied work and educational backgrounds. They may find that little in their previous training or schooling has prepared them for their current duties.

For the most part, training for fleet safety directors consists of short courses presented by industry safety directors guided through the work of the National Committee for Fleet Supervisor Training and Certification. A few colleges and universities offer degree instruction in the basics of loss prevention (see Appendix E, Bibliography and Additional Resources). In addition, some state trucking associations offer fleet safety courses.

The National Safety Council, through workshops and its Safety Training Institute, offers the following transportation safety courses:

- Instructor Training: HAZMAT Transportation Modules
- Hazardous Materials Transportation Workshop: Ground
- Dangerous Goods Transportation Workshop: Air
- Motor Fleet Accident Investigation
- Principles of Fleet Administration Safety
- Defensive Driving Course—Car and Small Truck
- Defensive Driving Course—Professional Truck Driver

In addition, safety directors whose backgrounds include either education or work experience in business administration, human relations, traffic, or law enforcement will find their knowledge and experience valuable in their new positions. The most successful directors have supplemented this type of background with courses in management, safety engineering, writing, speaking, and other valuable subjects.

One characteristic that distinguishes *fleet safety* from general safety is the emphasis on the human element. Because direct control and supervision of drivers is impossible, workers must be trained and motivated to do their jobs safely. As a result, safety directors will find that training or practical experience in human relations can prove vital for success.

TYPICAL JOB DESCRIPTIONS

The following two examples of typical job descriptions provide some insight into the varied talents needed to manage a loss-prevention program effectively.

Job Description 1

POSITION DESCRIBED: Director of Safety
DEPARTMENT: Operations (division of)
REPORTS TO: Vice President of Operations
SCOPE: Entire System
FUNCTION: Initiate general and specific safety programs, and oversee operation for compliance with management's safety policies. Provide management and supervision with information and techniques to prevent motor vehicle accidents, personal injuries, and other preventable losses. Supervise inspections of all locations for potential accident risks including buildings, grounds, vehicles, tools, and work areas. Maintain liaison with outside agencies to acquire new knowledge to improve our present program.

Specific Duties

A. Reports and Recordings

- Properly report all accidents to company officers, insurance carrier, and appropriate state and federal agencies.
- Keep individual accident and injury reports on all employees.
- Analyze this information to recommend corrective action.
- Receive driver violation reports and/or arrest notifications and forward to proper supervisor for action.
- Prepare monthly recap for management, listing persons who had accidents during the month. Classify all reports as to "preventability." (See Chapter 9, Driver Training, for a definition of "preventability.") Update the safety information on facility bulletin boards.
- Maintain individual safety award records (safe driving and no work injury). Process and present awards.
- Prepare required Office of Motor Carriers (OMC) reports of accidents. Also send required accident reports to state agencies.
- Process any OMC driver equipment compliance reports arising out of federal road inspections.
- Check on trailer interchange policies and techniques to ensure they are in compliance with federal regulations.
- Maintain perpetual inventory of all fire extinguishers and other safety equipment in vehicles, and ensure that workers follow maintenance schedules and do servicing.

B. Investigations

- Investigate all serious accidents, injuries, and fatalities. Direct investigations by local supervision of others.
- Investigate all instances of rough handling or reported abuse of equipment.
- Make recommendations to responsible parties of solutions to the problems found.
- Follow up on recommendations, and report any difficulties to management.

C. Personnel Practices

- Personally interview all prospective or new employees after initial screening by the appropriate manager. This is done prior to the individual's being employed or before the 30-day probationary period has expired.
- Review all references returned from previous employers, public agencies, and other sources. Check information and review against original application for accuracy.
- Make decisions from this information and notify the manager concerning the desirability of hiring or retaining applicant.
- Periodically check employee files in various facility locations to review information being retained.
- Personally interview employees to compliment them for unusual or outstanding conduct or service.
- Attend and occasionally chair meetings of local supervisors to determine disciplinary action to be taken.
- Process all physical examination reports.
- Review driver personnel files for federal compliance where appropriate.

D. Services

- Prepare and distribute information pertaining to new or revised company safety rules or personnel policies.
- Prepare and distribute information about new or revised laws that relate to drivers or their activities.
- Distribute bulletins and literature furnished by the National Safety Council, insurance companies, and other appropriate associations/organizations.
- Follow up with drivers and supervisors concerning the regular use of safety belts by all drivers.
- Follow up by seeing that drivers and dispatchers fulfill their required hours of service, and that drivers get sufficient rest.
- Order safety equipment.
- Maintain a tickler file and provide notification to appropriate personnel to keep drivers' physical examinations up to date.

- Make available current issues of federal regulations to all interested personnel along with information on the safe handling and transport of dangerous articles.
- Conduct safety meetings with drivers, supervisors, and other employees.
- Counsel employees through personal interview.

Job Description 2

The following job description shows the complex responsibilities required of the safety director of a large utility fleet that also operates a community transit fleet.

POSITION DESCRIBED: Staff safety specialist in prevention of employee injuries

In the motor fleet safety function, a staff safety specialist's primary responsibility is to prevent mishaps to motor vehicles, passengers, merchandise, and the general public. Sizeable savings can be achieved in this area.

If the staff safety specialist must also set up and administer an effective employee injury-prevention program, he or she will probably do the following:

- Stay informed about employee accident-prevention techniques, including health hazards and their control.
- Teach accident prevention to both employees and supervisors. This responsibility will require some classroom instruction and the use of visual aids.
- Help foremen, supervisors, and superintendents establish and maintain effective safety programs within their jurisdictions.
- Provide continuous assistance to foremen, supervisors, superintendents, and safety committee chairmen so they can direct such activities effectively.
- Encourage foremen, supervisors, superintendents, and safety committee chairmen to attend the annual National Safety Congress and regional, state, and local safety conferences and safety equipment exhibitions. Attending these functions will help them stay abreast of the latest techniques and safety aids.

If any other key company personnel would benefit from attending these safety meetings, the staff safety specialist should encourage them to go to specific events. This responsibility may also include coordinating transportation, hotel reservations, and preconference registrations; preparing a list of suggested conference sessions; and encouraging a daily critique of what was learned that could be applied on the job. Upon return from safety conferences, the staff safety specialist should coordinate or file an activity report on pertinent topics and techniques covered in a conference.

- Develop a schedule of mutually agreeable meeting dates for safety committee meetings in departments, divisions, sections, shops, stations, or garages.
- Attend all company safety committee meetings—in the role of counselor or advisor.
- Attend general safety meetings. At such meetings, the safety specialist will:
  A. Give a brief summary of the company's safety record. Include any outstanding record of employee hours worked without a disabling injury or extended fleet records.
  B. Assist members of management and others in the presentation of safety awards. Prepare fact sheets to be used by management in their speeches or remarks at these presentations.
  C. Report the facts concerning an employee injury or motor vehicle accident that is of particular interest and is to be discussed at the meeting.
  D. Exhibit and demonstrate new items of safety equipment.
  E. Introduce safety films and provide background information.
- Coordinate purchase and use of safety posters for the safety department and for foremen, supervisors, or safety committee chairmen. Assign responsibility for changing posters, which should be changed at least semi-monthly.
- Procure safety training materials used, such as motion pictures, videotapes, filmstrips, slides, safetygraphs, and exhibits.
- Maintain an up-to-date library of safety reference publications, such as the National Safety Council's *Accident Prevention Manual for Business & Industry*, pertinent selected lists of *Occupational Safety and Health Data Sheets*, and other fleet safety resource materials.
- Advocate membership in the National Safety Council and participation in the volunteer activities of the Motor Transportation Division. Include purchase of suitable administrative units for key personnel.
- Keep management informed of progress—or lack of it—made in preventing accidents.
- Prepare suggestions to determine hazardous conditions, and/or unsafe practices or procedures related to employee injuries or motor vehicle accidents.
- Prepare a guide for the safety inspection of plant and equipment.
- Encourage setting up an effective employee safety suggestion system.
- Prepare articles for publication in a company magazine or newspaper related to off-the-job accidents. If no company magazine is published, safety information can be prepared in bulletin, memorandum, or e-mail form for distribution to all concerned.
- Prepare publicity concerning safety awards. The articles or press releases should emphasize the number of times such awards have been earned, their significance in terms of injuries avoided, and the safety-minded teamwork required to earn the awards.
- Prepare material suitable for the company's annual report. Such material could include a photographic reproduction of any safety achievement awards received during the preceding calendar year and a brief summary of the company's safety record—both motor vehicle and employee.
- Arrange for suitable forms of Safe Driver and Safe Worker recognition, including certificates and emblems. Provide rules governing how and to whom such forms will be awarded.
- On behalf of eligible employees, apply for membership in the Wise Owl Club of America (eyesight saved), and the Golden Shoe Club (foot injuries avoided), and other safety award programs.
- Counsel employees on their personal accident prevention problems. For example, arrange for the purchase of safety glasses made to the individual's prescription.
- Represent the company to the National Safety Council, state and local safety councils, the American Society of Safety Engineers, industry associations, and other groups.
- Work with the company's casualty insurance carrier.
- Cooperate with the company medical office.
- Coordinate safety matters between the safety department and the training department.
- Act as safety liaison between the safety department and all other departments of the company.
- Assist in selecting first-aid equipment. Help set up a replacement material control program to ensure that first-aid kits are always complete and correctly stocked.
- Coordinate the selection of adequate firefighting equipment.
- Supervise and direct the work of safety subordinates.
- Prepare the annual safety department budget and approve such expenditures.
- Stimulate interest in accident prevention work throughout the company. Stimulate pride in group safety achievements at all levels. The staff safety specialist should handle the paperwork necessary to apply for any awards these achievements might merit. The specialist will maintain updated records of fleet miles traveled safely by the company and by each

subordinate group. He or she will arrange to display all awards, plaques, and trophies in a prominent location and to get maximum publicity concerning them.

- Participate as much as possible in community safety work. Provide outside leadership as an authority on motor vehicle accident prevention.

These two job descriptions clearly show that the safety function is based on proven techniques of loss prevention and requires academic training and preparation. For maximum effectiveness, the techniques of loss prevention must be channeled through line supervision to every level of an organization. The safety of workers can be achieved only through the actions of their immediate supervisors. To the extent that executive managers fail to make the individual supervisor accountable for safety, they must also share the responsibility for any resulting accidents. Everyone must be responsible for safety if the program is to be successful.

DUTIES OF A FLEET SAFETY DIRECTOR

At various stages in the creation or maintenance of an accident loss-prevention program, a fleet safety director possesses the following qualifications and performs the following functions.

Preparation for the Job

The safety director's preparation or qualifying period consists of formal education, special safety training, and pertinent work experience. However, preparation is also an ongoing process. The fleet safety director must use all available means to keep abreast of changing science and technology, new products and procedures, and new federal and state regulations. This endeavor includes reading professional journals and trade publications, attending conferences and seminars, and participating in the activities of various safety organizations. Keeping up-to-date may even mean going back to school to study special subjects required by specific safety conditions or problems.

The National Safety Council's *RegScan MCS* (Motor Carrier Safety) is an example of a computerized tool that can help the professional stay current with the industry. The full text of the *Federal Motor Carrier Safety Regulations* is available on a basic personal computer or laptop. The software, which is updated monthly, allows global searches and printing of any part of the regulations. This is just one of a variety of uses that makes a personal computer essential to modern safety management.

Another indispensable tool for the fleet safety director is an updated safety library that touches on all aspects of

the job. Appendix E, Bibliography and Additional Resources, of this manual provides a broad selection of publications that will give the fleet safety director a good foundation. Membership in the National Safety Council includes free use of the Council's extensive library.

Aside from the formal sources of information, the fleet safety director can also network with colleagues who have similar job functions. The American Society of Safety Engineers, American Trucking Associations, or the National Safety Council are all good places to seek fellow safety professionals who are willing to share knowledge and experiences. The National Safety Council has developed a structure to encourage this interchange.

The Motor Transportation Division of the National Safety Council was established in 1959 with the mission to determine motor transportation safety needs and develop innovative solutions. In that effort, the Division responds, when appropriate, to legislative issues affecting the membership. It also coordinates accident prevention methods among fleets in business and government, insurance companies, trade associations, safety councils, and other interested groups. Over 1600 organizations are represented. Under the Division, four sections—Commercial Vehicle, Mass Transit, School Transportation, and Fleet Administrator—deal directly with specific types of vehicle fleets.

Commercial Vehicle Section members are typically motor carriers, insurance company personnel, and others who are affected by the safety regulations of the U.S. Department of Transportation (DOT). Carrier groups include both private and for-hire, van, specialized, tank, and others. The members focus their attention on safety compliance and driver training to help prevent motor vehicle accidents, injuries, and fatalities.

The Mass Transit Section unites a diverse group of safety professionals. Their disciplines include systems; operational and occupational safety; fire, environmental, and construction safety; and industrial hygiene. The section has developed programs and materials to prevent injury and death to drivers, passengers, employee groups, and the public.

The School Transportation Section gives members the opportunity to meet with other school transportation professionals and school bus manufacturing representatives who share mutual safety concerns.

The Fleet Administrator Section was established to provide safety and regulatory assistance to fleet administrators responsible for fleets of cars, vans, and light-duty trucks. The employee group managed includes sales representatives, service representatives, and other administrative personnel driving these smaller vehicles.

Membership in the appropriate section offers organization members the opportunity to promote safety beyond the limits of their companies. At the same time, by associating with their peers, the members are growing professionally and increasing their value to their companies.

Investigation: Problems and Prevention

The fleet safety director must not only investigate incidents, but also determine where the company should focus its safety efforts. Such investigations involve examining accident records and current job procedures, and inspecting company facilities and equipment.

The investigative function will probably begin with a thorough examination of fleet accident records, including insurance and police reports. Analysis of past accidents (for several years, when available) should indicate types of high-frequency incidents and their locations, causes, and other factors. The fleet safety director should also investigate all accident review committee judgments on previous preventable accidents. Quite often accident reports will not reveal all pertinent information. Safety personnel may also need to interview the involved parties and personally examine the evidence.

The fleet safety director also should visit all plant, building, dock, and similar facilities and examine work procedures, job instructions, and routine supervision activities. He or she must review OSHA Form 200 to determine occupational accident frequencies and types as well.

Planning

Once armed with information from accident investigation, inspections, and personal interviews, the fleet safety director can analyze the data and assemble a suggested plan of action. This task may require changing company procedures, work habits, and supervision, and providing for proper employee training. The plan is the blueprint to obtain management consent for action; therefore, suggestions must be complete, understandable, and practical. The more carefully prepared the plan, the better chance for success.

Plans must also be flexible. Not only should they include alternative courses of action, they should be designed to allow revision. Changes often are dictated by new experience, procedures, or practices developed within a company or by the industry.

At this point, the fleet safety director may wish to verify any conclusions by sampling opinions or by seeking the advice of other experts. Consulting veterans in the business (within or outside the organization) can help the director avoid costly mistakes.

Selling the Program

Once convinced that the most effective action has been planned, the fleet safety director must convince, or sell, management to undertake such a program. The chief executive officer of the organization must be apprised of the program and agree with its recommendations. This is true whether the safety administrator reports to this executive or to some other manager.

The best way to sell management on supporting a safety program is to present it in a factual, businesslike manner. Too often, a fleet safety director expects management to buy the safety program simply because it's the "right thing or moral obligation" of a firm to do so. Actually, this is a weak reason for management to support any business function. Any manager worthy of the job examines a proposal on the basis of its anticipated costs and its relative value to the organization. The manager then decides whether to go ahead with the program and delegates subordinates to work out the details.

To determine the costs and benefits of a safety program, the fleet safety director may find help by consulting the organization's insurance carrier. The director should be sure that the estimated benefits include reduced direct and indirect accident costs, reduced insurance costs, increased employee productivity, and so on.

Training for Safety

In most organizations the safety director acts as advisor to top management, executive staff, and line supervisors. As an advisor, the safety director must institute training plans, either directly for the classroom or as a guide for management.

All job training, job specifications, and work procedures should be reviewed by the fleet safety director to make sure they meet current regulations. No matter who does safety training—the line supervisor or a training specialist—the materials and procedures must be checked by the fleet safety director. In fact, from a practical viewpoint, such training will probably originate from the safety group.

Training for accident prevention begins with line supervisors. All too often the first-line supervisor is the "forgotten person" in the training effort. Because they are a vital link between management and the employee, line supervisors must be trained carefully if the safety program is to succeed with the employees.

Supervisors must be given a chance to examine all new safety procedures and plans. They will need time to become thoroughly familiar with these items and to question them. "Sell the supervisor on the plan and you'll sell the employees" is an axiom of successful safety training. The supervisor not only should be kept informed of all safety training, but also be instructed on the best way to present accident prevention information to employees, and on how to coordinate it with other training the employee may receive.

Orientation training usually is done by the training specialist, although sometimes the fleet safety director handles it. The training of drivers, including employees whose driving is incidental to their regular employment, must be carefully planned and outlined in the training procedures.

Follow-Up to Safety Programs

A safety program requires periodic follow-up, which can include:

- A monthly memo or report of worker absenteeism due to accidents; this information can be obtained from payroll records to ensure that injury or vehicular accident reports are being submitted.

- Regular safety inspection by committees; this process determines how well supervisors are complying in such matters as housekeeping, personal protective equipment usage, and vehicle maintenance.

- Incomplete accident reports returned for additional information.

- A compliance check when remedial action is indicated.

- Continuing analysis of accident and injury records to ensure that the program is getting results. If it is not, the reasons should be determined as quickly as possible to modify the program.

Reporting Safety Results

At regular intervals, the fleet safety director must report all safety achievements and problems to management and to all employees. These reports should be informative and businesslike, and prepared using accepted accounting methods, when applicable. The fleet safety director should prepare the reports using company formats and organizational divisions familiar to company executives.

Employee reports should emphasize the object lesson. For instance, it is not as important for employees to know that Bill Smith was involved in an intersection collision as it is for them to know that the accident was caused by the driver's failure to approach the intersection carefully.

Reports must be fair and accurate, but they should not soft-pedal mistakes. Mistakes can cause accidents. Sharing mistakes can help motivate others to work more safely.

ACCIDENT PREVENTION

An accident prevention program must include the following basic elements: standards, motivation, training, and supervision.

Setting Standards

The most common standard used to judge professional driving performance is the ability to avoid *preventable* accidents. The National Safety Council has developed this brief definition of a preventable accident:

> A preventable accident is one in which the driver failed to do everything that *reasonably* could have been done to avoid the accident.

In other words, when a driver commits errors and/or fails to react *reasonably* to the errors of others, the National Safety Council considers the ensuing accident to be "preventable." When the driver has done everything reasonable to avoid the situation that may have contributed to the accident, the Council considers the accident to be "nonpreventable."

One of the keys to a successful fleet safety program is for the organization to set its own standards for safe driver performance. The ideal standard should be for employees to drive without becoming involved in *any* preventable accidents. Many companies use the National Safety Council's guidelines for motor vehicle accident preventability to set their own standards for safe driving performance. The appropriateness and fairness of the standards that are set will ultimately determine the success of the program. Once adopted, the standard must be distributed and thoroughly explained to all employees, and it must be strictly and fairly administered and enforced.

Motivating Employees

Because drivers cannot be personally supervised every minute, they must be motivated to police their own driving. This means that they must understand what is correct performance. Many drivers learned how to operate a vehicle from a friend and may not know the correct way to drive safely. Once they are trained in techniques, drivers can be motivated through pride of workmanship, skill, or other factors to do a superior job. To avoid the appearance of harassment or discrimination, motivational methods and disciplinary actions must be carried out in accordance with established and *published* company policies.

On the other hand, drivers with a long accident-free record can be lulled into a false sense of security and can become careless about safety. The fleet safety director can help to overcome this problem by using incentive programs, periodic retraining, and consistent demonstrations of the importance of safety. These techniques will be discussed later.

Training

Once the safety standards have been announced, every effort must be made to train employees to achieve them. Remember that a standard, by itself, cannot prevent accidents—it represents a goal to be achieved through constant training and supervision.

The training process should include safeguards to ensure that preaching about the rules does not substitute for job instruction. Rules must be obeyed out of respect for and understanding of the principles behind them. Good driving is an art that requires intelligence, not blind obedience.

Supervision

A regular system of checking driver performance includes accurate and timely accident reporting. Without such a system, it is difficult and often impossible to determine whether company training is effective and in compliance with the standard.

All drivers should be checked periodically without waiting for accidents to reveal which drivers may be high-risk employees. Only those drivers who are known to stretch the rules are usually checked extensively. Management should make sure that such drivers receive intensive follow-up remedial and rehabilitation training until there is evidence that their performance meets or exceeds company standards. The company can use their computer programs to keep track of employees' performance and driving records.

In general, spot checks for all drivers are needed to disclose problem areas in their performance and to help in training and retraining workers.

SAFETY PROGRAM

The following example of a safety program proposal uses costs that are fairly typical for a large over-the-road carrier company operating in the mid 1990s.

Proposal to Start a Safety Program

I. Problem
  A. Average of 1,500 workdays lost through disabling injuries during each of the last three years: Salary loss equivalent to about $252,000 a year (figured at $21.00 an hour).
  B. Five permanent disabilities in current year, four in previous year, and three in year before that. (Describe these, such as lost eye, finger amputation, 30% loss of use of left arm.)
  C. Two employees killed in motor vehicle accidents. (Tell where and how.)
  D. Liability insurance premium $6,000 per vehicle, compared with rate of $5,000 per comparable vehicle in competitive operations.
  E. Workers' compensation premium $21.00 per hundred dollars of payroll, compared with industry rate of $17.00 per hundred.
  F. Estimated excess costs of accidents compared to industry average:
    Liability insurance (100 vehicles @ $1,000 each): $100,000
    Workers' compensation (100 drivers @ $4 per $100 of payroll): $174,720
  G. Direct Costs $274,120
  H. Estimated indirect costs (calculated by this firm to be a 3 to 1 ratio): $824,160
  TOTAL EXCESS COSTS: $1,098,880

II. Cause
  A. Lack of a system to select, train, and supervise workers and drivers.
    EXAMPLE: Selection system does not include check of previous driving experience or examination of driving ability.
  B. Drivers put to work without orientation training.
  C. Supervisors lack accident prevention expertise.
III. Solution
  A. Reorganize employee hiring procedures. Provide one additional clerk to check references and check state vehicle department and license revocation records. This person will also process and analyze accident reports and records. Approximate salary: $ 20,000
  B. Employ full-time safety specialist to organize and develop loss control program, including training of drivers and key supervisory personnel. Approximate salary: $50,000
  C. Secretary-clerk in safety department. Salary: $25,000
  D. Provide facilities for safety department and training program (furniture, office supplies, etc.) Annual charges: $4,000
  E. Staff time (average 20 hours at $20 an hour per employee for first year: $40,000
  F. Provide transportation for safety specialist (car purchase or lease and expenses): $14,000
  G. Outside services, memberships, material: $5,000
IV. Costs
  A. TOTAL COSTS OF SAFETY PROGRAM: $158,000
  B. Estimated direct dollar reduction in accident losses annually: $274,720
  C. Net cost of safety program: $116,720
  D. Estimated savings in indirect losses (same ratio as calculated for costs—3 to 1): $824,160
  E. ANTICIPATED NET ANNUAL SAVINGS: $940,880

NOTE: The above is based on the premise of reaching an industry average within one to two years. It should be explained that better-than-average results could be obtained over a longer period and that the active cash outlay for insurances may not change immediately. The full effect of the savings may be delayed up to three years due to the lag time in rating systems.

In actual practice, this proposal would be more detailed and would include a step-by-step description of the program, including suggested training materials, training schedules, and other details. Also, the cost figures used will vary widely according to the type of operation.

SAFETY BUDGETING

Progressive fleet organizations have established budget costs relating to accidents. They hold the departmental or divisional manager just as responsible for cost over-runs in this budget as they would for other items (such as salary, production costs, and maintenance). When accident losses are regarded as part of a supervisor's or manager's operating efficiency (on which he or she is rated for salary increases and promotion), the individual is far less likely to shift the responsibility to a fleet safety director or other "scapegoat."

To provide accurate records for management's use and guidance, the safety professional should set up cost controls that provide sufficient information to make valid comparisons. It is easy to overlook pertinent items or deliberately to omit costs that could be disguised under some other operating category.

Many costs are revealed in a superficial examination of the records. Among these are salaries and wages lost due to accident absenteeism and doctor, hospital, and other fees. Hidden costs, however, can be considerable and often involve a manager's judgment and "guesstimates" to calculate.

For example, when an experienced employee is replaced by an inexperienced one (even temporarily), there is usually an appreciable difference in productivity that can be categorized as a loss due to the accident.

Other factors, such as lost productivity when other employees stop to help, watch, or discuss an accident, are more difficult to measure. In addition, injured workers often continue to receive fringe benefits, such as family medical insurance or coverage, paid holidays, vacation, and pension contributions, while they are off the job. These costs can represent a sizeable expense to the employer.

Finally, all supervisory time spent in reporting and investigating an accident, as well as time spent in cleanup, and in ordering and obtaining replacement or repair of machinery, equipment, or vehicles, should be charged against the accident that triggered the series of events in the first place.

It is rare, however, that an organization will examine every accident (vehicular or occupational) in terms of its absolute cost. To do so would require an elaborate and expensive investigative system. It is easier to spot check accident reports periodically to determine fluctuations in the total costs of typical incidents. These costs—direct and hidden—can then be applied (by ratio) to the complete accident record.

As can be seen, the fleet safety director's job involves far more than just driver training programs and safety slogans. It requires an individual whose primary mission is to make safety part of the daily operations of an organization and to obtain a high level of safety performance from all employees.

CHAPTER
4

Motor Fleet Accident Data

"All accidents have a cause" is the first axiom of accident prevention. The second axiom might well be "Accidents can be prevented by removing or controlling their causes." A large part of a fleet safety director's job is (a) identifying accident causes and (b) recommending ways to remove them or to guard against them to protect the employee.

Many facts about accident causes are found in published motor vehicle accident statistics, in summaries and reports of the Office of Motor Carriers, in records of highway and roadway agencies, and in special studies released by insurance companies, trade associations, and the National Safety Council. Safety directors can use these sources for background information when planning a safety program and accident-reporting system.

As valuable as these reports may be, however, they can never reveal the exact distribution of accident causes in any one particular fleet. Nor can general reports pinpoint specific accident causes. Yet such knowledge is essential to any effective accident prevention program. Therefore, a system of accident reporting, recording, and analysis must be carefully planned and intelligently used.

This chapter discusses the analysis of accident causes and how to collect, record, and analyze accident-causing data. It also shows how these data can be used to establish a system that will pinpoint the specific causes in a company and provide effective follow-up for prevention.

HOW ACCIDENTS ARE CAUSED

An accident is "caused" whenever a vehicle collides with a person, another vehicle, or any other object. Moreover, the accident usually results from several factors working together. The following example illustrates this principle.

Bill was dispatched to transport a load of freight to a distant city. He recognized that his tractor was hooked up to a different trailer from those he usually pulled. Bill noticed that this particular trailer had an unusually high center of gravity. The entire capacity of the trailer—from front to rear and from bottom to top—was loaded with knocked-down cardboard cartons, which elevated the center of gravity still further.

A rookie driver was assigned to accompany Bill on the trip. Seeking to impress this new driver, Bill negotiated a right turn faster than he should. To make matters worse, the road was crowned. The combination of speed, load, crown of road, and centrifugal force worked together to create an accident situation. The accident was triggered by Bill's desire to "show off a little."

If this accident had to be attributed to one factor, then "speed too fast for conditions" would usually be recorded. Unfortunately, "speed too fast for conditions" is not sufficient analysis on which to base corrective

action unless the complete story is told. The complete analysis of Bill's accident could result in many changes besides a simple recommendation that drivers reduce their speed in certain conditions. Some of these additional changes might be:

- Use a trailer designed with a low center of gravity and appropriate for the type of material hauled.
- Establish a company rule to lower speeds at right or left turns.
- Provide refresher training for drivers who are training new drivers.

ORGANIZING AN ACCIDENT RECORD SYSTEM

Accident prevention consists of determining the factors that could cause an accident and then controlling or eliminating them by planning ahead. Although accidents usually result from several contributing factors, accident prevention activities are based on the premise that removal of one or more of those factors, in any accident situation, may have prevented the accident. Therefore, the primary purpose of an accident reporting, recording, and analysis system is to determine all the factors contributing to the accident and to eliminate or control as many of these causes as possible.

The organization and operation of such a system must include (a) gathering accident data, (b) analyzing the data, and (c) applying the data to develop countermeasures and to administer an accident prevention program.

Gathering Accident Data

A carefully planned system for gathering all pertinent information about fleet accidents is essential not only to determine and eliminate accident causes but also to take the following actions:

- **Obtain the best defense in a court action.** There is always the possibility that the employee-operator of the vehicle will be cited to appear in traffic court or be indicted in a criminal action as a result of an accident. The thoroughness with which accident data has been gathered may determine the result of any traffic court or criminal court action. Complete data are the first line of defense in a civil court action. Many cases have been won because of the thoroughness with which a company obtained the facts about a particular accident.

- **Place responsibility where it rightfully belongs.** When gathering information, company investigators should never try to "white-wash" the actions of the firm's driver. Any attempt to do so defeats the whole value of the process. Only by knowing the full facts, whether favorable or unfavorable to the organization, can the necessary corrective action be taken.

- **Promote good labor relations.** Vehicle operators involved in an accident should know that their safety record, as well as their security of employment, will be handled fairly. Likewise, labor union representatives are far more likely to agree that a driver should be discharged if the factual evidence given to them by the company supports such an action.

Completing the Accident Report Form

The basic tool of an accident data-gathering system—the accident report form—provides a blueprint for the information-gathering process. It lists the types of facts to be gathered for every accident that will be made available later when the accident is thoroughly analyzed. Because the form serves as a checklist to ensure that all essential information is obtained, it should provide for accurate recording of important accident information yet be as easy as possible to complete and to analyze. The person reading the report should be able to visualize exactly how the accident happened.

The National Safety Council's Driver's Accident Report is suggested as one model of a report form (Figure 4–1). Various insurance company report forms may also prove adequate for company accident prevention administration. Accidents reported to local or federal authorities will probably need to be made on specific governmental forms. Although most companies have their own special forms, any form can be modified to meet the needs of a particular organization. The person starting a safety program may want to look over report forms used by similar organizations and incorporate some of their ideas.

Following Accident Reporting Rules

It is essential that every company supervisor understands what has to be reported and makes sure it is done. If complete and uniform reporting is not carried out by everyone, lax supervisors will win safety contests simply because they report fewer accidents. Thorough reporting by workers and supervisors must become routine before the company can award incentives for improved safety records.

Management should devote sufficient time to develop accident reporting discipline during the driver and supervisor training sessions. Supervisors should review reports and have drivers revise their incomplete reports. Drivers should be instructed how to complete an accident report on the designated report form for every incident coming under the following definition:

> Any incident in which a company vehicle is involved (whether in motion, temporarily stopped, parked, or being unloaded or loaded) that results in personal injury and/or property damage, regardless of who was hurt, what property was damaged, or who was responsible.

Most companies require that drivers also report any claims by other people that the drivers were involved in an accident, even if they were not involved. The company also may require drivers to report complaints, the witnessing of an accident, the rendering of aid, or any other unusual incident arising from the operation of their vehicles.

Many company policies state that a driver's failure to report an accident is considered grounds for dismissal. The enforcement of the rule to report all accidents requires continuous attention by management and workers alike. When strict compliance is obtained, the company is said to have "good accident reporting discipline." This rate of compliance is also a good index to a company's overall safety discipline.

Good accident reporting discipline requires not only the reporting of every incident but also the submission of complete and well-written accident reports. To accomplish this goal, supervisors should be required to submit complete accident reports and to train their drivers how to conduct themselves at the accident scene, with emphasis on their data-gathering responsibilities. Incomplete reports should be returned to the supervisor, if necessary, to be filled in. When drivers fail to report an accident or alleged accident, no investigation can be made by supervisors or the insurance company. As a result, a claim for damages may be imposed by default.

All accident data should be recorded and preserved in a format that makes the information of the greatest possible value in the accident prevention program. Accident data should be transferred to permanent accident record forms, a procedure that is essential for efficient accident control.

Maintaining the Accident Register

Most fleets maintain an accident register (Figure 4–2a and b) that provides a journal of information on all accidents in chronological order. As a checklist for follow-up, the register ensures that the fleet operator will have a single record of all accidents.

In large fleets, the register may be kept at the office that has direct supervision over the driver involved and that is also responsible for initially receiving the driver's report of the accident. In small fleets, records are usually kept by the persons responsible for loss control. Information from accident reports should be transcribed to the register and kept up to date as follows:

- **Accident date.** This is the date the accident occurred, not the date the accident was reported. File chronologically.

- **Accident number.** In this column, enter the number that has been assigned to the accident file. This number serves as an excellent cross-reference to the file itself.

- **Driver's name.** This is another excellent cross-reference to the master file because it will identify the accident and refer back to the number of the master file.

(*Text continues on page 32.*)

National Safety Council

(For office use)

File No. _____
- ☐ Preventable
- ☐ Not Preventable
- ☐ Reportable
- ☐ Not reportable

_____
_____

COMPANY _____

DIVISION _____ ADDRESS _____

ACCIDENT INFORMATION

DATE OF ACCIDENT _____ , 19 ___

DAY OF WEEK _____

TIME _____ A.M. P.M.

M O V I N G
- ☐ Another com'l vehicle
- ☐ Passenger car
- ☐ Pedestrian
- ☐ _____

F I X E D
- ☐ Building or fixture
- ☐ Parked vehicle
- ☐ _____

T Y P E
- ☐ Head On
- ☐ Sideswipe
- ☐ Right Angle
- ☐ Rear End
- ☐ Other (Describe) _____
- ☐ Front End
- ☐ Non Collision (Describe) _____

LOCATION

PLACE WHERE ACCIDENT OCCURED:

ADDRESS OR STREET ON WHICH ACCIDENT OCCURED: _____

☐ AT INTERSECTION WITH: _____

CITY/TOWN, STATE _____

☐ NOT AT INTERSECTION: _____ FEET N S E W ☐☐☐☐ OF _____

Nearest Intersecting Street/Road; House Number, or Landmark: Bridge, Milemarker, etc.

POLICE

PRESENT? ☐ YES ☐ NO

Name of Force _____
☐ Local ☐ County ☐ State

Officers Name _____

Badge No. _____

Report No. _____

Tickets/Arrests   Driver   1 ☐   2 ☐

Other _____

DRIVER / PASSENGER / PEDESTRIAN INFORMATION

DRIVER VEHICLE ONE

Driver's Name:	Company I.D. Number:
Driver's Address:	City/State:
Phone No.:	Driver's License Number:
Vehicle Number(s):	Run:	Route:
Date Of Birth:	Employment Date As Driver:	Hours Since Last 8 Hours Off:
Parts Of Vehicle Damaged:	

Was Street Lighted? ☐ Yes ☐ No
Was Vehicle Lighted? ☐ Yes ☐ No

DRIVER VEHICLE TWO

Driver's Name:	Phone No.:
Driver's Address:	City/State:
Driver's Occupation:	Driver's License Number:
Age:	Insurance Co.:
Make Of Vehicle:	Year:	Type:	Vehicle License No.:
Registered Owner:	
Owner's Address:	
Parts Of Vehicle Damaged:	
Others In Vehicle:	

Was Vehicle Lighted? ☐ Yes ☐ No

PASSENGER / PEDESTRIAN

PASSENGER ☐
PEDESTRIAN ☐
NO. 1

Name	Address, City, Zip	Home Phone
Passenger In Vehicle #	Date Of Birth	Sex	What Was Pedestrian/Passenger Doing:

PASSENGER ☐
PEDESTRIAN ☐
NO. 2

Name	Address, City, Zip	Home Phone
Passenger In Vehicle #	Date Of Birth	Sex	What Was Pedestrian/Passenger Doing:

INJURIES

	INJURED: YES	NO	DESCRIBE INJURIES	INJURED TAKEN TO/BY
DRIVER VEHICLE 1				
DRIVER VEHICLE 2				
PASSENGER VEH ___				
PASSENGER VEH ___				
PEDESTRIAN 1				
PEDESTRIAN 2				
OTHER				

Figure 4–1. Driver's Accident Report.

VEHICLES/PEDESTRIANS/PASSENGERS

(CHECK ONE OR MORE FOR EACH DRIVER)—YOU ARE No. 1	PREVIOUS TO ACCIDENT		WHEN FIRST IN DANGER		AT IMPACT	
	No. 1	No. 2	No. 1	No. 2	No. 1	No. 2
Going straight ahead	☐	☐	☐	☐	☐	☐
Slowing	☐	☐	☐	☐	☐	☐
Stopped in traffic	☐	☐	☐	☐	☐	☐
Park or stopped in zone	☐	☐	☐	☐	☐	☐
Backing	☐	☐	☐	☐	☐	☐
Starting	☐	☐	☐	☐	☐	☐
Passing	☐	☐	☐	☐	☐	☐
Being passed	☐	☐	☐	☐	☐	☐
Changing lanes	☐	☐	☐	☐	☐	☐
Turning left	☐	☐	☐	☐	☐	☐
Turning right	☐	☐	☐	☐	☐	☐
Entering zone/Pulling to curb	☐	☐	☐	☐	☐	☐
Leaving zone/Pulling from curb	☐	☐	☐	☐	☐	☐
Other (explain)	☐	☐	☐	☐	☐	☐
YOUR SPEED	___ MPH		___ MPH		___ MPH	
SPEED OF OTHER VEHICLE	___ MPH		___ MPH		___ MPH	
DISTANCE YOUR VEHICLE FROM OTHER VEHICLE	___ FEET		___ FEET			

DID YOU SOUND HORN? ☐ YES ☐ NO HOW FAR AWAY? ___ FEET
DID YOU APPLY BRAKES? ☐ YES ☐ NO HOW FAR AWAY? ___ FEET

AFTER IMPACT—VEHICLE MOVED	AFTER IMPACT—OTHER VEHICLE MOVED
___ FEET	___ FEET

GIVEN CONDITIONS, WHAT WAS SAFE SPEED FOR:

VEH. 1 _____ MPH   VEH. 2 _____ MPH

VEHICLE

1	2	
☐	☐	Did not have right-of-way
☐	☐	Following too closely
☐	☐	Failure to signal intentions
☐	☐	Speed too fast for conditions
☐	☐	Disregarded traffic signs or signals
☐	☐	Improper passing
☐	☐	Improper turning
☐	☐	Improper backing
☐	☐	Improper traffic lane
☐	☐	Improper parking
☐	☐	No improper driving
☐	☐	Defective brakes
☐	☐	Defective steering
☐	☐	Defective lights
☐	☐	Defective tires
☐	☐	No defects
☐		_____
	☐	(Specify other)

PEDESTRIAN

- ☐ Walking with traffic
- ☐ Walking against traffic
- ☐ Coming from behind parked vehicle
- ☐ Crossing at intersection
- ☐ Crossing not at intersection
- ☐ Alighting from a vehicle
- ☐ Working in roadway
- ☐ Playing in roadway
- ☐ _____
  (Specify other)

PASSENGER

- ☐ Boarding vehicle
- ☐ Alighting from vehicle
- ☐ Caught in doors
- ☐ Seated
- ☐ In motion in vehicle
- ☐ Other (describe)
  _____
  _____
  _____

ENVIRONMENTAL CONDITIONS (CHECK ALL THAT APPLY)

WEATHER (check one)
- ☐ CLEAR
- ☐ CLOUDY
- ☐ RAINING
- ☐ SNOWING
- ☐ FOGGY
- ☐ OTHER
_____

SURFACE (check one)
- ☐ DRY
- ☐ WET
- ☐ ICY
- ☐ SNOWY
- ☐ OTHER
_____

TRAFFIC CONTROL (check one)
- ☐ STOP SIGN
- ☐ YIELD SIGN
- ☐ TRAFFIC SIGNAL
- ☐ FLAGMAN
- ☐ NO CONTROL
- ☐ OTHER

LIGHT (check one)
- ☐ DAWN
- ☐ DAY
- ☐ DUSK
- ☐ DARK-NO LIGHTS
- ☐ ARTIFICIAL LIGHT
- ☐ OTHER

ROADWAY No. of Lanes
- ☐ DIVIDED ___
- ☐ UNDIVIDED ___
- ☐ ASPHALT
- ☐ CONCRETE
- ☐ GRAVEL
- ☐ OTHER ___

ALIGNMENT (check one)
- ☐ STRAIGHT
- ☐ CURVE
- ☐ BRIDGE
- ☐ INTERSECTION
- ☐ RAMP
- ☐ RAILROAD

- ☐ OVERPASS
- ☐ UNDERPASS
- ☐ LEVEL
- ☐ UPHILL
- ☐ DOWNHILL

WITNESSES

NAME	ADDRESS	PHONE

INDICATE ON THIS DIAGRAM WHAT HAPPENED

Use one of these outlines to sketch the scene of your accident, writing in street or highway names or numbers.

1. Number each vehicle and show direction of travel by arrow: →[1]<[2]

2. Use solid line to show path before accident →[2]; dotted line after accident →[2]

3. Show pedestrian by: ———○
4. Show railroad by: ++++++++++++
5. Show distance and direction to landmarks; identify landmarks by name or number.
6. Indicate north by arrow, as: (↑)

INDICATE NORTH BY ARROW

ACCIDENT DESCRIPTION

DRIVER'S ACCOUNT OF ACCIDENT _____
_____
_____
_____
_____
_____
_____
_____

This report is accurate to the best of my knowledge   DRIVER(S) _____   DATE _____

Figure 4–1. (continued)

National Safety Council

MOTOR TRANSPORTATION

ACCIDENT REGISTER

PERIOD COVERED ____________ TO ____________

ACCIDENT NUMBER ____________ TO ____________

COMPANY ________________________________

LOCATION ________________________________

NATIONAL FLEET SAFETY CONTEST

KEY CODE NO. ______

DIVISION OF CONTEST ____________

	ACCIDENT DATE	ACCIDENT NUMBER	DRIVER'S NAME	DRIVER'S HOME TERMINAL	VEHICLE NUMBER	ACCIDENT TYPE	SHOW NEAREST CITY & STATE
1							
2							
3							
4							
5							
6							
7							
8							
9							
10							
11							
12							
13							
14							
15							
16							
17							
18							
19							
20							
21							
22							
23							
24							
25							
26							
27							
28							
29							
30							
31							
32							
33							
34							
35							
36							
37							
38							
39							
40							

Figure 4–2a. Accident Register (vehicles).

THIS FORM CAN BE CONVENIENTLY FILED IN A
THREE RING BINDER. TEAR OFF THIS FLAP AND FOLD
AS INDICATED AND THE PAGE IDENTIFICATION WILL
WILL BE UNCOVERED FOR REFERENCE.

FOLD

← TEAR OFF HERE →

ACCIDENT LOCATION			OBJECTS, PERSONS OR VEHICLES INVOLVED	ESTIMATED COST INFORMATION						USASI D-15						
URBAN	SUBURBAN	RURAL		COMPANY		OTHER PARTY		TOTAL	REPORTABLE	NOT REPORTABLE	REPORTS FURNISHED					
				PERSONAL INJURY	PROPERTY DAMAGE	PERSONAL INJURY	PROPERTY DAMAGE				CO. HDQTS.	INS. CO.	POLICE	BMCS		
																1
																2
																3
																4
																5
																6
																7
																8
																9
																10
																11
																12
																13
																14
																15
																16
																17
																18
																19
																20
																21
																22
																23
																24
																25
																26
																27
																28
																29
																30
																31
																32
																33
																34
																35
																36
																37
																38
																39
																40

Figure 4–2a. (*continued*)

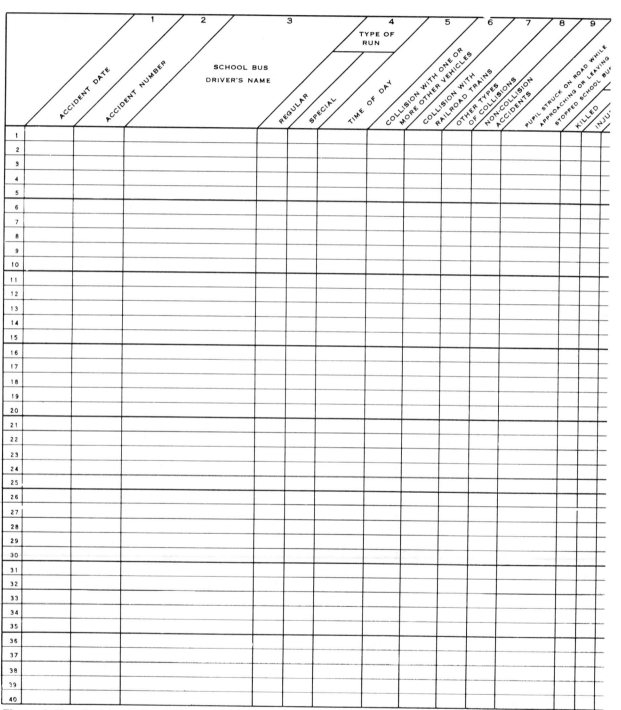

NATIONAL SAFETY COUNCIL
FORM VEHICLE 9

SCHOOL BUS TRANSPORTATION

ACCIDENT REGISTER

SCHOOL DISTRICT _____

ADDRESS _____

Figure 4–2b. Accident Register (school buses).

30

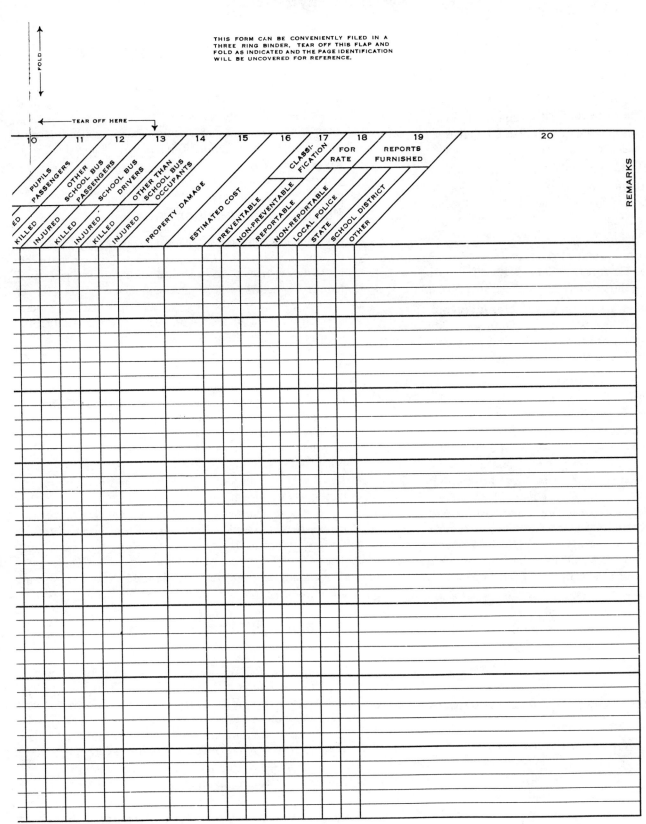

THIS FORM CAN BE CONVENIENTLY FILED IN A THREE RING BINDER. TEAR OFF THIS FLAP AND FOLD AS INDICATED AND THE PAGE IDENTIFICATION WILL BE UNCOVERED FOR REFERENCE.

Figure 4–2b. (*continued*)

• **Driver's home terminal.** When a control register is maintained at the organization's general office, this column helps to locate accidents by terminal and provides a quick review of the accidents that occur.

• **Vehicle number.** The vehicle number assists the maintenance, operations, and safety departments. Whenever practical, the numbering system should indicate the type of vehicle involved.

• **Accident type.** This is the first major categorization of accident type. The breakdown should include head-on, sideswipe, right angle, front end (your vehicle), rear end (your vehicle), overturn, other.

• **Accident location.** Location data of a general nature can be used later for accident analysis. These data can indicate where the majority of accidents are taking place.

• **Objects, persons, or vehicles involved.** Here, as in the section above, descriptive information should be recorded that can be analyzed by categories, such as truck and car, bus and pedestrian, taxi and utility pole.

• **Estimated cost information.** A company must know what accidents are costing or might cost. Accurate estimates furnish the data for making realistic financial projections.

• **"Reportable" or "not reportable."** To be compared on an equal basis, all fleets must use the same standard of accident reportability. The National Safety Council's National Fleet Safety Contest uses American National Standards Institute (ANSI) standard D15.1–1976, *Method of Recording and Measuring Motor Vehicle Fleet Accident Experience and Passenger Accident Experience,* as do other national contests. (ANSI D15.1–1976 has been withdrawn but is still available through the National Safety Council's Motor Transportation Department.)

• **Reports furnished.** In some cases, specific reports must be furnished to company headquarters, the insurance company, the police and the DOT's Office of Motor Carriers. This section provides a checkpoint to make sure that such reports have been made.

Using the Award and Accident Record Card

The safety record of each driver is important to the evaluation of overall job performance. A special Council form, Award and Accident Record, lists dates of all accidents and summarizes the essential facts about each one (Figure 4-3). The card also records performance commendations and dates of safety awards earned. The cards may be kept in a special file or included with the driver's other personnel records. The driver's accident record may be kept with those of all other drivers in an index file or entered into the computer as part of the personnel or payroll master file.

ANALYZING ACCIDENT DATA

Accident analysis involves studying accident data to determine what actions will result in the greatest improvement in a firm's safety efforts. This analysis requires breaking down every accident into its component parts and tallying the information so that it can be viewed objectively. Accident-causing factors must be isolated so that a company can try to eliminate or control them.

Purpose of an Accident Analysis

Accident investigation reports are of little use if they are merely placed in the files and forgotten. They must be properly evaluated. Analysis of accident causes pinpoints high-risk situations and suggests remedies.

For example, if the analysis indicates that equipment problems, such as defective brakes, is a contributing factor to accidents, then there may be shortcomings in the maintenance program or in a mechanic's performance. Should the analysis show that a large number of accidents occur at intersections, the safety director could conclude that drivers need additional education and training. Similarly, if several drivers are shown to be accident repeaters, then the person who is responsible for driver selection may not be using adequate selection techniques. Analysis also may point out discrepancies between a problem and any action taken to remedy the problem and may indicate a better way to implement corrective action.

Accident analysis provides fleet operators with "advance warning" of what accident experience is likely to be. Because the analysis relates the times, places, conditions, causes, and other factors that most often contribute to accidents, it indicates which action should be taken to prevent the accident or to reduce the accident frequency.

Frequency of Accident Analysis

An analysis should be made whenever the number of accidents indicates a trend or reveals a need for any change in accident prevention activities. The intervals between accident analysis reports generally depend on the size of the fleet operation. A ten-vehicle operation that has few accidents may not warrant an accident analysis summary more than once a year (or possibly every two years), unless accidents increase. In a much larger fleet, a summary may be warranted once a month.

Mechanics of an Accident Analysis

Analysis is the process of breaking something down into its individual parts. In the analysis of a group of accidents, the separate factors in each accident are isolated and counted. This is largely a routine process; once the analysis

MOTOR TRANSPORTATION AWARD AND ACCIDENT RECORD

National Safety Council

Form Vehicle 6

JAN	FEB	MAR	APR	MAY	JUN	JUL	AUG	SEP	OCT	NOV	DEC

Company ....

Address ....
     Number   *Street*

Name ....
     Last   *First*   *Middle*

Location ....

Badge Number ....
Date Employed ....
     Month   *Day*   *Year*
Age ....
     At Emp.

SAFE DRIVER AWARD RECORD

Earned .... Year N.S.C. Award during period

from .... to .... with

Company ....

Certified by ....

DRIVING TESTS

Date	Score	Remarks

Award earned	Certificate Number	Date Award earned	Preventable Accidents		Non-Driving Time	
			File No	Date	From	To

REMARKS: ....

....

....

....

....

....

....

2M 385

Printed in U.S.A.

Stock No. 229.36

ACCIDENT RECORD

Accident File No.	Date of Accident	Co. Veh Number	Type of Company Vehicle	Type of Accident	Location	Preventable or Not-Preventable	Violation

Figure 4–3. Award and Accident Record (front and back).

system has been designed, it can easily be programmed into a computer that will store and count the factors. To establish this system, the safety director must decide (a) what accident facts to analyze and (b) what subcategories to use for each factor to show either its presence, absence, or relative effect.

Selecting factors to be studied. Because an accident can be highly complex, it is difficult to record for study all the factors that may have brought it about. Therefore, guidelines such as the following must be established to select which factors should be recorded.

What information is available and how easily can it be obtained? Because analysis is usually confined to those items on the Driver's Accident Report, all the items that are to be analyzed should be completed.

At times, many factors surrounding an accident may or may not be associated with its causes; to study all factors would complicate the analysis and render it too costly. For example, an operator's height, weight, and hair color are unlikely factors to be related to accident causes. Even if they were, probably nothing could be done about them. The safety director should limit the analysis to those factors which, if they did contribute to the accident, are subject to some control.

The following are some of the accident factors usually selected for accident analysis:

- date of accident
- date reported
- name of driver
- age of driver
- length of service of driver
- hours on duty
- driver's home terminal
- weather conditions
- light conditions
- road conditions
- accident location
- direction traveling
- type of accident
- vehicle type
- vehicle number
- time of day of accident
- traffic violation
- other vehicle type
- vehicle speed versus posted speed limit
- pedestrian(s) involved
- property damage
- vehicle or object struck

- driver striking vehicle or object
- responsibility for accident
- any failure by company driver
- cost of accident

Selecting an analysis tool. With the cost of a basic desktop computer at less than $1000, there is no justification for continuing to use hand-sorting methods for accident analysis. A simple database can be constructed with a menu for the input clerk. Input, analysis, and report generation can be selected by mouse or a keystroke. Commercial programs are also available. The National Safety Council's ACCUSAFE MV software is an example of a program designed specifically for motor vehicle incident tracking. Through the reports generated, the objective is to identify trends and specific cost factors so that corrective action can be taken early.

Constructing the classification. Once you have decided what factors to analyze, construct a system of classification by categorizing each factor. For example, to study the pedestrian factor requires only two categories: "Pedestrian" and "No Pedestrian." More detailed information about pedestrians can be obtained by constructing a classification composed of the categories: "Male (age)" and "Female (age)."

Because the value of a classification depends entirely on how useful it is to the safety director, the following considerations should help in constructing categories:

- The categories should be *mutually exclusive*—that is, a certain weather condition should be classifiable into only one category. Categories must also be *collectively exhaustive*—that is, there should be an appropriate category for every type of weather condition. A classification whose categories are not mutually exclusive and collectively exhaustive is defective and can introduce many errors into the analysis.

- The classification should be sufficiently detailed to provide as much specific information as needed. If categories are too general, they become worthless. For example, a classification by time of day into "A.M." and "P.M." categories is too general to be meaningful. A better classification would be into categories made up of 24 one-hour time brackets, 12 two-hour brackets, or 6 four-hour brackets.

- The classification should not be *too* detailed. Because the purpose of an analysis is to arrive at a useful generalization about the fleet's accident experience, it is used to search for a trend or a constellation of factors. It would be difficult, if not impossible, to discover such a trend if the classification were excessively detailed.

With the reduced cost of hard drive storage and system memory, managers can use the computer to handle the task of categorization where possible. In the past, items had to be coded to save memory; now it is possible to use a scroll bar to select the appropriate category name or to use a database of acceptable terms to check a typed entry. Managers should avoid the temptation to fit data into groups during input. Instead, they should let the software sort individual data into categories. This approach minimizes errors and maintains the detail that may be needed later.

One classification useful in guiding the training program is by type of accident. When well constructed, such a classification provides a certain amount of built-in analysis and a fairly ready-made answer to the questions: "What are we doing wrong?" and "What must we do to correct it?"

The simplest and most widely used classification by type of accident is composed of the following categories:

- head-on
- sideswipe
- right angle
- front end (your vehicle)
- rear end (your vehicle)
- backing
- overturn
- other
- noncollision

Other classifications may be according to the movement of each vehicle (for example, straight ahead, turning, or changing lanes) or according to the incorrect act of the driver when the accident has been judged as preventable.

APPLYING ACCIDENT DATA

After painstakingly gathering the facts about all fleet accidents and carefully analyzing them, the safety manager knows the "what," "when," "where," "who"—and to a large extent, the "how" and "why"—of the fleet's accident experience. These data can now be used to guide accident prevention programs.

Every accident, even if minor, must be treated as a matter of importance. Management cannot afford to dismiss an incident as being "a necessary part of doing business," "bad luck that could happen to anybody," or "regrettable, but just one of those things." Any display of indifference on the part of management or supervisors will suggest to drivers that safety is not important and will inevitably result in lower safety performance.

Although a strong attitude toward safety must be impressed on every driver, management cannot go to extremes and fire a driver simply because of one incident. How management handles drivers who have had a motor

vehicle accident can help determine whether a driver learns anything from the experience and improves his or her performance, or whether the incident, by being ignored, will reinforce an operator's unsafe driving habits.

Reports for Management

Reports on accident data should be made to management monthly. The reports should show the actual number of accidents and the accident rate for the separate terminals, divisions, or company locations, as well as company-wide totals.

So that management can have some basis for comparison, a graph of the moving average for the previous 12 months should be presented. This type of chart helps smooth out the month-to-month variation and shows clearly whether the long-term trend is rising or falling. The actual monthly performance can be overlaid on the moving average chart to demonstrate seasonal shifts or other factors affecting the rates. The information should be prefaced by a brief written summary that points out the most noteworthy facts in the report.

Again, the versatility of today's computer software allows data that are input one time to be used in many ways. For example, data input to a database can be imported to a spreadsheet for analysis, then transferred to a word processor as a graph for use in a letter to the staff. The possibilities are unlimited—another reason why the safety director must be computer literate.

Other information might be included in monthly and annual accident experience reports to management. For example:

- accident rates by type of equipment and type of accident
- high-accident locations
- accidents by seniority groups
- miles operated per accident
- accident costs per mile

The company can create a powerful competitive safety tool if the monthly reports are ranked to show which company divisions or locations have the best improvement in accident rates. Copies of the reports can then be distributed to all locations. Others will see the improvement record of each location and be able to measure their own performance against these results. Because upper management receives the monthly reports, it would be a shortsighted supervisor who did not try to better his or her team's standing on the next report.

Carrying this effort further, the results on the monthly summary can be tied to each employee's incentive programs. The report can show actual or average accident cost savings.

Using Incentive Awards—Pitfalls to Avoid

Sharing a portion of the savings gives every employee a stake in doing better. These incentive awards should be distributed when the fuel economy, perfect attendance, and other awards are given. The incentive programs are a way of telling employees about management's priorities.

In any incentive program, management should avoid trying to compare locations that are not truly similar. For instance, a terminal in New York City can hardly be compared to one in Helena, Montana. But both terminals can be compared to the insurance rate performance of other similar fleets in their respective regions. Even more importantly, they can be compared to their own performance over time. If a terminal cuts its insurance costs by 20% and the regional rates stay constant, a portion of the savings could be distributed to the best performers as an incentive for improved safety. If the regional performance rate improved by the same 20%, the insurance commissioners' rate change might be the cause, and no improvement incentive would be appropriate.

What would prevent a driver from sharing in the incentive? A preventable collision would be one reason. The formula for computing incentive awards should consider traffic violations, driver's daily log violations, vehicle abuse as reported by the trip recorder, and any other safety-related factors that will be perceived by all to be fair. A fairly administered safety program is the most important consideration when awarding incentives.

Another pitfall to avoid is to reward only improved performance. When the incentive is given solely for improvement, performance will deteriorate after a specified high performance level is achieved. Sustained high performance levels should also be rewarded.

OTHER USES OF ACCIDENT DATA

Accident data gathered can also be used in the following ways.

Driver Selection

Management should use accident data to check on the safety performance of the drivers hired. If some drivers do poorly on the job and leave the company or have to be discharged, this information should be reviewed to improve the company's ability to select better drivers.

Driver Training Programs

The training program for new drivers should educate them to drive safely. A company's accident records may indicate that the fleet drivers were not given enough instruction in some specific area, for example, how to avoid backing accidents. As a result, the training program should be altered to correct this deficiency. The training program should be reevaluated routinely so that it deals with the type of accident problems encountered in the fleet.

Safety Meetings

If regular safety meetings are a part of the safety program, the content of such meetings should be based on current accident data. Accident prevention efforts should always be aimed at the most appropriate cause. If accident records indicate that a certain location, weather condition, or type of accident accounts for most incidents, safety meetings should focus on showing drivers how to avoid or manage these conditions or types of accidents. (Appendix B provides more details on these efforts.)

Awards and Incentives

Accurate accident records serve a positive function as the basis for fleet contests, driver awards, and incentive systems. The operation of award and incentive plans is discussed in Chapter 10, Driver Supervision, under the section Encourage High Performance.

Management Support

Interest in and support of the safety effort will be high only if all managers and supervisors are kept informed of safety achievements within the company. The rate of motor vehicle accidents is based on the number of reportable accidents per million vehicle miles driven. The ANSI standard D15.1, *Method of Recording and Measuring Motor Vehicle Fleet Accident Experience and Passenger Accident Experience,* should be used to compute rates. (Call the Motor Transportation Department, National Safety Council, for a copy.)

Fleet accident data not only tell management and employees how the company is doing regarding safety efforts but also what the organization needs to do to improve its safety record.

CHAPTER 5

Accident Investigation

Accident investigation is more than filling out the proper forms, as important as they are. It is a system of collecting and documenting factual evidence. The accident investigation system includes training drivers in the correct conduct at the scene of an accident and in the procedures for notifying the authorities and the company, obtaining witness statements, marking the accident site, protecting the vehicle and its cargo, and doing the necessary paperwork.

For the safety specialist, accident investigation includes all this plus accurate field investigation; evidence gathering; witness statement recording; site and vehicle diagramming; and training, interviewing, and retraining drivers.

This chapter gives a comprehensive overview of the accident investigation system.

DRIVER'S PROCEDURES

A driver involved in an accident must take specific action immediately, because he or she is usually the only representative on the scene at the time of the accident.

It is crucial that all drivers be trained to follow the correct procedures in the event of an accident. The National Safety Council Accident Report Packet lists on its envelope tasks to be done in order of importance (Figure 5–1 front and back). (Similar envelopes are available from many insurance carriers.)

Courtesy cards can be used to get names and addresses of witnesses without frightening them away (Figure 5–2). A card can also be used to obtain an exonerating statement from the responsible motorist while he or she is still apologetic and wants to make amends (Figure 5–3).

Steps to Follow

1. Protect the scene of the accident. To keep the effects of the accident from becoming worse, the driver should immediately place warning signals and devices at the scene to ensure the uninterrupted safe flow of traffic around the accident.

2. Protect the injured. If possible, the driver should request medical assistance from authorized sources (police, fire fighters, hospital, etc.).

3. Report the accident. Depending on your local reporting requirements, call the local police or state police and notify the designated company representative. A procedure should be established whereby the driver can talk to the person who will be responsible for the accident investigation. A previously prepared telephone checklist is invaluable in recording the information reported by a driver

(Figure 5–4). With its information, the company can decide whether to dispatch equipment, another driver, a mechanic, or additional staff to the scene of the accident. Management can make arrangements for whatever help will be needed with a minimum of delay and confusion. A prominent notice on the dashboard of the vehicle should state who to notify if the driver is incapacitated by the accident.

4. Obtain information. All drivers should carry an accident report packet that will help them gather information at the scene (Figure 5–1). Instructions are printed on the outside of the packet, and the accident memorandum inside will guide the driver in recording details. The packet should also contain a sharp pencil, paper, courtesy cards, a lumber crayon, coins or a phone credit card for phone calls, and other materials as needed. The driver should follow the steps on the outside of the packet, including passing out courtesy cards (Figure 5–2).

Everyone who was in the area at the time of the accident should be asked to fill out one of these cards and return it to the driver, whether or not he or she actually saw the accident occur. The cards can be used later to determine who actually saw the accident. Also, at times, a statement that an individual did *not* see the accident might prove valuable in court. Although these cards are sometimes referred to as witness cards, people do not like to be "witnesses," so they should always be called courtesy cards.

Another card that should be filled out, if possible, is the exoneration card (Figure 5–3). If the other driver is willing to admit fault, the driver should promptly ask for the admission in writing. It may not seem likely that a driver would admit guilt, especially in writing. But experience has shown that guilty drivers are more forthcoming at the scene of the crash than they tend to be days or weeks later.

Accident Memorandum

At this point, the operator is in a position to fill out the Accident Memorandum (Figure 5–1 back). This will provide important information that may not be available later.

A few things need to be emphasized about filling out the accident report:

- It should be filled out completely and legibly because it may ultimately serve as evidence in court.

- Facts should be definite and specific.

- There should be no question as to its accuracy.

- It should identify all vehicles involved.

- It should supply the correct full name of everyone involved.

- It should include addresses of all persons involved in the accident.

National Safety Council
Form Vehicle 2 Rep. 03

ACCIDENT REPORT PACKET
KEEP THIS ENVELOPE IN YOUR VEHICLE
OPEN ONLY IN CASE OF ACCIDENT

FIRST —

Stop Immediately and determine damage. Avoid obstructing traffic if possible.

Place emergency reflectors, flares, lanterns or flags.

Aid the injured and see to it that they receive medical attention as soon as possible.

Report accident to local police and your company.

SECOND —

Get witnesses to sign courtesy cards.

Record information on reverse side of this envelope at scene of accident, and give this envelope to an authorized representative of your company.

IMPORTANT —

Make no statement to anyone except:

A. An officer of the law.

B. Your company's representative.

C. Your insurance company's representative. Make no settlements. Do not argue about the accident.

If the accident involves an unattended vehicle or fixed object, take reasonable steps to locate and notify the owner. If the owner cannot be found, leave a notice in a conspicuous place on the vehicle or object, listing your name and address, the company name, and a brief description of the accident, with date and time. Whenever possible get a witness signed statement.

TURN ENVELOPE—FILL IN INFORMATION

Figure 5–1 (front). Accident Report Packet with Accident Memorandum on back.

ACCIDENT MEMORANDUM

Date of
Accident . . . . 19 . . . .   Day of
Week . . . .   Hour . . . . . .   a.m.
p.m.

☐ CITY
☐ SUBURBAN
☐ RURAL

PLACE WHERE ACCIDENT OCCURRED

County . . . .   City, town
or township . . . .

If accident was outside city limits
indicate distance from nearest
town. Use two distances and two
directions if necessary.
{ . . . . miles . . . . north-south
  . . . . miles . . . . east-west }
of
{ ☐ limits of
  ☐ center of }
. . . .
City or Town

ROAD ON WHICH ACCIDENT OCCURRED . . . .
Give name of street or highway number (U.S. or State)

☐ AT ITS INTERSECTION WITH . . . .
OR
Name of Intersecting street or highway number
☐ NOT AT INTERSECTION
(Check and complete one)
{ . . . feet . . . . north-south
  . . . feet . . . . east-west }
of
Show nearest intersecting street or highway, house
number, curve, bridge, rail crossing, alley,
driveway, culvert, milepost, underpass, numbered
telephone pole, or other identifying landmark.
Show exact distance, using two directions and two
distances if necessary.

OTHER DRIVER'S NAME

ADDRESS

CITY	STATE	DRIVER'S LICENSE No.

OTHER VEHICLE OWNER'S NAME

ADDRESS

CITY	STATE	VEHICLE LICENSE No.

TYPE VEHICLE	MAKE	YEAR	No.

DAMAGE TO OTHER VEHICLE AND/OR PROPERTY

INJURED PERSONS	Age	Sex	Injuries
Name			
Address			
Name			
Address			
Name			
Address			

POLICE Name	Badge No.

BE SURE WITNESS CARDS ARE COLLECTED   *PLACE THEM IN THIS FOLDER*

INDICATE ON THIS DIAGRAM WHAT HAPPENED

INDICATE
NORTH
BY ARROW

SHOW POSITION OF VEHICLES

DRIVER'S SIGNATURE

Figure 5–1 (back).   Accident Report Packet with Accident Memorandum on back.

Figure 5–2. Ask people at the scene to fill out and return a courtesy card.

- Date, day of week, and exact time of day should be recorded.
- The location of the accident should be described so specifically that the memo could be used later to find the exact spot.
- The diagram of the accident should show the direction of travel, the exact location of the vehicles on the street or roadway, obstacles, traffic signs, signals, and

Figure 5–3. If a driver clearly admits guilt at the crash scene, ask him/her to fill out an exoneration card. Reprinted with permission from the American Trucking Associations, Inc. ("ATA"). For more information or to order a copy of the Exoneration Card as part of ATA's Accident Reporting Kit, call ATA's toll free telephone number (800-ATA-LINE) and ask for Item # C1960.

other pertinent objects. The diagram should show exactly what happened and where.

- The accident memorandum, courtesy cards, and other pertinent data should be carefully secured and preserved.

This memorandum report is usually all of the information that a company can expect its drivers to obtain at the scene of an accident. Some companies require their drivers to fill out a much more detailed Driver's Accident Report. Other companies prefer that this report be filled out later, under the supervision of a company official (Figure 4–1).

ACCIDENT INVESTIGATOR'S PROCEDURES

Every company should have an accident investigator who can be dispatched to the scene of an accident, take charge of the company's interests, direct the activities of the driver, and gather data concerning the accident to supplement the data provided by the driver. The accident investigator must be trained in the specifics of conducting a detailed investigation.

Investigator's Role

Frequently, in a city operation or in a small company, no supervisor will be available to investigate. *Company officials should make it clear that accident investigation is a job for the highest local supervisor and takes precedence over sales or other operations responsibilities. It is not to be delegated to noncompany personnel, such as adjusters, mechanics, or tow truck operators.*

If a company driver is killed or disabled in an accident, a responsible company representative must show up promptly to take charge. Even if the driver is not disabled, the company should not rely solely on the driver's account of what happened. Also, good drivers have accidents so rarely that they do not acquire experience in dealing with an accident situation. But an accident investigator who has presided over the cleanup of a number of accidents should have the skill and poise to deal with the situation effectively.

Aside from gathering useful accident prevention information, the trained accident investigator can:

- Keep costs to a minimum. An investigator who arrives quickly at the scene can prevent further damage, protect company property, and prevent looting.
- Prevent excess costs. Efficient handling of an accident provides management control and reduces the opportunity for fraud.
- Expedite the movement of traffic at the scene.
- Preserve vital information. Complete investigation of

DRIVING SUPERVISOR'S ACCIDENT REPORT CHECKLIST

1. Driver's Name:_____   2. Can you talk freely on the phone?_____
3. Where are you?_____
4. Where can you be reached by telephone? _____
5. Are you hurt?_____   6. Are other people hurt?_____
                    (nature of injury)
                                                        7. Is help on the way? _____
8. Have police been called? _____   Where?_____
9. What was the time of the accident? _____ A.M. P.M. 10. What was the exact location of the accident?
_____
11. What happened? _____
_____
12. How bad is the damage to the other vehicle? _____
_____
13. How bad is our equipment damage? _____
14. What are the tractor and trailer unit numbers?_____
_____
15. Do you have witness names? _____ 16. Did you use the exoneration card? _____
_____
17. What equipment will be needed to bring our unit and cargo in? Wrecker?
_____
18. What is the cargo? _____
     Out of: _____ To: _____
19. Is the unit safe in its present spot until a supervisor can get there?_____
     DO NOT MOVE THE UNIT UNLESS ABSOLUTELY NECESSARY.
20. Did you get the other driver's car license, address of owner, insurance carrier, operator's
     license number, etc.? _____
_____
21. Where will you be when the supervisor gets there?_____
22. Driving Supervisor's instructions to the driver: _____
_____
23. Time of call: _____ A.M. P.M. 24. Date:_____ 25. Received by: _____

26. TWX: Safety Dept. on fatal accidents.   27. Phone: Call insurance adjuster.
     Dispatch Dept. on extensive loss or
     delay to explosives, hazardous, and
     radioactive shipments.

Figure 5–4. A telephone checklist helps organize the information received.

the situation is necessary for claims protection. Keeping a consistent record of each accident provides a comparison base for future analysis.

The investigator needs to use the Driver's Accident Report or a similar form to make sure all the necessary data are obtained to protect the company and to help complete the accident reports, the Office of Motor Carriers report, and any other records that may be required.

Because each accident is unique, it may not be practical for the investigator to follow the checklist item by item. The particular situation may necessitate entering facts as they arise. However, as many items as possible should be completed before the investigator leaves the accident scene.

It should be remembered that an accident investigation is a search for facts. The investigator should have an open mind and an unbiased attitude. The investigator is responsible for determining what factors may have contributed to the accident, not merely filling out an accident report. The accident investigator's job is not complete until the following data have been collected:

- all of the factors that contributed to the accident
- how the accident occurred
- all the physical evidence that might have a bearing on

the case
- sufficient information that he or she can reconstruct the entire accident later

What to Investigate

Ideally, all accidents involving vehicles operated by the motor carrier should be investigated to determine their basic causes. In practice, limitations of time and staff, the scope of the company's operations, or other factors may preclude the complete investigation of every accident. However, every accident serious enough to require a report to the Office of Motor Carriers or state regulatory authorities must be investigated.

Accidents involving the following should be investigated thoroughly:

- fatalities and/or personal injuries
- extensive property damage
- transportation of explosives and other hazardous materials, particularly where the nature of the cargo might have contributed to the seriousness of the accident
- vehicles or loads of abnormal dimensions and/or weight
- unusual circumstances

A series of accidents involving factors that suggest a pattern should also be investigated. Such patterns include but are not limited to those involving:

- a single driver, particularly in a relatively short period of time or under recurrent circumstances
- a particular locale
- special types of cargo
- certain types or makes of vehicles (or combinations of same)
- factors in common, such as a particular type of accident

Tools for Investigation

A complete field equipment kit is essential to accurate accident investigation. Factual evidence surrounding an accident site will not stay put for long, and the safety specialist needs to document the evidence quickly and accurately. An initial investment in investigation tools can pay for itself many times over because the tools will clearly document accident damages and sites for insurance claims.

The equipment purchased should be reliable and durable. A well-outfitted equipment kit includes the following:

- **Recording device.** A cassette tape or other recording device is needed for recording driver and witness statements.
- **Photographic equipment.** A camera kit should include a 35mm single-lens reflex (SLR) camera, a 50mm or 55mm lens with macro capability, a wide-angle 24mm or 28mm lens, a high-powered electronic flash unit, spare batteries and film, and a carrying case large enough to store all the equipment. A camcorder is useful to establish the setting of the collision. A videotape of witnesses' first impressions could also be a powerful tool in future litigation.
- **Measuring equipment.** A measuring wheel with a 6-inch or larger wheel (the greater the diameter, the more accurate the measurement), a 100-foot fiberglass or steel tape, 12- and 25-foot "wide body" measuring tapes, a tire tread gauge, and tire pressure gauges are desirable.
- **Accident investigation report kit.** Reporting forms and checklists, paper, pens and pencils, clipboard, courtesy cards (Figure 5–2), business cards, coins or a telephone credit card number for phone calls, lumber crayons, chalk and chalk line, and masking and sealing tapes are important items for the kit.
- **Auxiliary lighting equipment.** Be prepared for after-dark investigations by having floodlights and flashlights with spare batteries.
- **Emergency equipment.** The minimum is a multipurpose dry chemical agent fire extinguisher, a first aid kit, blankets, and a tow rope.
- **Warning devices.** Begin with triangles, reflectors, flares, flags, fusees, and strobe lights; add other approved warning devices as necessary.
- **Tool kit.** In addition to the basics, such as a hammer and pliers, include nails, spikes (to hold the far end of the measuring tape), a plumb bob, a broom, and a shovel.
- **Equipment cases.** Use a sturdy, compartmentalized case large enough to protect all your equipment from damage, weather, and loss. A well-organized equipment case speeds the investigation process and cuts down on equipment loss.

Clothing for Investigation

Many accidents occur during inclement weather. The fleet safety specialist should consider purchasing appropriate protective clothing that stresses comfort, maneuverability, safety, and visibility. These include:

- **Safety vest.** A fluorescent orange safety vest with retroreflective striping can help keep the fleet accident investigator from becoming the cause or victim of a second accident (Figure 5–5).
- **Rain gear.** Coat, boots, and hat in fluorescent orange or another highly visible color are useful, as is a covered clipboard with water-resistant ink pens.
- **Cold-weather gear.** Insulated boots, parkas, and insulated pants in fluorescent orange are available from sports shops.
- **Gloves.** Insulated gloves should be flexible enough

to allow the investigator to use tools and writing materials. Ordinary work gloves can be worn during warmer or dry weather.

Postinvestigation Reporting Aids

The fleet safety specialist must organize the field investigation data into an accurate, concise report. To do so, the specialist will need:

- an accident diagramming template
- a calculator
- architectural scales
- straight-edge rulers

Others Aiding the Investigation

Frequently, the investigator coordinates efforts so other experts can help. The investigator may go to the scene with the insurance adjuster, who will preserve evidence and obtain statements from the participants. The local company maintenance supervisor (if there is one) should be called on to help resolve mechanical questions and get the damaged equipment ready to be brought in. Other drivers or loaders may be needed on the scene and may contribute valuable insights into the causes of the accident.

The following detailed procedure assumes that the investigator will be doing the entire job alone and that the accident is serious enough to warrant a great deal of investigative time. The basic procedure can be modified for simpler accidents or those where other experts will perform some of the work.

Steps in the Investigation

Arrival at scene. The investigator should park where his or her vehicle will not obstruct traffic or contribute to another accident. At night, the vehicle can be parked so the headlights illuminate the scene but do not blind oncoming motorists.

The investigator should make sure triangles, flares, fusees, or other approved warning devices have been placed in accordance with regulations and to ensure maximum protection. The investigator should be wearing a fluorescent orange safety vest with retroreflective stripes or other outer garment in a highly visible color. The investigator should then:

- Show identification to the police at the scene, or when they arrive, and give them full cooperation.
- If necessary, assist in protecting the injured until medical aid arrives. (Use caution and judgment to avoid aggravating an injury.)
- Check the bystanders for possible witnesses and volunteer helpers.
- Take steps to protect company property from theft or damage.
- Examine the area carefully for any possible hazards, such as spilled gasoline, flammables, or broken electrical cabling.
- Look for any evidence that may be associated with the

Figure 5–5.   The value of retroreflective strips on work vests is apparent in these day and night photos. Courtesy 3M Scotchlite ™ Reflective Material.

accident and have it guarded until it can be properly examined.

- Locate the driver of the company vehicle, provide identification, and take charge of the situation. Take possession of all reports and any information the driver may have.

Information gathering. To pursue a step-by-step accident investigation (such as shown in Figure 4–1), the investigator should bear in mind the following:

1. Time. Record the exact date, day of the week, and hour of the day the accident occurred. If the vehicle is equipped with a tachograph, the chart will show these. If not, every effort should be made to determine the exact time when the accident happened.

2. Accident location. Be specific enough so that a complete stranger could take the report later and go directly to the scene where the accident occurred. It isn't enough to say "accident occurred in the county of Fulton, 10 miles north of Atlanta on U.S. Route 29." Add more specific information: "355 feet south of utility pole No. 647328" or "550 feet north of the north end of a bridge abutment where U.S. Highway 29 crosses Rising Creek." The diagram should reference these specific points. (Data should agree with the accident memorandum, previously filled out.)

3. Accident involved. Describe exactly what was involved in the accident. If there was another vehicle, determine (a) its type and (b) whether the vehicle itself (not just the action of its operator) contributed anything to the accident by virtue of its type, color, or other characteristics. If any pedestrians were involved, indicate the contribution of each to the accident. If there is a fixed object involved, describe it in detail, including the location, size, shape, marks, and any other pertinent data.

4. Type of accident. Determine the accident type (Figure 4–1, Driver's Accident Report form) and record it in the accident report. Any information with regard to type not covered in the accident report should be described completely to avoid doubt or indecision.

5. Drivers. Identify the driver of each vehicle by complete name, exact address, operator's or chauffeur's license number, and any other information necessary.

6. Vehicles. Identify all vehicles involved in the accident by type, make, model year, vehicle identification number (VIN), company number (if any), and state and number of the license. Describe the damage to the vehicles and the damage to cargo or other property. Any estimates should be as accurate as possible.

7. Injured. List the exact name and the address, age, and sex of every injured person. However, do not antagonize an injured person by persistent questioning in public. Wait until a better time presents itself, such as at the hospital or the person's home. Describe the injuries as completely as possible. The injuries can be verified and any changes made in the notes when you visit the doctor's office or hospital. Specify whether the injured persons were drivers of vehicles, passengers, or pedestrians. Give their relationship to the accident.

8. Witnesses. Seek out witnesses as soon as possible. They are not obligated to remain at the scene and may leave before you have a chance to question them. First, record their license numbers so you can contact them later if needed. Witnesses may often be found talking to a driver, discussing the accident with each other, or examining the damage. Check the courtesy cards turned over by the driver. The complete name (accurately spelled) and address of every witness is important. Make note of how these persons can be contacted at work or any other place they might be.

Indicate any interest the witness may have in the accident—whether as investigating police officer, bystander, passenger in a company vehicle, passenger in the other vehicle involved, or any other designation. The driver of a vehicle that escaped damage may well have been involved in the situation leading to the accident. Get statements from such persons.

All passengers involved should be interviewed, especially in serious accidents. It may be helpful to determine their relationship to the driver to detect possible bias. Establish the passenger's position in the vehicle to determine if the passenger could actually have seen the accident occur. Also find out what the passenger was doing at the time of the accident. Make sure the witness actually saw the accident happen. Note only facts, not the opinions of witnesses.

Double-check exactly what the witness is saying. For instance, if the witness says a vehicle was traveling "fast," determine what he or she considers fast. Similarly, if the witness says "a long distance," determine approximately how long.

To enhance the reliability of witness testimony:

- If your insurance adjuster is available, ask him or her to question the witnesses; adjusters are usually experts at this.
- Show every witness courtesy and consideration at all times.
- Interview each witness separately, with no other witnesses present, whenever practical.
- Get the witness's full story before asking questions or citing any contrary or conflicting statements made by other witnesses.
- If it serves a useful purpose, quote other witnesses' statements, but never use their names.

- Never attempt to coerce witnesses who refuse to make a statement.
- Never engage in any controversies with witnesses.
- Never retaliate against hostile witnesses.

9. Movement. Describe the exact movements of all vehicles, passengers, and pedestrians at the moment of the accident. In many cases, more than one box should be checked for each vehicle involved. Make an effort to show exactly where each pedestrian was in relation to the accident. Identify any passengers involved, whether or not they were injured.

10. Conditions.

Drivers and pedestrian(s). Use this section of the report to describe completely the condition of every person involved in the accident. Check all appropriate boxes; use additional space if necessary. Look for any evidence of intoxication or physical defects in pedestrians, drivers, and other witnesses.

In attempting to determine the driver's condition prior to the accident, take into account such items as prior delays, coffee stops, arguments, fatigue, and schedules. The original copy of the driver's data logs or tachograph charts can help establish the driver's mental alertness and disposition just before the accident and suggest future remedies for the particular type of accident. It may be helpful to establish how much sleep the driver had one to four days before the accident.

Upon returning to the office, secure the following information about the driver from the fleet's personnel files:

- length of employment
- training
- overall driving experience and experience in driving the particular type of vehicle involved in the accident
- attitude toward job
- record of physical examinations
- illnesses and personal problems
- accident record
- record of traffic violations
- commendations or disciplinary actions

Vehicles. Determine whether the mechanical condition of each vehicle involved may have been a contributing factor in the accident. The thoroughness of the check at the accident scene should be based on the extent of damage to the vehicle. If possible, perform a road test to determine brake performance, including a test of the braking system for leakage or inoperative parts. Check thoroughly the steering mechanism, noticeable damage to wheel alignment, engine performance, and any other mechanisms affecting the safe operation of the vehicle.

Company maintenance supervisors should assist in this evaluation.

If, as a result of the accident, the condition of the vehicle does not permit a road check at the accident scene, investigate it thoroughly upon its return to the storage or repair location. Use extreme care when attempting to determine whether a vehicle part or system was inoperative before the accident or as a result of the accident. In very serious accidents where lawsuits can be expected, it pays to hire a reputable independent expert who can later testify about the evaluation.

Weather. Note the weather conditions at the time of the accident. Also indicate whether any previous weather condition may have contributed to the accident. For instance, sun glare can blind a driver and obscure signals, pedestrians, and other vehicles.

Roadway. The roadway itself contributes to a number of accidents. Note this on the accident report, then record a more detailed description of the roadway on extra paper.

11. Contributing factors. Usually several factors contribute to an accident, so in most cases more than one box should be checked for each vehicle involved.

- Speed. As a contributing factor to many accidents, speed is important enough to warrant special consideration. Fill out this section of the report carefully, estimating the speed of each vehicle involved as accurately as possible. Here again, if the report does not have sufficient space to describe the situation completely, use extra paper.
- The trip. Investigate the origin, destination, and related distances of the trip on which the accident occurred. If the total trip extends over more than one day, note the point at which driving began that day, as well as the origin and destination of the entire trip. Also note the distance from the point of origin to the accident scene. List stops en route, time spent at each, and the driver's activities at each stop. Retrace the driver's activities for at least 24 hours prior to the accident, showing time spent on and off duty. Investigate the driver's activities over a longer period of time preceding the accident if it appears desirable.

The original copy of the driver's log record for the same period should be placed in the company's accident file. If the vehicle was equipped with an operations recorder, examine the chart, especially for speed and stops en route, and compare it with the driver's log. The original chart should be a permanent part of the accident file.

Insofar as possible, reconstruct the activities of other drivers or persons involved to determine whether their actions or physical and mental conditions contributed to the accident. This investigation should also cover at least 24 hours before the accident. Information on the activities of other persons will generally have to be developed through direct inquiry. Their answers may have to be verified.

12. Accident diagram. The accident diagram should be comprehensive enough to show at a glance exactly what happened. Graph paper can enhance the accuracy of the diagram. A plotting device, such as the Northwestern University investigator's traffic template, will help diagram the accident site. (The traffic template is available from the Traffic Institute, Northwestern University, Evanston, IL 60204.) In drawing the accident scene, record both primary and secondary factors.

The following primary factors should be. available from actual measurements taken at the accident site:

- Width of roadway, including condition and type of pavement. Indicate whether the roadway is new, slippery from oil deposits, covered with deposits of sand, gravel, or stones, or full of holes or ruts.
- Width and number of traffic lanes; assign numbers to each lane.
- Width and condition of shoulder (berm) of road, including any dropoff from the pavement edge to the shoulder. Record the depth and running length of this "lip" accurately.
- Point of impact, as indicated by physical evidence. Describe that physical evidence.
- Dimensions of any intersecting street, roadway, alley, or driveway.
- Location and direction of travel of each vehicle before the impact, at impact, and after impact.
- The exact location of the accident so its site can be definitely located later. You might identify a number on an adjacent utility pole, such as "three feet east of center line, 50 feet northeast of utility pole number 16847." Or you might designate any permanent object, such as "three feet east of center line, 300 feet north of the north side of Cain Creek Bridge, Highway 41, six miles north of Citizenville, IL."

The following secondary factors should be available from actual measurements:

- Length of skid mark for each wheel.
- Exact position and physical description (for example, size and height) of any objects that might have obstructed the vision of any driver, such as buildings, trees, embankments, or billboards.
- Exact location of debris, spilled liquids, marks, scratches, or gouges in the pavement made by any of the vehicles involved. Mark the location of liquid spills and stains and other temporary debris with a lumber crayon after taking the photo for the accident report.

- Exact location of any traffic sign, signal, or other traffic control device. Indicate whether or not devices were working at the time of the accident. If a driver's view of the device was obstructed by foliage or other objects, defaced by markings, or obliterated by road film, note this on the diagram (and report).
- Location of fixed objects near the scene or debris that appears in the photographs, as well as any measurements related to these objects.
- Exact points from which photos were taken. Two diagrams may be necessary if many of the above items are noted.

The following measurements are usually needed:

- skid marks
- sight distances
- point of impact and final resting position of the vehicle(s)
- location of dead or injured victims
- point at which vehicle ran off the road
- distance to fixed objects from which photos were taken

To increase accuracy, take all measurements with a measuring tape or measuring wheel. Find witnesses who can verify their accuracy if called upon. Triangulation and coordinates are the standard methods of location measurement.

Triangulation. To locate objects in the accident diagrams by triangulation, simply find two fixed points, such as a utility pole or tree and a utility cover on or near the road. Then measure from the object to be located to each of these points. To finish the triangle, measure the distance between the fixed points (Figure 5–6).

To later locate the exact spot at which the accident occurred, use the distances measured and swing two arcs

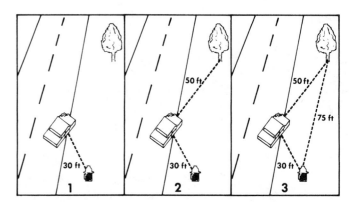

Figure 5–6. To pinpoint location by triangulation, (1) measure from debris to a fixed object (in this figure, a fire hydrant), (2) measure the distance to another fixed object (a tree), and (3) measure the distance between the fixed objects.

from the fixed points. Clearly identify all fixed reference points so that anyone returning to the accident scene could determine the exact points referenced in the accident diagram.

Coordinates. The coordinates method of location measurement uses two reference lines, usually at right angles to each other. The two lines are chosen from the natural features of the accident site, such as roadway edges, berms, center lanes, and railroad tracks.

The intersection of the two reference lines is the reference point. Measure along the reference lines from the reference point to the spot nearest the vehicle or object. Then measure a right angle from the reference line to the object (Figure 5–7).

Detailed explanations of both the triangulation and coordinates systems of measurement can be found in J. Stannard Baker's *Traffic Accident Investigation Manual* (see Appendix E, Bibliography and Additional Resources).

13. Driver's account of accident. This section of the investigation requires the driver's own statement regarding how the accident occurred. Interview the company driver carefully, while the facts are still fresh, to obtain a detailed account.

Find out how the driver attempted to avoid involvement in the events leading to the accident. Establish whether the driver could possibly have avoided the accident. Obtain his or her observations and a statement of actions leading up to the accident. Through tachographs, logs, and schedules, establish the driver's approximate operating speed before the accident situation developed. Learn when and how the accident situation was first noticed.

14. Suggestions. This portion of the report asks for the driver's opinion as to how he or she can prevent future accidents of this type.

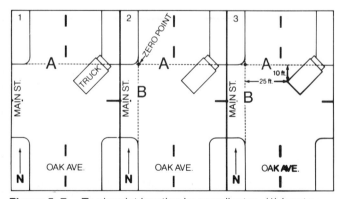

Figure 5–7. To pinpoint location by coordinates, (1) locate and trace a reference line A from an easily identified feature at the accident site, (2) locate and trace reference line B, not necessarily at a right angle, and (3) measure the shortest distance at right angles to each of the two reference lines.

15. Photographs. Photography is an excellent way to record facts and preserve evidence that may be needed in the future. It can also record details the investigator may fail to notice. Photos should be taken of the accident scene as soon as possible to record (a) the position of the vehicles before they are moved; (b) debris such as broken glass, oil stains, or hubcaps before they are moved or obliterated; and (c) skid marks.

- For the most complete record, take several photos of the accident scene: (a) in each direction from the point of impact; (b) from each approach to the point of impact, showing the view each driver had approaching the key point of the accident, as well as road alignment; (c) a close-up of the scene, showing the point of impact; and (d) an overall view of the scene.

- For each vehicle, show the extent of damage. Try to establish the angle of collision and the movement of each vehicle while in contact.

- Photograph debris, skid marks, or any other physical evidence of vehicular movement before and after impact.

- Photograph any broken vehicle parts. Try to establish whether the accident caused the damage or the damage preceded the accident.

- Take any other photos that will preserve data such as road defects, improper signage, obstructions, foliage that blocks the view, or other physical conditions that may have contributed to the accident. Identify on each photo time and date taken, direction in which taken, and location from which taken. Use measurements to pinpoint the location.

Follow-up. The next step in the accident investigation involves clearing the scene. This should be done as quickly and completely as possible, even to the extent of sweeping the roadway to remove debris.

Follow-up also involves removing damaged cargo to a place where it can be salvaged or recouped; transporting undamaged cargo to its destination (in the case of a bus accident, this would be passengers, baggage, and any express); and arranging for disabled vehicles to be removed to the proper repair agency for detailed estimates of damage and ultimate repair or wrecking.

Obtain a copy of the investigating police agency's report for the accident file. This report should provide all factual information determined by the investigating police officer, as well as any citations or summons given. In some states, this report will not reveal the investigating officer's opinion, but this is not a problem because such opinions are not admissible as evidence. If the case goes to court, the investigating officer can testify only to the factual information in the report.

Contact the physician who attended the injured person(s) for detailed information about the nature and extent of injuries. If the injured were hospitalized, hospital author-ities should also be contacted. Decide whether or not to visit injured persons while they are in the hospital based on company policy and the insurance adjuster's wishes.

THE POSTACCIDENT INTERVIEW

As soon as possible after an accident, the driver should be interviewed by the supervisor and/or the terminal man-ager. The safety director can give advice, but supervisory personnel must conduct the interview to avoid diluting management authority.

Objectives of the Interview

The objectives of the postaccident interview are to:

1. Impress upon the driver the importance of driving safely.

2. Determine whether the accident was preventable or not, in accordance with company standards of safe driving practice.

3. Help the driver learn from this accident how to pre-vent similar accidents.

Preparation

The supervisor should prepare for the interview by study-ing the driver's entire past safety record. For example, the driver's record may show three years' driving experience with tractors and semitrailers before the date of employ-ment. In the 29 months since coming to the company, he has driven the same type of equipment. The card shows one other accident while driving for the company, 11 months ago, and one summons for failing to stop at a stop sign.

The current accident occurred at dusk, four hours' driving time away from the terminal. The truck was side-swiped as the driver was pulling away from the curb after a temporary stop. According to the accident report, the driver was attempting to maneuver into the center lane to make a left turn at an intersection. He signaled, but not soon enough to warn the car behind.

In the previous accident, which occurred shortly after sundown after about four hours of driving, the company vehicle was struck from the rear while turning out to pass another vehicle that had slowed abruptly. The accident report showed that, although a quick turnout was neces-sary to avoid striking the vehicle ahead, the company driver had been following too closely and going too fast for the conditions of visibility and had not allowed suffi-cient time to signal the vehicle behind.

The supervisor will note the factors common to both accidents—they occurred at twilight after a period of steady driving, both involved failure to watch out for vehicles behind when entering a different traffic lane, and both involved improper signaling. The supervisor will plan the interview to emphasize these points.

In the preparation phase, the supervisor should also note all nonpreventable accidents the driver has had. An informal tabulation can show how many preventable and nonpreventable accidents the driver has had compared with the group average of the fleet. The supervisor can also tabulate the costs of this driver's accidents and project them over the years remaining before the driver's retire-ment. This information will make the driver aware that the accidents reflect on his driving ability and cost the com-pany money. The safety director can be of real service here.

The supervisor should also study all materials avail-able on the current accident and arrive at a tentative decision as to whether it was preventable or nonprevent-able.

Conducting the Interview

The postaccident interview should be conducted in a place where the supervisor and driver can have complete privacy and as much time as they need. Although the interview should be conducted with an air of objectivity, the interviewer should project a spirit of friendly helpful-ness.

Even if the accident was a minor one, it's important to discover whether any faulty driving habits were involved. If so, point out to the driver that the habit which caused this accident could cause a much more serious accident in the future if not corrected.

After impressing upon the driver the importance of safe driving, comparing ratings with those of other drivers, and projecting the cost of accidents that could be expected in the future, the supervisor should turn to a dis-cussion of the present accident. The supervisor already has studied all available information about the accident and the driver. The supervisor and the driver "think through together" the details of the accident: what was (or was not) done, what might (or might not) have been done, and what should (or should not) have been done. In this part of the interview, the driver does most of the talking; the supervisor guides the discussion by means of a question or observation now and then.

After the accident has been thoroughly discussed, the supervisor should ask the driver whether he or she could have prevented it with better defensive driving. If the driver says no, the supervisor should ask, "Does this mean that if you are permitted to continue to drive, every time this situation occurs, you will be involved in an accident?" To answer this key question, the driver is forced to view the accident more objectively in terms of its preventability. Therefore, this question is crucial.

In concluding the interview, the supervisor should sum up the accident details, announce the decision as to preventability, explain why that decision was made, and point out what the driver can do to prevent a recurrence. If a sound decision has been made and the interview was conducted properly, the driver will agree with this decision and accept it with good grace. The driver will leave the interview feeling that it was fair and reasonable and having acquired a heightened respect for safe driving.

If the driver does not agree with the supervisor's decision as to preventability, some companies provide for a review of the accident and a decision by an accident review committee. If the driver is still not satisfied (or the company itself is not sure how the accident should be classified), the accident facts can be submitted to the Motor Transportation Department of the National Safety Council for a decision. (Contact the Council for procedures and costs of submitting an accident for review.)

Preventability should be decided by a trained local supervisor wherever possible, or at least by some authorized person at the location where the driver works. The decision should be made as soon after the accident as possible. Time tends to blur the details and importance of an accident. Drivers will learn more from the interview and be more accepting of a "preventable accident" decision when the accident is fresh in their minds. The supervisor should state the decision as his or her own and not hide behind such phrases as, "The company treats all accidents as preventable," or "I could never get the main office to accept this accident as being nonpreventable."

Trained supervisors can make sound decisions on accident preventability regardless of their own driving experience. Supervisors may not have as much road experience as some of the veteran drivers, but they have made a careful study of the concept of accident preventability. They have acquired an authoritative grasp of the essentials by reviewing and discussing numerous accidents with different drivers.

ACCIDENT REPEATERS

One of the most important functions of an accident record system is to spot drivers who are accident repeaters so they can be brought to the attention of management and the safety department for remedial training. Fleets differ in their definition of an accident repeater, but usually it means someone who has a second accident within six months, nine months, or a year. City drivers are allowed a shorter period of time between accidents than are intercity drivers due to the greater hazards of city operations. The real key is the average preventable accident frequency per driver of the group as a whole. A driver's below-average performance points to an accident repeater.

After a second accident, drivers are given the regular postaccident interview, but they may also receive additional attention:

1. They are sent a warning letter, with a copy to the union if the driver is represented by one.

2. A driver trainer or supervisor is assigned to ride with them and report on their driving habits.

3. Special safety meetings or training courses, such as the National Safety Council's Defensive Driving Course, are scheduled periodically for all accident repeaters. New approaches to learning, new films, and new techniques can keep the meetings from seeming more like a penalty than a learning experience.

A number of other corrective procedures are sometimes used, including special physical examinations and counseling. When drivers continue to have accidents in spite of such efforts, the company has no recourse but to reassign them to nondriving jobs or to discharge them. Accurate and complete accident records are vital in case a driver takes the company's decision to arbitration.

CHAPTER
6

Employee Injury Record Keeping and Analysis

The objective of an occupational injury reporting and investigation program is to eliminate from the workplace all unsafe practices and conditions that could cause personal injury or property damage. If these hazards are removed, then employee injuries can be controlled. In spite of safe conditions, however, accidental injuries can still occur. When they do, companies should attempt to learn what factors caused these accidents to prevent them from happening again.

Various reasons have been given as to why some workers get hurt and others do not. Some reasons are valid, such as lack of experience and lack of attention. But only an accurate description of the actual causes can indicate what proper corrective or preventive action should be taken. There is little reason to determine the basic cause(s) of a personal injury if there is no commitment to set up practical measures for preventing injuries from similar causes in the future. Why investigate if no action will be taken?

This chapter discusses the most important responsibilities of an injury investigation committee. The committee must gather all the facts, evaluate them to determine the cause or causes of an injury, and finally, propose ways to eliminate or reduce the frequency of occurrence and reduce the severity of injuries.

RECORD-KEEPING SYSTEM

To determine the leading causes of accidents over time, a company must develop a record-keeping system. The Occupational Safety and Health Administration (OSHA) has mandated a record-keeping system that should serve as a first step toward developing an individualized company system. Although data gathered for OSHA have limited usefulness in a company's comprehensive accident prevention program, such information is a legal requirement. Poor record keeping was the second most common source of OSHA citations in fiscal 1993. In its *Record-keeping Guidelines for Occupational Injuries and Illnesses,* OSHA states, "The relatively simple OSHA recording boundaries assure a valid, consistent, and uniform record-keeping system that is capable of producing reliable statistical information."

Objective of the System

The objective of the record-keeping provisions is to generate accurate statistics. However, a system designed for all employers must be, by necessity, somewhat general. The problem for the safety professional is that general information does not solve specific problems.

Thus, relying on OSHA record-keeping regulations is not sufficient to help a company develop an effective accident prevention program. OSHA recognized this shortcoming in its Voluntary Protection Program. "It has long been recognized that compliance with its standards cannot by itself accomplish all the goals established by the (OSHAct of 1970)."

With these limitations in mind, a short discussion of OSHA record keeping is still in order. The company should obtain OSHA's record-keeping guidelines and *A Brief Guide to Record-keeping Requirements for Occupational Injuries and Illnesses.* The forms required include OSHA No. 200 and OSHA No. 101. Both the publications and the forms are free from the nearest OSHA office, Bureau of Labor Statistics regional office, or participating state agency.

Classification

Flowcharts are the simplest way to visualize the record-keeping requirements. Use the flowchart titled "Guidelines for Establishing Work Relationship" (Figure 6–1) to properly categorize an incident.

The first question is whether an injury or illness was work related. This question provides the answer to the first decision block in the flowchart (Figure 6–2). Most of the remaining decision blocks are self-evident, but two require special attention.

The decision on whether a case involves first aid or medical treatment is not as simple as it may seem, but requires a careful reading of the guidelines. If an antiseptic is applied during a second or subsequent visit to medical personnel, the injury must be recorded. Because many firms use the OSHA recordable frequency rate for comparison in competition, there is a tendency to "work around" the definitions.

For example, OSHA revised the definition of medical treatment to include specifically "butterfly adhesive dressing(s) or Steri Strip(s) in lieu of sutures." Some firms had used these adhesives to avoid the recording requirement presented by sutures. This deception did not help the employees, the accident prevention program, or the accuracy of OSHA's statistics.

The other troublesome decision block is the "Restriction of Work or Motion." In OSHA's own example, a laceration to the knuckle that required only a small bandage would probably be classified as recordable for a typist but not for an executive. The difference is that the executive might be inconvenienced but the typist might have to do other work until the wound healed.

Such differences may seem insignificant, but large firms have received six-figure fines for systematically underreporting recordable injuries and illnesses.

OSHA Forms

Once the injury/illness is classified as recordable, the safety director should document the facts in the case on

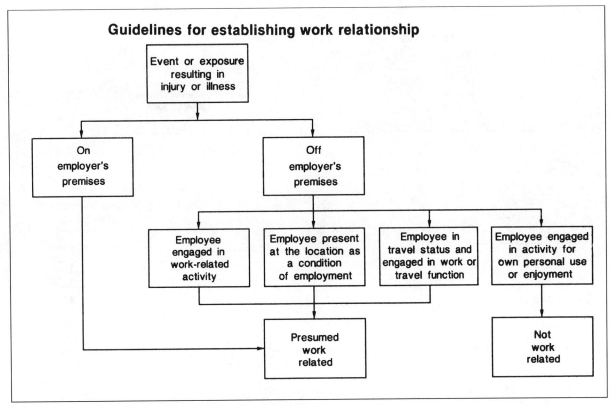

Figure 6–1. Guidelines for establishing work relationship.

OSHA Form No. 101 (Figure 6–3) or an equivalent method. To minimize both the paperwork and duplicate efforts to gather the information this form requires, the safety director should incorporate the information into other required documents at the same time. Examples include data that must be recorded on workers' compensation reports of injury, insurance forms, and existing injury report forms. The ideal method would be to enter this information directly into a single data base. The computer could then generate all of the required documents from a single entry.

With OSHA No. 101 complete, it is time to enter the injury on the OSHA 200 Log (Figure 6–4). The entry must be made within six days of notification of the injury. Because this log will be part of any OSHA inspection activity, accuracy is essential. The information should be entered to the proper columns for each recordable injury.

If an injury is later reclassified as not recordable, the entry should be voided with a single line drawn through it. Neither correction fluid nor erasures should be used to void entries. The documentation justifying the removal should be retained with the original Form No. 101. This form may be maintained at another location on computer, but a copy must be available at the site where the update was made within 45 calendar days.

Each year, a summary of OSHA Form No. 200 must be posted. The portion to the right of the arrows must be posted by February 1 and remain until March 1. The Bureau

of Labor Statistics may mail selected firms a copy of OSHA No. 200–S. Any firm receiving one of these forms must complete it and return the form within three weeks. The front of the form contains general information about the firm. The reverse side repeats the data from the posted portion of Form 200.

After working through all of the required reports, the safety professional will see that a great deal of information is available. The company's overall safety performance can be compared to the performance of other firms. But the data are not in a usable form for detailed analysis of the cause(s) of accidents—recordable and not recordable. The next section will provide a structure for that essential analysis.

DATA ANALYSIS

For information to be analyzed in a meaningful way, it must be organized in a convenient form. The analyst seeks clusters of common factors that can be used to draw conclusions regarding cause.

Classifying Factors

When an analysis is conducted, factors must be classified or categorized according to a workable scheme, whether the sorting is done by hand or by computer. The objective

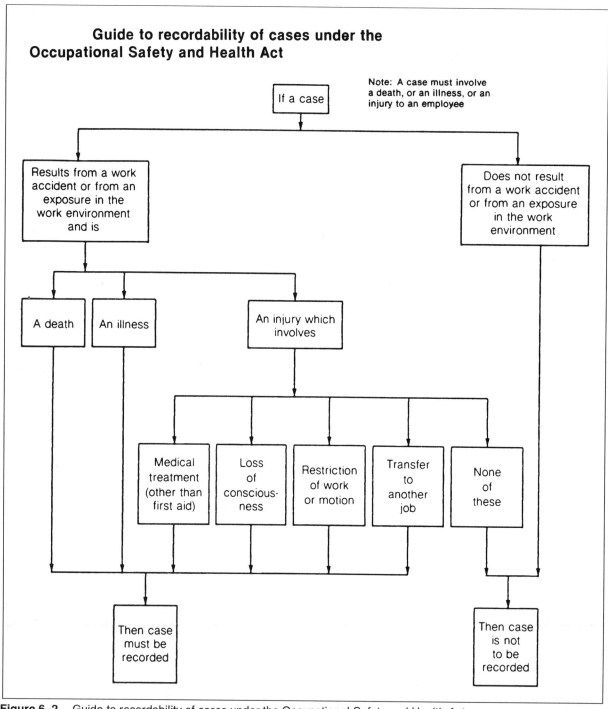

Figure 6–2.   Guide to recordability of cases under the Occupational Safety and Health Act.

is to describe the factors as specifically and unambiguously as possible. The approach is very much like the accounting system's chart of accounts. There, too, proper categorization is key to accurate records.

For instance, the nature of an injury must be categorized. Injury types include burn, laceration, puncture wound, and fracture. These types can be classified into more specific categories. Fractures, for example, can be subdivided into hairline, undisplaced, displaced, and compound.

The part of the body is another categorization that will be useful in determining type of injury and causes of accidents. Examples include head, torso, upper extremity, and lower extremity. Subdivide the upper extremity to the hand, then further to the finger, and more specifically to the phalanges (finger bones), if necessary. However, the

Bureau of Labor Statistics
Supplementary Record of
Occupational Injuries and Illnesses

U.S. Department of Labor

This form is required by Public Law 91-596 and must be kept in the establishment for *5 years.* Failure to maintain can result in the issuance of citations and assessment of penalties.	Case or File No.	Form Approved O.M.B. No. 1220-0029

Employer

1. Name

2. Mail address *(No. and street, city or town, State, and zip code)*

3. Location, if different from mail address

Injured or Ill Employee

4. Name *(First, middle, and last)*   Social Security No.

5. Home address *(No. and street, city or town, State, and zip code)*

6. Age   7. Sex: *(Check one)*   Male ☐   Female ☐

8. Occupation *(Enter regular job title, not the specific activity he was performing at time of injury.)*

9. Department *(Enter name of department or division in which the injured person is regularly employed, even though he may have been temporarily working in another department at the time of injury.)*

The Accident or Exposure to Occupational Illness

If accident or exposure occurred on employer's premises, give address of plant or establishment in which it occurred. Do not indicate department or division within the plant or establishment. If accident occurred outside employer's premises at an identifiable address, give that address. If it occurred on a public highway or at any other place which cannot be identified by number and street, please provide place references locating the place of injury as accurately as possible.

10. Place of accident or exposure *(No. and street, city or town, State, and zip code)*

11. Was place of accident or exposure on employer's premises?   Yes ☐   No ☐

12. What was the employee doing when injured? *(Be specific. If he was using tools or equipment or handling material, name them and tell what he was doing with them.)*

13. How did the accident occur? *(Describe fully the events which resulted in the injury or occupational illness. Tell what happened and how it happened. Name any objects or substances involved and tell how they were involved. Give full details on all factors which led or contributed to the accident. Use separate sheet for additional space.)*

Occupational Injury or Occupational Illness

14. Describe the injury or illness in detail and indicate the part of body affected. *(E.g., amputation of right index finger at second joint; fracture of ribs; lead poisoning; dermatitis of left hand, etc.)*

15. Name the object or substance which directly injured the employee. *(For example, the machine or thing he struck against or which struck him; the vapor or poison he inhaled or swallowed; the chemical or radiation which irritated his skin; or in cases of strains, hernias, etc., the thing he was lifting, pulling, etc.)*

16. Date of injury or initial diagnosis of occupational illness   17. Did employee die? *(Check one)*   Yes ☐   No ☐

Other

18. Name and address of physician

19. If hospitalized, name and address of hospital

Date of report	Prepared by	Official position

OSHA No. 101 (Feb. 1981)

Figure 6–3. Supplementary Record of Occupational Injuries and Illnesses, Form No. 101.

Bureau of Labor Statistics
Log and Summary of Occupational
Injuries and Illnesses

U.S. Department of Labor

For Calendar Year 19 _____

Page _____ of _____

Form Approved
O.M.B. No. 1220-0029
See OMB Disclosure
Statement on reverse

NOTE: This form is required by Public Law 91-596 and must be kept in the establishment for 5 years. Failure to maintain and post can result in the issuance of citations and assessment of penalties. (See posting requirements on the other side of form.)

RECORDABLE CASES: You are required to record information about every occupational death; every nonfatal occupational illness; and those nonfatal occupational injuries which involve one or more of the following: loss of consciousness, restriction of work or motion, transfer to another job, or medical treatment (other than first aid). (See definitions on the other side of form.)

Company Name
Establishment Name
Establishment Address

Case or File Number

(A) Enter a nonduplicating number which will facilitate comparisons with supplementary records.

(B) Date of Injury or Onset of Illness — Enter Mo./day.

(C) Employee's Name — Enter first name or initial, middle initial, last name.

(D) Occupation — Enter regular job title, not activity employee was performing when injured or at onset of illness. In the absence of a formal title, enter a brief description of the employee's duties.

(E) Department — Enter department in which the employee is regularly employed or a description of normal workplace to which employee is assigned, even though temporarily working in another department at the time of injury or illness.

(F) Description of Injury or Illness — Enter a brief description of the injury or illness and indicate the part or parts of body affected.

Typical entries for this column might be: Amputation of 1st joint forefinger; Strain of lower back; Contact dermatitis on both hands; Electrocution-body.

Extent of and Outcome of INJURY

Fatalities — Injury Related — (1) Enter DATE of death. Mo./day/yr.

Nonfatal Injuries

Injuries With Lost Workdays
(2) Enter a CHECK if injury involves days away from work, or days of restricted work activity, or both.
(3) Enter a CHECK if injury involves days away from work.
(4) Enter number of DAYS away from work.
(5) Enter number of DAYS of restricted work activity.

Injuries Without Lost Workdays
(6) Enter a CHECK if no entry was made in columns 1 or 2 but the injury is recordable as defined above.

Type, Extent of, and Outcome of ILLNESS

Type of Illness

CHECK Only One Column for Each Illness
(See other side of form for terminations or permanent transfers.)
(a) Occupational skin diseases or disorders
(b) Dust diseases of the lungs
(c) Respiratory conditions due to toxic agents
(d) Poisoning (systemic effects of toxic materials)
(e) Disorders due to physical agents
(f) Disorders associated with repeated trauma
(g) All other occupational illnesses

Fatalities — Illness Related — (8) Enter DATE of death. Mo./day/yr.

Nonfatal Illness

Illnesses With Lost Workdays
(9) Enter a CHECK if illness involves days away from work, or days of restricted work activity, or both.
(10) Enter a CHECK if illness involves days away from work.
(11) Enter number of DAYS away from work.
(12) Enter number of DAYS of restricted work activity.

Illnesses Without Lost Workdays
(13) Enter a CHECK if no entry was made in columns 8 or 9.

PREVIOUS PAGE TOTALS

TOTALS (Instructions on other side of form.)

Certification of Annual Summary Totals By _____ Title _____ Date _____

POST ONLY THIS PORTION OF THE LAST PAGE NO LATER THAN FEBRUARY 1.

OSHA No. 200

Figure 6-4. Log and Summary of Occupational Injuries and Illnesses, Form No. 200.

analyst should avoid creating too many subdivisions within one category. For example, no one will argue against the value of analyzing oil expenses for large vehicles, but you will never see that cost noted in a corporation's annual report as a line item. Costs for oil are subtotaled into the accounts for truck maintenance, vehicle maintenance, fleet operating expense, and finally operating expense.

The safety director should be interested in the same objective of reducing costs and improving operations. Safety efforts should produce a reduction in death, injury, and property damage. Like the accountant with a single account for overall operating expenses, the safety director cannot analyze the causes of injury with statements like "organization had 20 injuries."

To provide more detail, a company needs a system of categorization similar to the bookkeeper's chart of accounts. The American National Standards Institute (ANSI) Z16.2, *Method of Recording Basic Facts Relating to Nature and Occurrence of Work Injuries,* is one such system. Although this standard has inactive status at ANSI, it is currently undergoing revision to bring it into line with the Bureau of Labor Statistics' *Occupational Injury and Illness Classification Manual.* Its definitions will be used here for demonstration purposes.

Whether a firm uses the ANSI standard or one of its own making, it should use the accounting analogy when purchasing or developing software. For example, an injury to the finger would be automatically subtotaled both to the hand and to the upper extremity categories.

Categories and Causes of Injuries

Categories that will aid the search for injury causes include:

- The *nature of injury* or illness identifies the principal physical characteristic(s) of the injury or illness.
- The *part of body affected* identifies the part of the body directly affected by the injury or illness.
- The *source of injury or illness* identifies the object, substance, bodily motion, or exposure that directly produced or inflicted the injury or illness.
- The *event or exposure* describes how the injury or illness was caused by the source of injury or illness.
- The *secondary source of injury or illness* is the object, substance, or person that generated the source of injury or illness or that contributed to the event or exposure.

For example, suppose a maintenance employee loses an eye while using a pedestal grinder. The *nature of injury* is loss of an eye. The *part of body* is obviously the eye. The *source of injury* was the pedestal grinder. The *event* was the shattering of the grinding wheel. The *secondary source*

of injury was the shop towel that was wrapped around the part being ground. It was pulled into the gap and jammed the part into the brittle wheel. Pieces of the wheel entered the employee's eye.

This type of information, gathered over time, will help management focus their resources on corrective actions to eliminate the causes of injury and illness. Two important management responsibilities are to ensure that safe work practices are taught and then monitored for compliance and to maintain a safe workplace free of unsafe conditions. The employee's failure to wear safety glasses, the missing eye shield on the grinder, and the half-inch gap between the tool rest and the grinding wheel certainly contributed to the cause of the incident.

Measuring management's effectiveness in maintaining safe conditions and practices is essential to improving safety performance. For that purpose, Figure 6–5 lists examples of unsafe conditions and practices that can lead to an employee injury. These items can be used as thought starters and modified to suit the hazards in specific operations.

OCCUPATIONAL INJURY REPORTING AND RECORD-KEEPING SYSTEM

Once an organization accepts the principle that accidents are caused, it has reached the point where it can determine the individual causes of accidents with ever-increasing skill and begin to prevent future accidents. Figure 6–5 is a useful checklist for reviewing hazardous conditions and unsafe procedures in a facility.

Records of occupational injuries are essential to efficient and successful safety work—just as records of production, costs, sales, and profits and losses are essential to the efficient and successful operation of any business.

The Occupational Safety and Health Administration (OSHA) requires that nonexempt, and some regularly exempt, employers prepare and file records of their employees' injuries and illnesses. The OSHA record-keeping and reporting requirements are different and separate from any state's workers' compensation recording and filing procedures (see the section on OSHA and injury records later in this chapter). For information on the OSHA requirements, write the U.S. Department of Labor, Bureau of Labor Statistics, Washington, DC 20212.

Accurate work accident records provide a safety director and management with an objective evaluation of their safety program. They identify those fleets, terminals, or departments with high injury rates and give the safety director the information needed to isolate the most significant causes contributing to such high accident rates.

Specifically, standardized work accident records are used to:

Hazardous Conditions

Defective, inferior, or unsuitable tools, machinery, equipment, or materials

Broken	Loose	Improperly designed
Cracked	Slippery	Improperly assembled
Corroded	Dull	Improperly constructed
Decayed	Rough	Improperly compounded
Frayed	Sharp-edged	Improperly maintained
Worn	Defectively insulated	Improperly lubricated

Dress or apparel hazards

Improper clothing; inadequate clothing; loose clothing; loose jewelry
No shoes; shoes defective or unsuitable
No goggles, face shields, eye shields, or safety glasses; unsuitable eye protection
No respirators; respirators unsuitable or defective
No gloves; gloves unsuitable or defective
No head protection; safety hats or caps unsuitable or defective
No body protection; aprons, jackets, etc. unsuitable or defective

Environmental hazards *(not elsewhere classified)*

Congested working space; inadequate aisle space, inadequate clearance
Improper illumination: general illumination inadequate; insufficient light at point of operation; poor lighting due to glare, shadows, dirty fixtures, etc.
Improper ventilation: lack of a ventilating system; ventilating system of wrong type or insufficient capacity; improperly installed; poorly maintained

Hazardous methods or conditions

Improper assignment of personnel; inadequate help for heavy lifting, etc.
Use of inherently hazardous methods or procedures
Use of inherently hazardous (not defective) materials or equipment

Placement hazards

Unsafely piled materials (overloaded; unbalanced; not crosstied)
Inadequately secured against undesired motion

Inadequately guarded

Unguarded mechanical or physical hazards
Inadequately guarded power transmission equipment; poorly guarded at point of operation
Uninsulated or ungrounded (electrical)
Unshielded or inadequately shielded (radiation)
Unlabeled or inadequately labeled materials

Hazards of outside work environments *(not public hazards)*

Defective premises of others; defective materials or equipment of others
Natural hazards: wild animals; poisonous plants or insects; exposure to the elements; hazards of irregular or unstable terrain

Public hazards *(encountered away from employer's premises)*

Unsafe Practices

Working on potentially hazardous equipment

Cleaning, oiling, adjusting, or repairing equipment that is moving, electrically energized, or pressurized

Failure to use available personal protective equipment

Goggles	Gloves	Aprons
Safety glasses	Hats	Shoes
Hoods	Caps	Lifelines

Failure to wear safe personal attire

Loose clothing	Neckties	Loose hair
Long sleeves	Jewelry	High heels

Failure to secure or warn

Failure to place warning signs, signals, tags, etc.
Starting or stopping vehicles or equipment without giving adequate warning
Releasing or moving loads, etc., without giving adequate warning
Failure to lock, block, or secure vehicles, switches, valves, or other equipment

Figure 6–5.   Guide for determining the hazardous conditions and/or unsafe practices related to an employee injury.

Improper use of equipment
  Using material or equipment in a manner for which it was not intended
  Overloading
Improper use of hands or other body parts
  Using hands instead of hand tools to feed, clean, adjust, repair, etc.
  Gripping objects insecurely. Inattention to footing or surroundings
Making safety devices inoperative
  Disconnecting, blocking, plugging, tying, or misadjusting safety devices
Operating or working at unsafe speeds
  Feeding or supplying too rapidly. Throwing material instead of carrying or passing. Jumping from elevations (vehicles, elevators, platforms, etc.)
  Running
Taking unsafe position or posture
  Unnecessary exposure to suspended or swinging loads
  Unnecessary exposure to moving materials or equipment
  Entering tanks, bins, or other enclosed spaces without proper supervisory clearance
  Riding in unsafe position: on platforms, forks of lift trucks, etc.
Unsafe placing, mixing, combining, etc.
  Creating a tripping, slipping, or bumping hazard
  Pouring water into acid
Using tools or equipment known to be unsafe
Driving errors *(by a vehicle operator on public roadways)*
Horseplay *(distracting, teasing, abusing, practical joking, showing off)*
Failure to follow instruction or proper job procedure *(not in revised code)*

Figure 6–5. *(continued)*

- Create interest in safety among supervisors by furnishing information about the injury experience of their particular division, terminal, department, or other subdivision.

- Determine the principal injury sources so that efforts can focus on reducing them.

- Provide information about the most frequent unsafe practices and unsafe conditions so that supervisors and safety committees can use their time and efforts to the greatest advantage.

- Judge the effectiveness of the safety program by showing whether the accident experience is improving or worsening and by comparing that experience of other organizations doing similar work.

MEDICAL TREATMENT AND FIRST AID

The medical and first aid program is closely tied to the system of accident records and reports. Because employees may be injured at any time, a company should establish efficient first aid and medical procedures to provide prompt, adequate treatment to injured workers. Every fleet location should have a qualified physician to provide essential emergency medical care for all employees. On-call or consulting services should be arranged to ensure adequate coverage. Drivers away from home should be trained in what to do in case of accident or illness.

Physicians—besides providing emergency medical care—can conduct preplacement physical examinations, periodic physicals, and at times exit physicals for employees who quit or are discharged. This is covered more completely in the *Accident Prevention Manual for Business & Industry, Administration & Programs* volume, published by the National Safety Council.

In many fleets or in outlying fleet operations, it is not practical to employ full-time professional medical personnel to treat minor injuries. A suitable first aid kit or a station administered by a trained first aid attendant who follows procedures and treatments outlined by the company's medical advisor should be sufficient. However, a physician should be on call or available on referral for emergencies. Many firms find it cost-effective to have a nurse on site to handle minor emergencies and to provide invaluable feedback should types of injuries change.

A first aid program should include the following:

- properly trained and designated first aid personnel on every shift and at every company location

- a first aid unit and supplies or first aid kit. (A physician should approve the contents and provide written instructions for use.)

```
                    Form IS-6
Case No._____                        Date_____
                First Aid Report
Name_____  Department _____
Male ☐  Female ☐  Occupation _____ Foreman _____
Date of              a.m.  Date of              a.m.
Occurrence____ Time___ p.m.  First Treatment____ Time___ p.m.
Nature of
Occurrence_____

Sent: Back to Work ☐   Doctor ☐   Home ☐   Hospital ☐
Estimated Disability____ days
Employee's Description of Occurrence_____
_____
_____
                        Signed_____
                                    First Aid
Issued by National Safety Council, 1121 Spring Lake Drive, Itasca, IL 60143-3201
```

Figure 6–6. First Aid Report.

- a first aid manual
- posted instructions for calling a physician and notifying the hospital that the patient is en route
- posted instructions for transporting ill or injured employees and instructions for calling an ambulance or rescue squad
- an adequate injury record system

First Aid Report

Some companies require medical personnel to fill out a report for any first aid treatment (Figure 6–6). This approach can increase the data used to analyze injury experience.

Employer's First Report of Injury

Every state requires a report of any occupational injury where there is medical treatment beyond first aid and/or time is lost from work beyond the current shift. State forms vary and are usually available from the company's insurance carrier.

Employee's Report of Injury

It is important to get a firsthand account of how the employee thinks the injury occurred. Because the employee is usually the best source of information about what happened, his or her story should be obtained as soon as possible.

Of course, a badly injured employee cannot be expected to make out a report immediately, but the report can usually be secured in a few days. Generally, the worker welcomes the chance to tell what happened.

Copies of the employee's report must be furnished to the employee and to the company insurance carrier or department. This form should be acceptable to company labor relations experts and to the insurance carrier, who will have suggestions for a usable format.

Supervisor's Report of Injury

Because the state injury report form does not analyze the injury, and the employee may not want or be able to give the full facts, it is valuable to have the immediate supervisor's version on file. This form does not go to a public agency, so the supervisor is more likely to discuss the case fully (Figure 6–7).

EMPLOYEE INJURY RECORD

To maintain a record of the injury experience of each employee, enter information about all injuries, first aid cases, and disabling injuries into a log or folder. Figure 6–8, Injury and Illness Record of Employee, can be used.

Supervisors cannot be expected to remember the experience of individual employees over time, but a periodic study of the injury record forms may reveal that some employees are having far more accidents than others. This may be a signal for individual corrective action such as counseling, retraining, or reassignment to a less hazardous job. Many companies issue warning letters or take other disciplinary action where the records show consistent disregard for the employee's own welfare and that of coworkers.

COUNTING INJURIES AND CALCULATING RATES

The fleet manager and the fleet safety director need some method of measuring whether the employee safety program is succeeding in reducing injuries. The problem with measurement is that safety performance is relative. Only when a fleet compares its injury experience with its own previous experience or with that of similar fleets can it obtain a meaningful evaluation of its achievement.

However, the OSHA incidence rates are one means of measuring overall performance. Incidence rates are based on the exposure of 100 full-time employees and use 200,000 employee-hours as the equivalent of 100 employees working 40 hours per week for 50 weeks per year. For each injury/illness category, an incidence rate can be computed by multiplying the number of days lost by 200,000 in the numerator of the formula. The denominator should be the total number of hours worked by all employees during the same period.

ACCIDENT INVESTIGATION REPORT

Case Number

Company _____ Address _____

Department _____ Location (if different from mailing address) _____

1. Name of injured	**2. Social Security Number**	**3. Sex** ☐ M ☐ F	**4. Age**	**5. Date of accident**

6. Home address
_____

7. Employee's usual occupation	**8. Occupation at time of accident**

9. Length of employment
☐ Less than 1 mo.   ☐ 1-5 mo.
☐ 6 mo. - 5 yr   ☐ More than 5 yr.

10. Time in occup. at time of accident
☐ Less than 1 mo.   ☐ 1-5 mo.
☐ 6 mo. - 5 yr   ☐ More than 5 yr.

11. Employment category

☐ Regular, full-time   ☐ Regular, part-time

☐ Temporary   ☐ Seasonal   ☐ Non-Employee

12. Case numbers and names of others injured in same accident
_____   _____
_____   _____

13. Nature of injury and part of body
_____

14. Name and address of physician
_____

15. Name and address of hospital
_____

16. Time of injury

A. _____ a.m.
       p.m.

B. Time within shift

C. Type of shift

17. Severity of injury

☐ Fatality

☐ Lost workdays—days away from work

☐ Lost workdays—days of restricted activity

☐ Medical treatment

☐ First aid

☐ Other, specify_____

18. Specific location of accident
_____

On employer's premises?   ☐ Yes   ☐ No

19. Phase of employee's workday at time of injury

☐ During rest period   ☐ Entering or leaving plant

☐ During meal period   ☐ Performing work duties

☐ Working overtime   ☐ Other _____

20. Describe how the accident occurred
_____
_____
_____

21. Accident sequence. Describe in reverse order of occurrence events preceding the injury and accident.
Starting with the injury and moving backward in time, reconstruct the sequence of events that led to the injury.

A. Injury event _____

B. Accident event _____

C. Preceding event #1 _____

D. Preceding event #2, 3, etc. _____

_____

Figure 6–7. This form for a supervisor's report of employee injury can permit recording of additional details from the supervisor's perspective.

61

22. Task and activity at time of accident

General type of task _____

Specific activity _____

Employee was working:

☐ Alone   ☐ With crew or fellow worker   ☐ Other, specify _____

23. Posture of employee

24. Supervision at time of accident

☐ Directly supervised   ☐ Indirectly supervised

☐ Not supervised   ☐ Supervision not feasible

25. Causal factors. Events and conditions that contributed to the accident.
Include those identified by use of the Guide for Identifying Causal Factors and Corrective Actions.

26. Corrective actions. Those that have been, or will be, taken to prevent recurrence.
Include those identified by use of the Guide for Identifying Causal Factors and Corrective Actions.

Prepared by _____

Title _____

Department _____ **Date** _____

Developed by the National Safety Council
©1995 National Safety Council

Approved _____

Title _____ **Date** _____

Approved _____

Title _____ **Date** _____

Figure 6–7. (*continued*)

INJURY AND ILLNESS RECORD OF EMPLOYEE

(Name)   (Employee Number)

Occupation _____ Department _____ Date Employed _____

Case Number	Injury or Illness	Date of Occurrence	Z16 Type (Fatal, Permanent, Temporary, Non-disabling)	Z16 Days Charged	Comp. and Other Costs	OSHA Type (Fatal, Lost Workday, Non-Lost Workday)	OSHA Lost Workdays

(Reverse side may be used for remarks)

Issued by NATIONAL SAFETY COUNCIL. 1121 Spring Lake Drive, Itasca, IL 60143-3201

Figure 6–8. This card illustrates a method for keeping an employee record of injuries and illnesses. (Original is 4x6 in.)

$$\text{Incidence rate} = \frac{\#\text{ of recordable injuries \& illnesses} \times 200{,}000}{\text{Total hours worked by all employees during period covered}}$$

or

$$\frac{\#\text{ of lost workdays} \times 200{,}000}{\text{Total hours worked by all employees during period covered}}$$

Two other formulas can be used to measure the average severity of recorded cases:

$$\text{Average lost workdays per total lost workday cases} = \frac{\text{Total lost workdays}}{\text{Total lost workday cases}}$$

$$\text{Average days away from work} = \frac{\text{Total days away from work}}{\text{Total cases involving days away from work}}$$

Using these broad macro measures in combination with the previously mentioned micro measures, management can define the status of its safety program and develop appropriate corrective actions.

With all of the discussion about gathering statistics, it may seem that no hazard escapes scrutiny. Unfortunately, that is not the case. It is true that the study of historical records will reveal in detail what has happened and what will probably continue to happen until changes are made in the system. But history cannot reveal what catastrophes have not yet occurred.

For example, a gasoline shipping terminal may transfer millions of gallons of fuel each week using a faulty untested grounding system for the trailers. This situation may continue for years until one day the right conditions occur that produce an explosion and fire. If a methodical review of high-hazard complex systems is overlooked, a disastrous accident may be the result.

System safety is one method that takes the broader view. Failure Mode and Effects Analysis (FMEA) and Management Oversight and Risk Tree (MORT) analysis are also macro system review techniques. Although these techniques are beyond the scope of this publication, many books discuss them in detail. Companies should make these techniques part of their safety system data base.

USING INJURY INFORMATION EFFECTIVELY

For safety to receive the same consideration from management as the budget, sales, marketing, and purchasing functions, it must use a common form of reporting. Safety information reported in a language the managers fail to understand will not achieve results.

The Pareto (bar) chart is a graphic tool that can be used to display the most common safety problems in a company. Management will understand the concept that 20% of the problems generate 80% of the cost. For example, a chart with a bar for each of a firm's five worst safety problems will focus attention on the areas with the greatest potential for improvement. The chart also reduces the daunting list of problems to a manageable few. As problems are solved, others will take their place on the worst five list to be dealt with eventually.

What makes a problem worthy of the top five list? Frequency of occurrence is one measure, but this should be used with caution. It may be interesting to list the top problems strictly by the numbers, but it doesn't make sense to focus resources on minor finger lacerations just because of their numbers.

Another approach is to rank injuries by severity, which can be determined by cost, workers' compensation payments, lost workdays, or some other ranking method. When management chooses the measure, it must be used consistently over time and among locations.

Once the Pareto chart identifies the injuries that justify taking corrective action, management should evaluate the causes of these injuries. This approach further narrows the focus so that the company's limited resources can be applied where they will do the most good. If handling brake drums is the leading cause of finger fractures, it makes sense to prevent worker injuries by providing equipment to handle the drums (see Chapter 12, Fleet Purchase and Maintenance).

When corrective action has been taken, the analysis is still not complete. The expected improvement must be measured over time. A new chart is needed to track accident experience for at least 12 months after the purchase of equipment. If, for example, the number of finger fractures does not decline, either the wrong solution was implemented or employees are not following the new procedures to make it work. In either case, additional corrective action is warranted.

On the other hand, if the corrective action has produced a marked reduction in the finger fractures, it is time to share the success. This is the ultimate validation of the safety effort. Support for future changes will come from showing management that a small investment in the shop produced a large cost savings. The first projects must be chosen carefully. They should be perceived by everyone as problems worth solving and be likely to yield dramatic results in a short time.

The injury statistics for drivers and nondrivers should be handled using the same concepts discussed earlier for vehicle accidents. The reporting structure to management should be designed to give equal weight to vehicle and nonvehicle incidents. The concept of preventability is equally valid for a rollover on an exit ramp or for a fall from a broken ladder.

At year's end, it is recommended that each company send the National Safety Council a summary of its accidental injury experience. (The Council will furnish the reporting forms.) More and more companies are showing such facts in their annual reports to stockholders, particularly when they have achieved outstanding safety records. Once a good record is established, it seems to inspire a still better one.

OSHA AND INJURY RECORDS

The Occupational Safety and Health Act of 1970 (OSHAct) has undergone many changes in the past 25 years. While the impact of the act cannot be reviewed here, certain aspects must be considered in every company safety program.

- Every company location must maintain a yearly log of occupational injuries on a form provided by OSHA. In the motor carrier industry, this has been interpreted to mean a separate log for each terminal. A separate shop building with an office probably does not need to keep its own log separate from the terminal's. If the log is readily available for a "site," the requirement is met.

- At year's end, the columns of the log are summarized. By February 1, the summary sheet (actually the right side of the log) must be posted where all employees can review it. At the end of the month, the posting may be removed and filed with the logs from prior years.

- OSHA inspectors may call on the terminal to inspect its records and facilities.

This book is not intended to address every issue relating to OSHA in detail. But there are some basic provisions that every employer is obligated to observe. This discussion will be limited to some basic administrative details, a mention of specific standards, and references later in the book to OSHA rules that directly affect the motor fleet industry.

In allocating resources, OSHA sets its priorities also. Circumstances that trigger an inspection include:

- **Imminent danger.** Imminent danger is a condition where serious injury or death can reasonably be expected to occur immediately or before the normal cycle of inspections.

- **Catastrophes and fatal accidents.** OSHA gives second priority to the investigation of accidents that resulted in at least one fatality or three employees being hospitalized. Incidents of this type must be reported to OSHA verbally within eight hours after the employer learns of them.

- **Employee complaints.** Employees' complaints about unsafe conditions or health hazards may trigger an inspection.

- **Programmed high-hazard inspections.** This is self-explanatory, but it is useful to know that the trucking industry is included in the high-hazard group.

- **Follow-up inspections.** A follow-up inspection is conducted to evaluate the corrective action taken to resolve a citation.

When the OSHA compliance officer arrives, management should check the person's credentials. The officer will ask for an employee representative to participate in the opening conference, the tour, and the closing conference. The management representative will not be allowed to listen in on every interview. Copious notes should be taken when possible through all phases of the inspection process. If the officer takes a photo, air sample, or sound-level reading, the management representative should be prepared to do the same. If the company needs to contest citations, thorough documentation is the only defense.

Some of the most common citations are for failing to post the OSHA notice, OSHA 200 injury summary, and OSHA citations. These are first on the compliance officer's checklist. If an operation fails to get some of the easy requirements right, the OSHA officer may decide to conduct a more thorough inspection.

Specific subparts of the act include:

Subpart	Title
• D	Walking-Working Surfaces
• E	Means of Egress
• F	Powered Platforms, Manlifts, and Vehicle-Mounted Work Platforms
• G	Occupational Health and Environmental Control
• H	Hazardous Materials
• I	Personal Protective Equipment
• J	General Environmental Control

Subpart	Title
• K	Medical and First Aid
• L	Fire Protection
• M	Compressed Gas and Compressed Air Equipment
• N	Materials Handling and Storage
• O	Machinery and Machine Guarding
• P	Hand and Portable Power Tools and Other Hand-held Equipment
• Q	Welding, Cutting, and Brazing
• R	Special Industries
• S	Electrical
• Z	Toxic and Hazardous Substances

Managers should think twice if they do not believe that many of these subparts apply to their operations. A torch in the shop falls under subparts M and Q. A hand drill is covered by subpart P, and a pedestal grinder by subpart O. Even if no one is injured all year, the company must still post an OSHA 200 log stating that fact.

Beyond the subparts, some hazards warrant their own special program with requirements for training, record keeping, auditing, and enforcement. These special programs include:

• hazard communication
• lockout/tagout
• electrical safety training
• confined space entry
• bloodborne pathogen
• fork-truck operator training
• hearing conservation

New programs include the ergonomics and motor vehicle occupant protection standards.

The following resources will help the safety professional through this regulatory maze:

• National Safety Council's RegScan OSHA software
• OSHA's *Record-keeping Guidelines for Occupational Injuries and Illnesses*
• National Safety Council training videos on hazard communication, lockout/tagout, bloodborne pathogens, and others
• local safety council chapters and trade associations
• vendors and manufacturers of the tools and materials purchased

The OSHA standards are constantly changing, similar to the DOT regulations, so the fleet safety manager must keep up with the latest developments. The price in terms of accidents and fines provides the incentive to do well. A simple failure to hang the OSHA poster costs a firm $1,000. Willful and repeated violations can cost $70,000 per incident.

CHAPTER
7

Employee Safety Program

Employers coming under the Occupational Safety and Health Act (OSHAct) must ensure that their establishments are as free from potential safety and health hazards as possible. To do so, companies must establish an employee safety program. This program requires studying every job operation in the fleet in order to know the hazards connected with each. For those hazards that cannot be engineered out of the operation, isolated, or otherwise mitigated, management devises safe work procedures to control them. Every employee is trained in the safety procedures connected with the job. Each supervisor checks for compliance with these safety procedures, and all those in management vigorously and continuously support the employee safety program to make it an important part of their successful fleet operation.

STARTING A SAFETY PROGRAM

To start an employee safety program, the safety director must make certain that management knows the basic theories of accident prevention and how the theories will be put into practice. The National Safety Council's *Supervisors' Safety Manual* and *14 Elements of a Successful Safety and Health Program* contain details on setting up and administrating an occupational hazard control program (see Appendix E, Bibliography and Additional Resources).

The following principles must be accepted by management and employees to ensure the success of a safety program.

- Everyone in the organization must assume personal responsibility for safety: management, each department head, each supervisor, and each individual worker and driver.

- Accidents can happen anywhere at any time. Management and workers cannot assume, therefore, that any department, job, or facility is safe. Everything must be studied to eliminate hazards.

- Accidents are not the result of chance, but are caused either by specific unsafe practices or specific unsafe conditions. Accidents can be prevented by learning what these specific acts and conditions are and then substituting safe practices and safe conditions.

- Unless unsafe practices and unsafe conditions are corrected, an accident will eventually result. If corrective action is still not taken, accidents will be repeated.

Developing the safety program involves four major steps: inspecting for hazards, establishing and training workers in safe procedures, enforcement and follow-up, and maintaining the company's interest in safety.

INITIAL INSPECTION

As soon as management knows what is to be accomplished, the safety director should see that management sets broad policies and clearly states their total support of safety. An employee/management safety committee can be formed. Other types of committees can also be created: company-wide or inter-terminal, terminal, department, supervisory, worker, joint labor-management, inspection, and "get-it-done" committees. Enlightened management should make policies and give moral and financial support to its safety committees.

System-Wide Inspection

After managers are trained in what to look for, they or the management committee should make a system-wide safety inspection to bring all facilities up to current safety standards. The composition of any committee will depend upon the size of the fleet, but should include personnel with the most knowledge of the methods, practices, and conditions that the committee will encounter.

Every building and every yard or facility of the company should be inspected according to the housekeeping and maintenance checklists shown later in this chapter. When local managers are involved in inspecting separate shops or terminals, they should be members of or join the committee for the local inspection.

The safety director should perform an initial safety inspection to evaluate the facilities. Once problem areas and training needs are identified, the safety director should train line and upper managers. Following are some of the techniques to be used in this initial inspection. They apply to all properties.

- Review and list in advance the anticipated mechanical, physical, or chemical hazards.

- Let the inspection follow the job process whenever possible. For example, when buses or trucks are to be serviced, note what equipment is being used as vehicles are being refueled, checked, and cleaned. Is any of this equipment unsafe to use?

- Make notes during the inspection or soon afterwards. A compact cassette recorder would be useful here. Talk with employees to include them in the process.

- Do not pass up an opportunity to instruct employees in safe procedures. Usually, it is best to bring the matter to the attention of the proper supervisor or superintendent after the inspection has been completed, unless there is an emergency that requires immediate action.

- Use all of the senses when making an inspection.

    —Look for signs of poor housekeeping, poor maintenance, inadequate tools, unsuitable equipment.

QUALITY OF SHOP, STATION (TERMINAL), OR GARAGE HOUSEKEEPING

1. Are yards and outdoor premises clean?
2. Are roadway markings, lane numbers, markings for parking areas kept freshly and neatly painted or outlined?
3. Are buildings kept attractively painted?
4. Are windows clean? Are missing, broken, or cracked window panes replaced?
5. Are skylights clean? Are missing, broken, or cracked panes replaced?
6. Are building entrances unobstructed?
7. Are indoor traffic lanes kept freshly painted?
8. Are floors kept clean of oil, grease, water, dirt, or trash?
9. Are aisles kept clear?
10. Are stairs kept clear?
11. Are fire escapes unobstructed?
12. Is loose material left around building columns or walls or under benches?

    Soft drink bottles

    Discarded lunch boxes

    Short pieces of pipe

    Defective automotive parts

    Timbers or wooden blocks no longer needed
13. Are approved container, waste, or trash cans or bins provided?
14. Are waste bins or containers emptied regularly and often?
15. Are automotive maintenance or overhaul pits satisfactorily clean?
16. Is the area under automotive hoists kept clean?
17. Are lighting fixtures clean?
18. Are work benches and tool carts kept satisfactorily clean?
19. Are tools kept in a designated place when not in use?
20. Is portable equipment kept in a designated place when not in use?
21. Is material stored or piled neatly and safely?
22. Is firefighting equipment kept in a well-known, well-marked place?
23. Is firefighting equipment kept free of obstructions?
24. Are old brooms, mops, ladders, and other gear disposed of when no longer usable?
25. Are bulletin boards cleared periodically of out-of-date notices, letters, greeting cards, and the like?
26. Are locker rooms, change rooms, rest rooms, and washrooms kept neat and clean?
27. Are there any protruding nails, bolts, wire, splinters, glass, or other sharp objects?
28. Are warning or caution signs in good condition?
29. Are flammable liquids stored properly?
30. Are compressed gases properly segregated and secured?
31. Are incompatible materials stored in separate locations?
32. Are hoses and portable electrical cords kept overhead to avoid becoming a tripping hazard?
33. Are sawdust or metal chips swept up regularly and not allowed to accumulate on the floor?
34. Are office areas kept neat and free of samples, experimental materials, defective parts, catalogs, and discarded clothing?
35. Are desks and shop work benches neatly maintained?
36. Are clock faces kept clean?
37. Is the area around soft drink dispensers and candy bar dispensers kept neat and orderly?

Figure 7–1. Checklist for safety inspections for mechanical and physical hazards. Establish the proper frequency of inspection for all items. Check OSHA and state requirements.

—Listen for sounds of escaping compressed air, steam, water, oxygen, and acetylene. Listen for unusual sounds like thumps, squeaks, and squeals.

—Feel for equipment or machinery that is vibrating unnecessarily. Carefully check for sharp points or edges that may cut, puncture, or tear. Check for hot surfaces that may burn or radiate, causing discomfort or injury.

—Smell for odors of leaking gas, spilled gasoline or diesel fuel, or other toxic or flammable gases or liquids.

The safety director should call in trained personnel or contract for their services for appraisal and inspection of fire extinguishing equipment and of elevators and pressure vessels, if this has not already been done. Such inspections are required by a city, county, or state ordinance or code, and by insurance carriers.

Chapters 3 through 10 of the National Safety Council's *Accident Prevention Manual for Business & Industry, Administration & Programs* volume, 10th edition, discusses safety organization and inspection methods. Appendix 1 in the same book lists United States and international private organizations and government agencies that offer help. Safety directors should consult this book for the nondriving safety aspects of fleet safety management.

Freight and Passenger Terminals

In freight terminals, specifically, check the condition of the docks, floors, floor loading, lighting, freight-handling equipment (such as forklift trucks, dollies, pallets, conveyors, hand trucks), weighing scales, storage racks, bins. (See Figure 7–1 for a sample checklist.)

QUALITY OF SHOP, STATION (TERMINAL), OR GARAGE MAINTENANCE

1. Are floors and stairways in good condition?

2. Are handrails provided on stairways and kept in good condition?

3. Are aisle and work area markings provided and well maintained?

4. Are machine tools kept well painted?

5. Are moving machinery parts well guarded?

6. Is materials handling equipment kept in good repair?

   Cranes

   Hoists

   Conveyors

   Forklift power trucks and pallets

   Hand trucks

   Wheel barrows

   Carts

   Dollies

7. Are ropes, chains, cables, and slings in good condition?

8. Are elevators and manlifts well guarded and in good repair?

9. Are platforms and scaffolds in good condition?

10. Are ladders in safe condition; equipped with safety shoes?

11. Are pressure vessels inspected as required by the state?

12. Is compressed air equipment and piping in good condition?

13. Is gasoline and diesel oil dispensing equipment in good condition?

14. Is lubricating and transmission oil dispensing equipment O.K.?

15. Is venting equipment in safe condition?

16. Is heating equipment in safe condition?

17. Is general overhead lighting system adequate? Well maintained?

18. Is pit, storeroom, and other special lighting adequate? Well maintained?

19. Is firefighting equipment adequate? Well maintained? Are fire extinguishers adequate (CO_2 or dry powder)? Fire hose? Overhead and "beneath vehicle" sprinklers?

20. Is safe storage provided for flammable liquids? Is the area well maintained?

21. Are there adequate and sufficient facilities for storage of used oils, lubricants, and solvents?

22. Are containers of solvent labeled to show hazards of improper use?

23. Are material safety data sheets (MSDS) for all hazardous materials readily available?

24. Have all employees who use hazardous materials been informed of the location of the corresponding MSDS and been trained in how to read and use them? Do they understand and have access to the preventive measures specified?

25. If a vendor is contracted to dispose of used oils, solvents, and other materials, is the vendor properly licensed?

26. Are doors and windows kept in easy operating condition?

27. Are sufficient work benches provided? Well maintained?

28. Are vises, grinders, and welding equipment in good condition?

29. Are portable electrical tools safely grounded? Checked periodically?

30. Are tool rooms provided, and are they properly supervised?

31. Is first aid equipment kept in an accessible place? Checked periodically?

32. Are washroom and locker room facilities adequate and well maintained?

33. Are storage tanks provided and well maintained?

34. Are tire storage facilities provided and well maintained?

35. Are waste disposal drums or bins provided and well maintained?

36. Is adequate personal protective equipment provided and well maintained?

   Safety hats or caps

   Goggles, safety glasses, eye shields, face shields

   Respirators

   Gloves

37. Is personal protective equipment being used by employees?

38. Is an effective personal protective equipment training program in place?

39. Are respirators properly fit-tested?

40. Do roofs leak?

Figure 7–2.   Checklist for maintenance in shop, station (terminal), or garage.

In passenger terminals, check the condition of baggage-checking facilities, ticket counters, waiting room, and office furniture and equipment. Usually, such inspections are made in conjunction with the inspection of public-passenger facilities in waiting rooms, rest rooms, and boarding and arrival areas. It is far better to seek and detect probable injury-causing conditions than to wait for an accident to reveal them.

More details are given in the section Establish Safe Practices. See Figures 7–1 and 7–2 for checklists. Be sure to establish the proper frequency of inspection for items on all checklists. OSHA, or particular states, may have established specific time periods for meeting compliance standards.

Following this inspection, the committee should summarize all unsafe conditions observed and make recommendations for their correction. The supervisor should then ensure that the necessary corrective actions are taken. The safety committee should follow up on each recommendation to make sure it is carried out within a reasonable time. The results of the audits and subsequent follow-up should be reviewed by the safety director.

ESTABLISHING SAFE PRACTICES

Certain fundamental safe practices should be followed by everyone. These practices should be formulated, published, and disseminated to all employees in the form of logical and enforceable safety rules. A rule that is not logical or that cannot be enforced may seriously impair the effectiveness of other rules. Once definite safety rules have been selected and made known to employees, the company's safety policy should state explicitly that they must be observed.

General Safety Rules

General safety rules should first stress the need for such rules to operate and maintain a safe fleet. They should cover the following subjects.

• **Employee's responsibility.** Employees should conduct themselves in a safe manner at all times, report to the supervisor all unsafe practices and unsafe conditions observed, ask the supervisor for specific instructions about unusual hazards not covered in the rule book, and observe all safety signs and notices.

• **First aid.** The rules should discuss available first aid facilities, essential telephone numbers (such as those for a doctor and for an ambulance), and the injury-reporting system. The company can offer courses covering the subjects of infection, bloodborne pathogens, artificial respiration, heat sickness, and all other first-aid information pertinent to terminal, garage, or highway safety.

• **Firefighting.** This includes the location and description of emergency firefighting equipment in the plant, how to reach the local fire department, the specific procedure to be followed in case of fire or other emergency, an explanation of the emergency alarm system, and information on fire prevention.

• **Electrical equipment.** This covers hazards associated with certain types of electrical apparatus, appropriate precautions to be taken during maintenance and repair of defective equipment, and how to deal with electrical fires.

• **Work clothing.** Detailed item-by-item descriptions should be provided of what is safe and unsafe work clothing; for example, wearing rings, necklaces, or other jewelry is prohibited in the work areas.

• **Personal protective equipment.** Eye protection, foot protection, respiratory equipment, hand protection, head protection, and so on should be covered. The rules should state whether specific items are recommended or required and the circumstances under which required equipment must be used. Respirator fit testing must be performed properly and be in compliance with the personal protective equipment standard.

• **Good housekeeping and personal cleanliness.** The rules should stress the hygienic use of toilet, shower, washroom, locker room, and lunchroom facilities; safe methods of piling material; and other aspects of good housekeeping.

The company rule book should be given to all employees and its contents discussed at one or more safety meetings. It should also be provided to new employees and its material incorporated in the company's training program.

A general safety rule book, however, cannot cover everything. Therefore, the immediate supervisor must assume responsibility for instructing employees in specific job-safety practices. Safety performance, on the other hand, is the responsibility of the employee.

To determine the specific job hazards, the safety director should use the systematic procedure known as a job safety analysis (JSA). All safety supervisors should also learn this technique. The reader will find details in Chapter 14, Job Safety Analysis.

Important Job Hazards

Some of the more important job hazards found in fleets are as follows:

1. Hazards to eyesight. Probably the most tragic injury short of death is total loss of eyesight. This need not occur if eye protection is required by safety rules and consistently used. This safety habit can be acquired.

Employees who must wear prescription eye glasses should be required to wear prescription safety glasses.

Figure 7–3. The potential for flying debris in a vehicle maintenance shop justifies mandatory eye protection. Courtesy Direct Safety Company.

Prescription safety lenses can withstand eight to twelve times the impact without cracking or shattering than can ordinary glasses. An alternative is the use of spectacles that fit over prescription glasses (Figure 7–3). Of course, they should meet the ANSI Z87.1.

Because glasses will not afford sufficient eye protection for every job duty, other types of protection are available. Here is a suggested list of the type of eye protective equipment that should be worn for specific job duties:

- Wear safety goggles or eye shields when:

  grinding

  using impact wrenches and air drills

  chipping, scraping, or scaling paint, rust, carbon, or other materials

  using punches or chisels

  cutting rivets

  cutting or breaking glass

  chipping or breaking concrete

  using chemicals such as paints, solvents, etc.

  servicing air conditioning equipment with refrigerants

  soldering

  cleaning dust or dirt from motors, generators, compartments

  removing hard putty from sashes

  using metal-cutting lathe, shaper, drill press, or power hack saw

  steam cleaning

  washing vehicles or parts with soaps or solvents

  working under vehicles

- Wear face shield over goggles when:

  working around battery acid

  pouring babbitt or other molten metals

  buffing with wire brush wheels

  repairing brake linings (asbestos exposure will require further protection)

  grinding body filler

- Wear safety goggles with lenses of the proper shade when:

  metallizing

- Wear hood with clear lenses when:

  sandblasting out in the open

  pouring acid from carboys

- Wear hood with dark lenses of proper shade when:

  cutting or welding metal

  doing electric welding or assisting an electric welder

2. Health hazards. The primary health hazards to garage employees are spray-painting, toxic solvent vapors, skin irritants, carbon monoxide, corrosive chemicals, hearing damage from noisy work, inhalation of metal fumes when metallizing, and inhalation of asbestos dust when working on brake or clutch linings.

Spray-painting hazards can be overcome through the design and adequate maintenance of a ventilated paint booth. Ventilating systems will remove most of the exhaust gases produced by gasoline or diesel engines operated within buildings. Solvent vapors can be controlled through the use of properly designed equipment. Proper gloves, aprons, and other protective clothing can shield the skin against solvent absorption. Wearing ear plugs or other noise attenuators will protect the ears from hearing damage caused by excessive sound. Again refer to the National Safety Council's *Accident Prevention Manual for Business & Industry* and *Fundamentals of Industrial Hygiene* for details of detecting and protecting employees against unacceptable exposures to chemicals. OSHA requires compliance with 29 *CFR* 1910.1001, Asbestos.

3. Hazards of lifting autos, trucks, and buses. Three major hazards are associated with hoisting or raising automotive equipment: (a) having a vehicle fall off a hoist or a ramp because it had not been properly positioned, (b) having a hoist drop suddenly due to a loss of pressure, or binding and dropping suddenly due to a stuck or jammed piston inside a hydraulic cylinder, and (c) striking one's head against some part of the hoist or the vehicle on the hoist.

Install only those hoists specifically designed to handle all automotive equipment used. Do not use makeshift setups. To minimize hoist failure, companies should conduct competent periodic inspection of all hoisting equipment and establish a high quality maintenance program.

To avoid head injuries, workers should wear a "bump-type" safety cap, which will not limit their ability to work in close quarters. Along with wearing suitable head protection, workers should also wear safety goggles, eye shields, or face shields to prevent eye injuries from dislodged dirt or other foreign matter. Vapor-proof lights should be used around these areas.

4. Burn hazards from chemicals, hot water, or steam. Oil-soaked, grease-covered, and dirt-covered machine parts have to be cleaned from time to time to permit accurate, efficient maintenance or overhaul of automotive equipment. Special steam-cleaning equipment is used for the purpose. The hazard of using steam has to do with its accidental misdirection or having a steam hose burst or come loose while under pressure.

Boilers and other pressure vessels must be constructed according to the *Boiler and Pressure Vessel Code* of the American Society of Mechanical Engineers (345 East 47th Street, New York, NY 10017). They must be properly installed and fitted with all required safety devices, and be inspected regularly and conscientiously as required by the insurance underwriter and state or local laws. Burns arising from accidental contact with hot surfaces can be avoided by workers using suitable insulation, barricades, railings, or enclosures. Check local codes also.

When a heated caustic solution is used for cleaning, it presents a chemical burn hazard. Workers can safeguard against this hazard by wearing suitable safety goggles, eyeshields or face shields or hoods, gloves, and aprons. Acid burns from handling, servicing, or charging of storage batteries can be prevented by using proper personal protective equipment such as hoods and rubber gloves and aprons. Those people handling cleaning chemicals can be protected from dermatitis by wearing similar protective gear. See the *Supervisors' Safety Manual* and *Fundamentals of Industrial Hygiene* for detailed information.

5. Hazards of removing or replacing very heavy unit parts. When workers handle engines, transmissions, clutches, front and rear axles, dual tires and rims and brake drums, air conditioning equipment, and all other heavy automotive parts, they should use jacks, dollies, hoists, or cranes (Figure 7–4). If workers use rope or steel slings or forklift trucks to handle these heavy loads, they should be trained and properly supervised when working with such equipment. The equipment must be safe and properly maintained to handle the heavy weights involved.

Many supervisors and workers overlook certain hazards when using powered materials-handling equipment. Employees must exercise caution when raising, lowering, and tilting the hoisting ram and guides of forklift trucks. The ram can pinch off fingers as it is raised or lowered unless all pinch points are well guarded.

Monorail hoists and traveling cranes must have their interlocks checked periodically to make sure the stop dogs will readily drop to prevent the equipment from running off the rail. Hoist load blocks and hooks should have a sheave guard to prevent fingers, hands, or arms from being caught between the sheave and the wire rope. When jacks or table hoists are used to raise or lower metal parts, metal-to-metal contacts may slip and permit movement of whatever is being raised or lowered. Use a piece of cloth or properly fitted wood blocks to separate metal from metal.

6. Hazards of mounting heavy-duty tires rims. The obvious hazard in mounting tires and rims is that of blowing off the rims, flanges, or lock rings as high-pressure, heavy-duty tires are being inflated. Blowoffs can occur with such violence that they can kill a person instantly. To safeguard against this, deflate tires before any other operations are performed, and use a correctly constructed metal cage to contain the lock ring should it accidentally blow off during inflation (Figure 7–5). For complete details on how to combat this hazard, see the OSHA requirements in 29 *CFR* 1910.177 and the OSHA publication 3086.

OSHA also requires that tire changers be trained in the proper procedure for servicing tires. In addition to the requirement for a tire inflation cage, the employer must also provide a clip-on chuck, an in-line valve with gage, and charts or rim manuals for the type of wheels being serviced. The air hose must be sufficiently long for the tire changer to stand outside of the trajectory of parts from a failed rim (Figure 7–6).

Another hazard associated with heavy truck and bus tires comes from mishandling impact wrenches used to loosen or tighten wheel lug nuts. In addition, the close clearance between tires and fenders frequently causes skinned knuckles and hands. Therefore, workers should keep their hands low when pulling tires and rims.

One ever-present hazard is that of being struck by a falling heavy-duty tire or by dual-mounted tires. These tires must be moved carefully and, if laid aside, must be left in a very secure position.

A somewhat unexpected hazard in tire servicing comes from temporary repair products. For example, some emergency inflation products contain flammable propellants. A spark from a tire-changing tool can cause an explosion. In other instances, there may be flammable material inside the tire. Fatalities have occurred when tire changers have squirted naphtha or other flammable solvent into the carcass of a tire and ignited it to seat the bead. The technique does work, but the outcome is so unpredictable and dangerous that any employee using it should be disciplined immediately.

7. Hazards of machine tools. Two principal sources of hazards associated with metal-working tools are:

Figure 7–4.   Maintenance personnel should use mechanical assistance like this brake service lift. Courtesy Safe Shop Tools, Inc.

Figure 7–5. A properly designed tire inflation cage will help retain pieces of a failed tire or rim. Courtesy Rubber Manufacturers Association.

- Power transmission equipment such as pulleys, sheaves, belts, gears, and clutches
- Point-of-operation hazards

Both hazards can be controlled by the use of well-designed and well-maintained guards or barricades. (The *Accident Prevention Manual for Business & Industry, Engineering & Technology* volume, contains many ideas about guarding.)

8. Hazards of welding equipment. Welding equipment can produce accidental burns (due to contact with the heat source or with hot metal), and eye injuries (due to exposure to ultraviolet light or popping slag). Fumes or vapors from certain metals like zinc can also produce ill effects. All of these hazards can be effectively guarded against when employees wear proper protective equipment (hoods, jackets, leggings, spats, gloves, goggles, and respirators) and have adequate ventilation in the work area.

Be sure all employees are protected from the radiation produced by electrical arc welding equipment. Welder's helpers must be required to wear tinted safety goggles.

Workers should erect screens and barricades around welding operations to reduce emissions of radiation to other areas. Welding booths must be ventilated adequately to protect those working inside. (More welding hazards are discussed in item 10 of this section.)

In addition, workers should wear clear lens flash goggles under the helmet to prevent hot slag from popping into their eyes when they temporarily raise their hoods. (See the section on hazards to eyesight in this chapter and Chapter 19, Welding and Cutting, in *Accident Prevention Manual for Business & Industry, Engineering & Technology* volume for more details.)

9. Hazards of powered hand tools. The use of portable electrical drills can result in eye injuries or electrical shock. Not only can hot chips or turnings cause burns, but the drill can puncture hands, arms, or legs. Therefore it must be handled with care.

To avoid accidental electrical shock from drills and other electrical hand tools that are not double insulated, workers must use a grounded tool with a three-wire electrical cord.

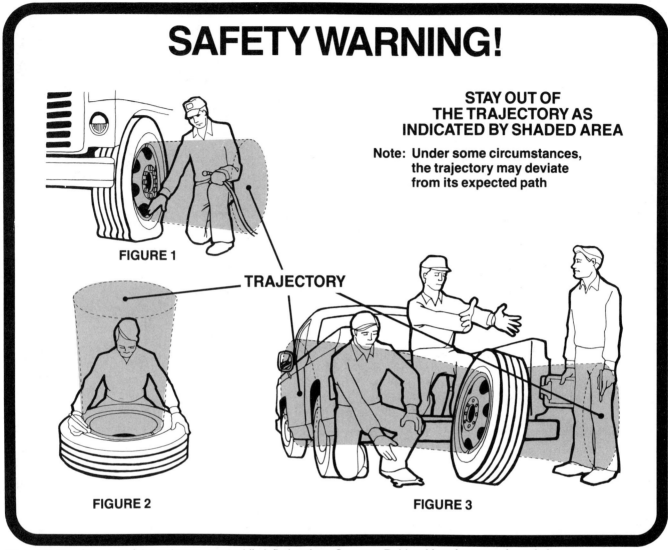

SAFETY WARNING!

STAY OUT OF THE TRAJECTORY AS INDICATED BY SHADED AREA

Note: Under some circumstances, the trajectory may deviate from its expected path

FIGURE 1

TRAJECTORY

FIGURE 2   FIGURE 3

Figure 7–6.   Stay out of the trajectory area while inflating tires. Courtesy Rubber Manufacturers Association.

In general, to eliminate tripping hazards, compressed air supply lines and electric extension cords should be suspended from the ceiling, if possible, and wound on automatic takeup reels.

10. Hazards due to explosive vapors. Both acetylene gas and petroleum vapors are highly explosive in critical air/gas ratios. But unless acetylene welding equipment has developed a leak, there should be no explosion hazard. Workers must handle welding hoses carefully to avoid cutting or burning a line.

Petroleum vapors can be extremely hazardous when workers weld a presumably "empty" oil drum or gasoline tank that is not completely free of vapors. Supervisors should prohibit the use of gasoline as a cleaning agent for automotive parts. Aside from the defatting effect on human skin, gasoline is also toxic when absorbed through the skin or spilled on clothing. During

the winter months, workers using gasoline could create an explosive mixture that might accumulate in confined areas and be ignited.

In place of gasoline, workers should use a safety solvent for cleaning. Even then, the solvent should be used as sparingly as possible and with adequate ventilation. There are many safety codes regarding this subject. See the *Accident Prevention Manual for Business & Industry,* and *Fundamentals of Industrial Hygiene,* for technical data.

11. Hazards of vehicle movement. Personnel must always watch the movement of vehicles inside garages, shops, and terminals as well as outside (Figure 7–7). Drivers must permit buildup of proper air pressure for the safe operation of air brake systems. Otherwise, there is always the possibility that a vehicle being moved may not only crash into the vehicle ahead, but also trap and crush someone between the two vehicles.

Figure 7–7. Blind spots at building corners and doorways can be eliminated by mounting convex mirrors. Courtesy K-10 Enterprises, Inc.

One particularly hazardous operation is washing the rear of motor vehicles. The person doing this job will be facing away from the next vehicle moving up the line. Workers must train themselves always to be alert for the movement of vehicles behind them. The penalty for failing to do so may be crushed legs or thighs.

Workers are also at risk for their legs being crushed when they work under a vehicle while on a "creeper." If a mechanic's legs and feet stick out, they can be run over by another vehicle, particularly one that is being backed up without a spotter assisting the driver. Make it a policy that other employees in the shop act as spotters for moving vehicles.

12. Other hazards to shop and garage personnel.
Employees encounter major sources of injury when they jump across open inspection pits, fall off ladders, hurt their backs while trying to move supplies and equipment, and use hand tools improperly. Prevention of all work injuries requires proper selection and training of employees, careful supervision of their work habits, review of all injury causes, and the creation of safety-mindedness in all employees, such as discussed in previous chapters.

13. Hazards in terminals.
Many of the hazards described in the previous section also apply to freight terminals and docks. Employees are in danger from the ever-present hazards of being crushed between a truck and a loading dock, of being crushed between two vehicles, of being hurt by falling merchandise or equipment, of being run over by forklift trucks, or being hurt on conveyors.

Appropriate use of "highway yellow" marking paint in and around freight terminals can minimize the possibility of drivers and freight terminal employees bumping objects or falling off places. For example, a yellow or white line painted six inches from the edge of a loading dock can deter a person from accidentally walking off the elevated area or driving freight-handling equipment off the edge of the dock.

Check the DOT and state regulations governing the contents and color mixes of marking paints before using a highway-type yellow paint in a public or municipal area.

Trailer movement. To reduce injuries to employees assigned to move freight in or out of truck trailers, the National Safety Council fully endorses and encourages the use of wheel chocks. Chocks provide an extra margin

Figure 7–8.   This 8 in. high heavy-duty cast aluminum chock provides secure chocking for trucks or trailers. Courtesy Worden Safety Products, Inc.

of safety against possible defects or deficiencies in the braking system of a trailer, which could interfere with safe loading operations. All trailers, including those with spring brakes, should be blocked or chocked at the dock (Figure 7–8.)

Trucks or trailers may edge away from the dock as a result of the movement of heavy freight in and out of the trailer or truck body or even from an accidental bump by a lift truck. Many dock workers have been seriously injured in falls between the vehicle and dock. In some cases, lift truck operators have actually fallen under the forklift. Wheel chocks, placed firmly ahead of the rear wheels, are the best safeguard against accidental trailer movement.

If sliding trailer tandems are left in a forward position, a heavy load, especially on a lift truck, may lift the front end of the trailer and force it away from the loading platform. This will affect the stability of the freight already in the trailer, the load on the lift truck, and the lift truck itself. Such imbalance can result in freight sliding in an avalanche toward the open end and possibly seriously injuring a dock worker. If sliding tandems are forward, the back of the trailer should be supported by stands to prevent the trailer from seesawing as freight is carried in and out of the trailer.

Whenever loading a trailer, workers must ensure that it is hooked up to a tractor or properly supported by jack stands (Figure 7–9). Too much weight ahead of the landing gear can cause the trailer to nosedive.

Likewise, mechanical failure of the landing gear can cause either a nosedive or tipping of unsupported trailers. These unexpected events may result in severe injury or death to the lift driver and others.

The most common cause of accidental trailer movement is the truck driver. Management should institute procedures that give the forklift driver control of the truck's

Figure 7–9.   Properly placed trailer stabilizing jacks will help prevent trailer tipping or falling. Courtesy The Aldon Company.

movement. A procedure as simple as having the lift driver place signs at the dock and in front of the truck may be adequate for some companies. Other firms may require a driver to give the truck keys to the material handler. With the keys secure, the forklift driver will not get an unexpected ride in one of the trailers.

If a procedural approach does not provide total control, more extensive measures must be taken. One firm went to the extent of interlocking the chocks and the dock doors. If the door is open, a magnet is energized to lock the chock in place. If the chock is forcefully removed, an alarm sounds. Another feature used by the firm is a chain on the jack stands that is locked to the glad hand on the brake lines. The lift driver has the only key, which gives good control of the situation.

Bridge plates. Bridge plates (dockboards or dockplates) used in loading operations pose a tripping hazard and affect the stability of freight and equipment moved

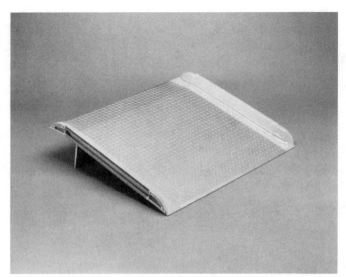

Figure 7–10. The bottom tang prevents this dock board from slipping. The side rails reinforce and serve as handles. Courtesy Magline, Inc.

across them. In addition, the edges of these plates become sharpened on concrete floors and can cause serious injuries if not kept flush with the surface of the dock and trailer. If they are not built in, loose plates may be driven away from the dock by the wheels of a lift truck or be knocked aside by cars, thus exposing workers to danger in the unbridged threshhold. Workers should not assume that the plate is secure just because it is properly positioned. They should make certain it is properly anchored (Figure 7–10).

Bridge plates should be kept clear of water, grease, ice, and other material that could create a slipping hazard and result in injury to a dock worker. Also, the bridge plates should be wide enough and able to support any load that crosses them. Power truck operators should be instructed to drive over them slowly. Portable bridge plates should have handholds, or other effective gripping devices for safe handling. Heavy plates should be moved by forklift.

Additional information on dockboards will be found in (a) American National Standard, *Loading Dock Levelers and Dockboards,* ANSI/ASME MH 14.1–1987, and (b) in the National Safety Council Industrial Data Sheet No. 318, *Dock Plates and Gangplanks.*

For a more permanent installation, powered levelers can be installed (Figure 7–11). Although they cost more, the cost can be justified by the labor savings.

If an ICC bar grab is used, an alternate plan should be made for nonstandard trucks (Figure 7–12). If the bar is damaged or designed so that the grab will not engage properly, it offers no protection to workers.

Interior trailer. Inadequate lighting within a truck-trailer will hide jagged edges, splintered crates, and various

Figure 7–11. This hydraulic dock leveler provides a barrier to prevent lift truck drivers from driving off the open dock. Courtesy Rite-Hite Corporation.

other hazards on the floor or walls. Many dockworkers have tripped over material in a dark trailer or cut their hands on rusty nails left in the floor where blocking timbers had been. If the front bulkhead of an empty trailer cannot be seen, or if a worker has difficulty reading labels on the freight being unloaded, the supervisor should arrange for more light inside the trailer.

When rigging additional lighting, workers should set up the equipment to minimize bulb breakage or other damage to the lighting fixtures. Wires should be placed where

Figure 7–12. This wall-mounted mechanical hook provides a supplementary means of keeping a trailer securely against the dock. Courtesy Rite-Hite Corporation.

they will not be run over. Also, all dock-workers should know where to obtain replacement bulbs and how to rig the portable lighting equipment, when needed.

Dockworkers must thoroughly inspect the trailer body before unloading or loading to spot hazards before they cause injury. The interior surfaces of a truck-trailer are not always smooth and uniform. Loose, dangling roof supports, jagged punctures in the sheet metal sides, holes in the floor, damaged posts, and holes in plywood side have caused many injuries. Such defects may be found even in the newest trailers. When defects are discovered, workers must take immediate action to minimize the danger until a permanent repair can be made.

In addition, dockworkers should be instructed to report all defects in the trailer to which they have been assigned. No damaged trailer should be loaded without first being repaired.

Some freight to be unloaded from a truck-trailer can discharge particles of matter, harmful mists, or vapors. After trailers have been sealed for a period of time, a high concentration of contaminants may build up within them. The effects on workers cannot always be predicted and can pose a serious health hazard.

As a result,. dockworkers should be. instructed to check the working atmosphere before entering any trailer.

Figure 7–13. Rail cars are securely chocked with this double-sided rail chock. The flag warns the train crew of its presence. Courtesy The Aldon Company.

Any worker who believes the air is contaminated should notify a supervisor.

Company policy should include detailed descriptions of the conditions under which contaminated trailers may or may not be loaded or unloaded. The policy should also establish the type and amount of protective equipment to be maintained at each terminal to handle such conditions.

Rail interfaces. Highway and rail transportation are frequently used together. If a carrier needs to transfer material or trailers to or from rail cars, a new set of standards applies. As with the truck, a rail car must be chocked to prevent unexpected movement (Figure 7–13).

Another similarity between highway and rail safety is the need for a properly secured dock plate. The blue flag requirement has no parallel in the truck rules. The intent is to notify the train crew that people are working in or around the rail cars. A higher level of protection can be achieved by mounting the blue flag on a derail mechanism (Figure 7–14).

The train crew is not only warned, they will have their unit derailed if they violate the danger zone. One firm received an unexpected visit from a train when some vandals threw a switch on the main line. The train entered the property but was laid over on its side by the derail mechanism and stopped before it could reach the plant.

Dock cleanliness. By keeping the immediate surroundings and the path over which materials are to be moved clean and free of obstacles, a firm can prevent injuries and lost time. Steel bands, splintered boards, and other trash can accumulate around the dock area and should be picked up. A neat, orderly dock allows operations to be

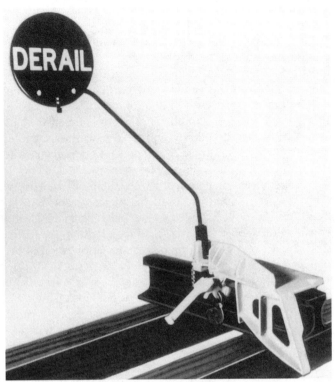

Figure 7–14. This lockable derail provides protection against unintended rail-car movement that the blue flag alone cannot. Courtesy The Aldon Company.

Figure 7–15. A sturdy, convenient ladder will eliminate the need to hop down from the dock to ground level. Courtesy The Ballymore Company.

efficiently performed and eliminates tripping and slipping hazards.

Managers and workers should be trained to keep working docks swept clean. Grease and other liquids must be cleaned off the floor immediately. There should be a specific place to put all materials handling equipment. When equipment is used, workers should be held responsible for returning it. This type of housekeeping should be done regularly, depending on the operation.

Illumination is also important. when moving freight. Be certain that appropriate lighting is available for all loading and unloading operations. Minimum recommended illumination on loading docks is 20 footcandles (decalux); inside truck bodies, minimum illumination is 10 footcandles (decalux), according to the Illuminating Engineering Society.

Good housekeeping should become a habit for workers and an important part of an effective fleet safety program.

Scattered debris. Freight and equipment are sometimes carelessly left lying in and around the working area by the previous shift. Unchecked freight, tools, wrappings, bottles, and loose dunnage are all traps for the wheels of a hand truck and for unwary feet. These traps have been the cause of almost every imaginable kind of personal injury from simple bruises and abrasions, to cuts and broken bones, to concussions.

Thus, the first duty of any dock worker, before beginning any actual work, is to make sure the work area is safe. This means that all dunnage and tools not in use should be placed in their respective storage racks; all trash should be deposited in the receptacles provided; and all unchecked freight should be checked and removed. Unloaders (strippers) should know that an "empty trailer" should be completely empty. Stripping is not completed until the floor of the trailer is swept clean of all trash, nails left in the floor have been removed, and the bridge plate has been pulled and stored..

Falls. Falls are a leading cause of serious injury in any industry, and freight handling operations are no exception. Workers are often injured when they move from the loading dock level to the truck well to place chocks. They frequently avoid the long walk to the ramp at the end of the dock by jumping off the dock. Properly placed ladders or stairs between dock doors can avoid this problem (Figure 7–15).

Workers also risk a fall when they walk on a flat bed trailer to secure the load. The highest risk for a crippling or fatal injury, however, occurs when workers must climb

Figure 7–16.   This 4 ft cantilever platform provides employees safe access to hatches on tank cars. Courtesy The Ballymore Company.

to the top of a tank trailer. Permanent platforms with guardrails at truck top height provide the most convenient protection for workers (Figure 7–16). Because this solution is not always practical, portable systems are available to safeguard workers when they climb.

Workers also can fall when simply climbing up to connect air lines and electrical connections. When ordering equipment, supervisors should specify that connections be located in a place that will not require climbing to reach them.

Cargo shifting. Companies who ensure that motor vehicles are loaded safely and who provide protection against shifting or falling cargo can do much to prevent highway and industrial accidents. Because trailers are designed for uniform load distribution, the cargo should be distributed equally between the rear tires and the fifth wheel. This arrangement transfers the trailer's load to the truck-tractor (Figure 7–17).

In addition, the weight of the freight should be distributed equally on each side of the trailer. A heavy load to one side will overload the springs and tires on that side. The cargo should be loaded so that its weight is equally distributed over the rear tires, which will prevent possibly twisting the frame and overloading the axle housing and wheel bearings. Heavy containers, equipment, or machinery large enough to occupy the width of the trailer floor should be loaded with their center of gravity positioned

over the center line of the trailer. Freight should be secured to prevent it from shifting.

Top-heavy articles, such as machinery and other equipment, should be blocked and braced to prevent them from tipping and damaging other freight or affecting safe operation of the vehicle. Such articles will generally require bracing near the top in addition to floor blocking. Blocks and bracing should be used to eliminate slack space. All cargo should be secured so it will not come in contact with trailer doors. This precaution prevents the load from shifting or rolling while in transit.

Properly seasoned and undamaged lumber, free of dry rot and knots, should be used for blocking and bracing freight in the trailers. Bracing and blocking material and construction should be capable of withstanding the forces that may act on them during emergency application of the brakes. Companies should observe the *Federal Motor Carrier Safety Regulations* for the safe loading of motor vehicles and protection against shifting or falling cargo.

For buses, the baggage, freight, or express cargo should be stowed and secured in a manner that will protect passengers from injury due to falling or displaced articles. The articles should not interfere with the driver's freedom of movement or proper operation of the bus. In addition, baggage or freight should not obstruct any occupant's access to any of the exits.

Materials handling. More workers in the motor transportation industry are injured by improper handling of shipping materials than from any other single source. Strains, sprains, and other injuries frequently cause long layoffs from work and can prove costly to both the worker and the company. Therefore, workers need to be trained in the area of materials handling. Personal protective equipment for hands and feet should be required on most jobs that involve handling materials. Some companies also require workers to wear goggles and/or safety hats as well.

The handling and stowing of objects and materials is not always as easy as it appears. As a result, workers should be taught to stop and reason out every intended operation before they begin the actual work. The fleet supervisor should instruct employees to estimate the weight of each load and to inspect it for slivers, nails, sharp edges, and weak bottoms.

If the load is too big to handle alone, the worker should be instructed to get help or to use equipment designed specifically to handle the load. When handling rough or sharp-edged objects, protective gloves should be worn. Also, workers should grip cartons away from the seams so that their hands do not come in contact with sharp staples. They should not let their bare hands come in contact with steel and wire banding. Because material can fall out of open or weak-bottomed cartons, workers should be encouraged to wear safety shoes.

WRONG

RIGHT

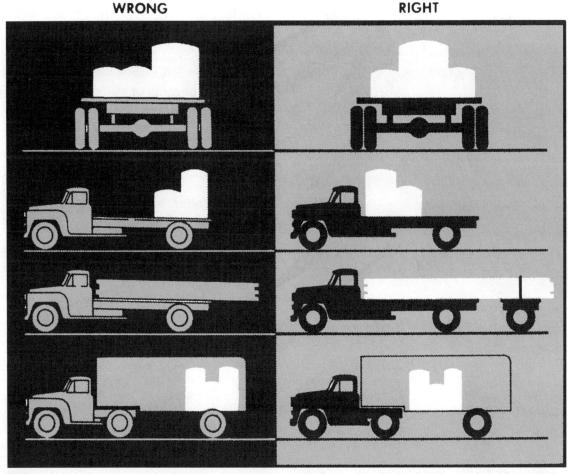

Figure 7–17. For proper load distribution, analyze . . . equalize . . . distribute. Analyze each truck or tractor-trailer unit according to tire size—the axle carrying capacity of the tires—and distribute the load accordingly. Equalize the loads on each axle according to the carrying capacity of the tires. Distribute loads on semitrailer units so each axle and the fifth wheel carries its share according to carrying capacities of the tires.

When lifting heavy objects, workers should be taught to keep their back straight, with their arms and elbows tucked into the side and their weight centered over their feet. They must lift with their legs, not their back muscles. Twisting during a lift is a common cause of back injury. Workers can avoid twisting injuries by simply turning their forward foot out and pointing it in the direction they intend to move.

Employees should m___ drums with a barrel truck whenever possible. Drums should not be rolled on edge because of the precarious balance such a maneuver requires. Avoid pinch points near the top of the drum, and keep feet clear of the bottom seam. Because drums often contain hazardous materials, workers must take great care to avoid puncturing the drum or spilling its contents. If a spill occurs, immediately contact the personnel trained to clean up such spills before it spreads.

In handling sacks (paper and cloth), caution workers to avoid cuts from wire stapling at the bound end. They should lift by gripping underneath the sack and using their legs to lift. If a large number of sacks are to be moved, two people should work together—one at each end of the sack. Do not throw sacks carelessly; keep the dust level down. If sacks are damp or warm, a chemical action may be taking place; workers should notify their supervisor at once.

When workers handle bundles, they should watch out for short, sharp ends of steel strapping used to bind the bundles. Train them to keep their fingers out from between the individual lengths in a bundle. Workers can use dock equipment to move bundles whenever possible; these objects are often coated with protective grease at the factory, which makes them hard to grip. When raising lighter bundles to load as top freight (for example, plastic tubing), try to keep both ends level; otherwise, an individual bundle is likely to slide back on the worker at the lower end, striking the person's face, chest, or leg.

Hand trucks. When handling freight with hand trucks, workers should place the "blade" of the hand truck

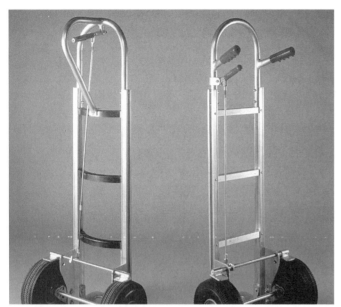

Figure 7–18.   A hand truck with brakes allows control of a heavy load on an incline. Courtesy Magline, Inc.

completely under the load, then pull it back slowly until the weight is entirely balanced over the axle. Always push, never pull, hand trucks (Figure 7–18) The freight should be loaded on the hand truck only as high as the top crossbar so that visibility is unobstructed. When pulling freight back to the siderails of the hand truck, workers should never grip the steel strapping, wire binding, or twine of the freight. Instead, tell them to reach across the top of the load and grip the far edge.

If workers are using barrel trucks, they should handle the freight in the same safe manner as the hand trucks. However, they must be particularly careful to center the weight of the drum exactly over the axle of the barrel truck. Liquid sloshing in the drum might destroy this balance, so move cautiously—especially at turns.

Freight should be loaded on four-wheel carts so that the worker can see over the top. Carts should be pushed so the leading edge of the cart cannot run up against another dock worker's heel. Workers should pull a cart only when moving downgrade, as when coming out of a trailer down an inclined dockplate. The dock worker, then, must face the car and brace against it for control. Two workers may be required to control heavily loaded carts.

Most "J" (Johnson) bar injuries occur when the handle is driven up with great force into a worker's face or jaw. The body should be kept in a position where it will not be struck if someone loses control of the handle.

Powered industrial trucks. All drivers of powered industrial trucks must complete a comprehensive training program to operate these machines safely. The supervisor and lift truck operator should be familiar with the safety

rules and regulations in the American National Standards Institute, *Safety Standard for Powered Industrial Trucks— Low Lift and High Lift Trucks,* ANSI/ASME B56.1–1993, and *Powered Industrial Trucks,* ANSI/NFPA 505–1995. OSHA 29 *CFR* 1910.178 still references the ANSI standard B56.1–1993.

14. Job hazards of truck and bus operators.   Bus and truck operators must not only avoid traffic accidents but also maintain good relations with the public. Defensive driving practices (described in Chapter 9, Driver Training) can generally prevent motor vehicle collisions; considerate, friendly dealings with the public can usually prevent any strained relations between outside people and the company (as discussed in Chapter 10, Driver Supervision).

Drivers also run the risk of being hurt in a nondriving accident. Operators are frequently injured when they fall while boarding or alighting from a vehicle, when they are within their vehicle, or when they fall at terminals and rest stops. Drivers should be taught always to have at least three limbs—two hands and one foot or two feet and one hand—in contact with the steps or hand holds when boarding or alighting from a vehicle.

Drivers can injure their hand, wrist, arm, shoulder, or back when their vehicle's front wheel strikes an object or drops suddenly into a depression, causing the steering wheel to jerk or spin. In addition, operators are frequently injured when adjusting the operator's seat, opening or closing doors, operating gear shift levers, or handling windows and ventilators and changing route and destination signs (if there are any).

If operators must handle merchandise, they must take care to avoid sprains or muscular overexertion, and to avoid foot injuries caused by falling or shifting objects. Safety shoes should be a requirement for freight handlers. If operators cannot handle themselves safely, how can they be counted on to handle passengers, merchandise, or freight safely?

To focus attention on driver safety records, management must maintain, review, and discuss accident statistics and make recommendations regarding how injuries can be avoided. If this procedure can be done in open safety meetings, group discussion will focus attention on injury-causing conditions or practices. If they cannot be handled this way, then the supervisor can discuss accidents and injuries with individual drivers. Accidents are only good for their educational value.

MAINTAINING INTEREST IN ACCIDENT PREVENTION

Companies cannot attain safe operation without working for it. As mentioned previously, the motivation and desire for a real safety program must originate with management.

A company can bring all its facilities up to high safety standards, subject all jobs to a hazard analysis, devise and enforce safe work procedures, and set up an accident reporting and analysis system. Yet one important task remains to be done—to stimulate employee interest in accident prevention. Employees should *want* to work safely at all times. Here are ways to accomplish this goal:

- **Management interest and example.** Management's sincere interest in accident prevention is one of the strongest incentives that will motivate workers to achieve a high level of safety performance. This principle holds true for all levels of management—each manager must reflect an interest in company safety objectives and set a good example of compliance with safety rules. Workers will believe in safety only to the extent they think their boss believes in it.

Supervisors should talk frequently to each of their subordinates about safety. Managers should seek every opportunity to be identified with the safety program, such as attending safety meetings and rallies and signing bulletins and announcements. Serious accidents should be personally investigated by management, and the affected employees interviewed by them. Above all, management personnel at all levels must set examples of safe action, both at work and off the job.

- **Safety meetings and rallies.** Periodic safety meetings and rallies keep worker interest in safety at a high level. Safety meetings should be small and conducted by employees or their immediate supervisors. Meetings should be confined to a definite subject and deal with specific problems. For example, a safety meeting for drivers and mechanics might be devoted to discussing the safe way of getting in and out of various vehicles. Meetings also can be held to explain a new safety procedure, announce a new contest or campaign, review a specific accident, or discuss the overall safety performance of the group.

Large rallies attended by all employees, including members of management, are helpful in celebrating safety achievements. These include winning an industry safety award or working a specified number of hours without a disabling injury.

- **Awards for work safety.** Employees like to be recognized individually for safe work performance. One good method is to establish a Safe Driver Award or Safe Worker Award program (Chapter 10, Driver Supervision). This program is available from the National Safety Council. Companies can also create their own.

Awards are usually presented for working a calendar year without a disabling injury. Workers who have a disabling injury do not receive an award for that year. Usually awards are cumulative, thus a worker can earn a one-year, two-year, three-year (or higher) award for going that many years without having a preventable accident or a disabling injury. (For publicity value, see Appendix A, Getting Publicity from Safe Driver Awards.)

- **Safety contests.** Various contests can be held—for example, working the highest number of hours without a disabling injury or achieving the lowest frequency rate within a specific period of time. Contests can be held among units within the same fleet or among fleets in different areas.

Contests should be well promoted for maximum interest. Workers should understand the method of scoring and be kept informed of the standing of the various contestants—either individuals or units.

There should be no contest penalties for reporting very minor injuries. Otherwise workers may fail to report them and run the risk of getting an infected wound.

Safety contests and award projects are a means of generating enthusiasm, cooperative effort, and safety awareness within the company. However, as effective as they are, contests and awards cannot substitute for a well-run safety program, established and backed by management, and administered by all levels of supervision in a firm and impartial manner.

- **Posters.** A good poster program can do much to maintain interest in safety—even the best employees need reminding about safety rules and procedures. Aside from the actual message of the poster, the mere fact that poster boards are well maintained with fresh posters tells employees that management has a continued interest in safety. In addition, such boards help give a terminal, dock, or driver room the look of a safety-minded company.

Special bulletin boards can also be used to promote various safety subjects. These boards can exhibit actual photographs of safety equipment that saved a worker's life or prevented crippling injuries, display award presentations, promote safety announcements, and show actual safety plaques and other awards.

Management can also use a special bulletin board to show the number of days worked since the last lost-time injury. Such a display can promote worker interest in safety as long as the figures are updated faithfully.

Planning and administering a good poster program requires careful consideration of (a) kinds of poster boards used, (b) number and placement of poster locations, (c) selection of posters, and (d) regular, frequent changes.

Poster displays. Mounting posters can be as simple as thumb-tacking them to a wall or as complicated as placing them in an illuminated, glass-enclosed bulletin board. The latter is more desirable because it is not only more dignified and attractive but it also protects the posters from damage or tampering.

Number and placement of poster locations. Posters must be seen to be effective. This means placing posters where employees work or congregate. Knowing the pedestrian traffic patterns in a company helps in planning poster locations. Management should consider these questions when selecting sites:

- Where will most employees see a poster most frequently?

- Will all employees see it during their normal workday?

- How many locations are needed to make sure that all employees are exposed to a poster program?

- Where are the most effective locations for posters that show specific work hazards? (Safe driving posters should be seen mostly by drivers; posters devoted to proper lifting techniques should be seen especially by dock and maintenance workers.)

At these optimum locations, place posters at eye level—centered about 53 in. (1.35 m) from the floor. Make sure the poster is in adequate lighting and is free from obstructions so that employees can focus their attention on it. Avoid placing posters at stairways, doorways, or other places where workers risk an accident if their attention is diverted. (See the National Safety Council catalog regarding available posters and order information.)

Changing poster displays. Posters are most effective when used one at a time and changed or alternated frequently. If posters are left in place too long, they become part of the workplace background and their message is diluted.

In general, it is better to use four posters per month—one each week—than to put all four in one location and leave them there for a month. Changing or alternating posters weekly gives a sense of urgency and timeliness to a poster program.

A capable employee should be assigned to administer the poster program personally. Periodically, the safety director should make sure that poster sites are kept in good condition and that posters are changed according to a prearranged schedule.

- **First aid training.** Many companies give all employees first aid and cardiopulmonary resuscitation training because they find employees work more safely when they are qualified to administer first aid. Also, OSHA requires personnel trained in first aid be on each work shift where emergency care is five or more minutes away. The National Safety Council's First Aid Institute offers courses in first aid.

First aid providers must also receive training for bloodborne pathogens. For instance, the medical director must determine which employees are likely to have occupational exposure to hepatitis B so they can be given the appropriate vaccinations.

CHAPTER 8

Driver Selection and Hiring

People differ in their ability to act and to drive safely. Yet little is known about *why* these differences exist or even how to rate a job applicant's future on-the-job safety performance with any degree of accuracy.

These facts present a real challenge to the fleet personnel officer, who is generally responsible for hiring drivers. Few occupations require a greater level of safety than that of motor vehicle operator, especially since much of the work is done almost without supervision. The personnel officer's choice of drivers can make a substantial difference in a company's overall productivity and financial performance. A properly selected, trained, and motivated driver has a greater chance of avoiding or preventing accidents that may damage property or injure people.

GENERAL ABILITIES AND APTITUDES

The general abilities and aptitudes required of a driver vary with the individual job. For example, the physical demands made on school bus drivers are very different from those made on delivery vehicle drivers. Figure 8–1 illustrates a method of grading the various abilities and aptitudes required in specialized driving jobs. The importance of correct driver selection is apparent after taking a closer look at items 6, 7, 8, and 12 on the Evaluation of Driving Job worksheet.

• **Responsibility for vehicle (item 6).** Every vehicle operator has the potential of damaging or demolishing a vehicle in an accident. The cost can range from several thousand dollars for a compact passenger car to several hundred thousand dollars for a city bus or line-haul trailer-tractor combination.

• **Responsibility for safety of cargo or passengers (item 7).** It is possible for a driver to damage expensive cargo or injure passengers. Many drivers of semi-trailers haul freight worth over a million dollars. A company's liability for passenger injuries can range from several thousand to several million dollars.

• **Responsibility for safety of pedestrians and other motorists (item 8).** Every vehicle operator has the potential to injure pedestrians and collide with other motorists. Again, the liability from such accidents can cost the company thousands or even millions of dollars.

• **Personal hazards (item 12).** It is certainly possible for any professional driver to be injured in a traffic accident. The time, productivity, and money lost because of such injuries can seriously affect company operations.

Because any driving job is potentially dangerous, the ability to avoid accidents is one of the most essential requirements for motor fleet drivers.

Accident Repeaters

Any discussion regarding individual differences to prevent or avoid driver accidents must first deal with the problem of accident repeaters. Although some drivers can work for years without incident, others seem to have many accidents during their work lives. It's also important to keep in mind that everyone is potentially an accident repeater—especially under certain conditions of stress.

Establishing the management-driver relationship. To avoid the problem of accident repeaters, the supervisor must select drivers with the best potential for driving safely, train them in the techniques of safe driving, and provide the kind of supervision that will help drivers maintain a very high level of safe driving. Thus, the relationship between management and drivers must be different from the ordinary one between management and employees or supervisors and the supervised. It is more like the relationship between the players and the coaches or managers of a big league sports team: club managers must not only select good players, but also work closely with individual players to keep them in good physical and psychological condition.

Likewise, a company's management must develop a group of carefully selected and highly trained safe drivers. The safety program and the supervisory program must keep the drivers conditioned and motivated to maintain a high level of safe driving.

Selecting safety-conscious drivers. Can the safe driving potential of an applicant be predicted at the employment office? The answer is a qualified "Yes." It is possible to screen out many of the poor risks. A selection program that succeeds in doing only this much has already made a substantial contribution to the firm's operations.

However, predicting safe driving ability is less exact. The best approach is to hire experienced drivers who have established records that can be verified.

Once the obviously poor-risk drivers have been screened out, the selection process should focus on all of the employee's skills and characteristics and not solely on the individual's potential ability to drive safely. Matching the total person to the total job offers the best promise for successfully screening out all potentially high-risk drivers.

Profile of the Good Driver

What are the characteristics and abilities of a good driver? An analysis reveals that the good driver must be able to

• avoid accidents
• follow traffic regulations
• perform pre- and post-trip inspections
• avoid abrupt starts and stops as much as possible

EVALUATION OF DRIVING JOB

Inter-City Truck, Semi-Trailer   Taxicab
Inter-City Truck, Straight   School Bus
Inter-City Bus   Passenger Car
City Truck, Semi-Trailer   Utility Truck
City Truck, Straight   Route Delivery Vehicle
City Bus   Other _____

	High		Average		Not Important
JOB FACTOR	1	2	3	4	5
1 Education					
2 Experience					
3 Technical Training					
4 Physical Demand					
5 Mental Visual Demand					
6 Responsibility for Vehicle					
7 Responsibility for Safety of Cargo or Passengers					
8 Responsibility for Safety of Pedestrians and other Motorists					
9 Contacts with Customers					
10 Responsibility for Company Funds					
11 Driving and Working Conditions					
12 Personal Hazards					
13 Supervision Received					

Figure 8–1. This form for Evaluation of Driving Job helps in making comparisons of relative abilities and aptitudes needed for various driving jobs.

- avoid schedule delays
- avoid irritating the public
- perform the nondriving parts of the job
- find satisfaction in the job
- get along with others
- adapt to meet existing conditions

Driving experience. Previous experience as a professional driver or as a private motorist is the best indicator of potential ability to drive safely. It has been fairly well established that a driver who has had frequent motor vehicle accidents in the past will continue to have frequent accidents in the future. This is one of the oldest and most reliable predictive factors. As a result, one of the most important items of information about an applicant is his or her record of motor vehicle accidents and citations for traffic violations. Because most high-risk applicants usually try to minimize or conceal a record of past accidents and traffic violations, their word alone is not sufficient evidence. Managers should consult an applicant's previous employers and state license records (MVRs) to find out the person's actual driving record.

Keep in mind that simply because an applicant has had past accidents, he or she should not be automatically disqualified for employment. Each instance should be discussed with applicants to determine their attitude toward the preventability of such accidents and the importance they attach to traffic rules and regulations.

How much previous driving experience should a company require of its applicants? This will depend largely on the scope of the company's driver training program and the fleet's personnel philosophy. Ordinarily, an applicant's previous driving experience should be viewed as a valuable asset in a new employee, particularly if the person has driven the same kind of vehicle the job requires. In many cases, fleets that lease equipment from owner-drivers do not have training programs. For these firms, it is even more critical for management to scrutinize an applicant's past driving experience, accident record, and demonstrated ability to drive safely.

Skill. The degree of driving skill possessed by the applicant can be determined to some degree from an examination of past driving experience and a review of Commercial Drivers License (CDL) endorsements. However, the only way to judge driving skill effectively is to put applicants behind the wheel of a vehicle and observe their driving ability over a prescribed course. (See Appendix C, Skill Drills and Test Courses, for an example of a skill course.)

Fleet safety administrators support two types of driving tests. One involves what is known as a "driving range test," which determines the driver's awareness of the physical dimensions and limitations of a vehicle. In this test, drivers demonstrate their ability to make starts, stops, turns, and various other maneuvers. For the second type of test, applicants must drive through traffic where they are exposed to various kinds of actual traffic conditions. In both cases, management must make every effort to standardize the testing procedures for each driver.

It must be borne in mind, however, that these tests simply show the applicant's skill in handling equipment. Available studies reveal that the results of these tests cannot be used to predict with any degree of accuracy the potential accident risk of any applicant.

The weight that a company places on an applicant's performance on these skill tests should depend on how much driver training the company provides. If no training is offered, the applicant's performance during the test may qualify or disqualify the individual for the job. If the company offers a comprehensive training program, then even a driver who shows below-average skill can be trained to perform the job.

Ability to avoid accidents. This characteristic is the main criterion for judging driving performance. No matter how well qualified a driver may be in other job requirements, repeated accidents can indicate a bad investment. Even a "star salesperson" can become a liability because of too many accidents. The capacity to avoid accidents is largely a result of the driver's natural ability, improved by training and conditioned by good supervision. The good driver also learns by observing the skills and mistakes of others.

Ability to follow traffic regulations. Observance of traffic rules and regulations is important to good driving. No company can afford to keep drivers who repeatedly violate traffic rules and regulations. Even though company policy may require the driver to pay any fines, an employee who violates the law is a public relations liability. In addition, studies have shown a close correlation between repeated traffic violations and repeated accidents.

Ability to care for the vehicle. Drivers differ in their ability to care for and conserve a vehicle on the road. Fleets that assign the same vehicle to the same driver every day have found that some drivers are able to coax more miles out of a vehicle and use less fuel than can others. When fleet operating costs are figured to the fraction of a cent per mile of operation, the ability to conserve a vehicle shows up as a substantial factor in fleet economics and a relevant measure of driving ability.

Ability to meet schedules. The fleet motor vehicle represents a capital investment whose purpose is to produce transportation service and resulting revenue. Time and distance are also critical elements factored into this service. A good fleet dispatcher knows what can be reasonably expected in terms of production output per vehicle per day. Thus, the driver who dawdles at stops, is unduly slow in negotiating traffic, and wastes time in other ways is not meeting production schedules and is not getting maximum return on the company's investment. In city bus service, for example, failure to stay on schedule creates difficulties and delays for other bus operators on the line and is a direct factor in producing accidents.

Obviously, schedules must be carefully drawn up with safety and traffic conditions in mind. Nevertheless, management should consider a driver's ability to meet schedules as a factor in rating driving skill.

Ability to avoid irritating the public. Most fleet vehicles are painted in distinctive colors and carry the company name. In effect, they are traveling billboards whose advertising value to the company, if duplicated in conventional advertising media, represents thousands of dollars. But if the vehicle is operated unsafely, this value can become a negative advertising factor, identifying a company that appears to care little about public safety. Discourteous and potentially dangerous actions such as tailgating, speeding through residential areas, racing the engine at traffic stops to hurry pedestrians out of the way, unnecessary use of the horn, and bulldozing through traffic can frighten, anger, and alienate the public. Thus, drivers must always operate company vehicles with courtesy and consideration for pedestrians and for other motorists.

Nondriving parts of the job. In many professional driving occupations, the nondriving responsibilities of the job take more time than the driving portion. These involve such tasks as meter reading, appliance servicing, food delivering, and route selling. Employees must be able to do the nondriving portion of the job well. If they are insecure or nervous about it, their attitudes may contribute to unsafe driving.

Ability to find satisfaction in the job. Employees who dislike their jobs generally perform poorly, quit, or must be discharged. The process of recruiting, selecting, and hiring a replacement can be costly. If the worker does not prove satisfactory and quits or is discharged after a short time, the company's investment in the person is lost. Added to this loss is the inevitable confusion and disruption that follows whenever a driver quits or must be discharged.

The selection process, therefore, can be considered a two-way street between potential employees and the company. Not only must the person be suited to the job, but the job must also be matched to the applicant's personal skills and characteristics.

When considering an applicant for the driving job, management should look at the person's minimum and maximum levels of ability. An applicant who is overqualified for a given job may be just as frustrated by his work as someone who is underqualified. Be sure the overqualified applicant is really seeking a driving job. Keep in mind, however, that it is not uncommon for highly educated people to be attracted by the higher pay that some driving jobs offer. If such candidates have a successful prior work history as drivers, they should be considered

as valued applicants with the potential to move up to management positions.

An applicant's needs for personal status also should be considered in the selection process. In most cases, an implicit level of status is attached to any given job. Management should consider whether the driving job offers an applicant a satisfying degree of status that may act as an incentive to keep the person on the job. If applicants indicate by words or actions that they feel driving is low-status work, they may not be good candidates for the fleet. People tend to resent or quit jobs they feel are demeaning.

Ability to interact with others. The ability to work well with others adds to a person's value as an employee and enhances total job performance. Hiring a new employee is an all-or-nothing proposition. One cannot hire merely skills and aptitudes; one hires the whole person, including all positive or negative personality traits. Personality is considered here in terms of the candidate's likableness and ability to get along with others. One negative person can upset an entire employee group.

Therefore, management should ask these questions during the selection process: How well will the applicant fit in with other employees? Will the applicant feel superior to fellow workers or accept them as equals? Will the workers accept the new employee? How well will the applicant get along with customers and other members of the public as a representative of the company?

The ability to evaluate clearly and quickly an applicant's potential usefulness to the company is a skill that hiring officers develop through experience. These officers can improve their evaluating capabilities by observing the firm's most competent employees. These workers often share common traits that indicate such qualities as personal responsibility and dependability. Fair-hiring laws have made it necessary for hiring officers to rely more heavily on factual assessments than on subjective evaluations of candidates' personalities and work skills.

Fair-Hiring Guidelines

For the safety director, or other hiring personnel, it is essential to have a working knowledge of fair-hiring laws before beginning the selection process. Because of antidiscrimination laws and possible lawsuits, the hiring officer should not request personal information from an applicant during the interview and on the written application. The only exception to this rule is when it can be proved that the answers are necessary to establish a candidate's occupational qualifications.

To help firms adhere to the law, state and federal agencies publish preemployment inquiry guidelines. These guidelines show how to phrase verbal and written questions so they conform to existing laws. For example, *Pre-Employment Inquiries,* published by the State of Illinois Department of Human Rights, suggests that the hiring officer should avoid asking questions regarding an applicant's citizenship or proof of legal entry status before hiring. After hiring the person, however, the officer can then ask the employee if he or she is prevented from lawfully being employed in this country because of visa or immigration status. The officer can then request proof of the employee's citizenship or legal entry status.

SELECTION PROCEDURE

Hiring a new driver is an important decision for any firm. Because it must be done carefully and thoroughly, the fleet manager should be willing to allocate as much time and personnel to this activity as it requires. Normally, the process should take from three days to several weeks between the time applicants first apply for a job and the actual date they are hired.

The selection procedure is designed to uncover facts about the applicant on which a decision can be made about his or her suitability for employment. These data come from a number of sources: what the applicant says, information from past employers and employment records, recommendations from business and personal associates, and the results of objective tests and medical examinations. Because gathering such information involves time and money, the selection procedure should be organized to screen out as quickly as possible applicants who do not meet the job requirements and can be eliminated from any further consideration.

Each fleet must find its own best sequence based on the number of techniques used in the selection procedure and the volume of hiring. However, the following steps can prove helpful in developing a selection procedure.

Step 1—Recruiting

It is a truism that a company can select applicants only from the group that applies for the job. For example, if only poorly qualified applicants apply for work, the most sophisticated procedure will still select a poor employee. The first step in any selection procedure, therefore, must be attracting an adequate number of well-qualified people to apply for employment. These candidates can be recruited from a number of sources.

• **Referrals from present employees.** Current employees can be an excellent source of applicants. Although many companies prohibit the employment of employees' relatives, this objection does not hold true for friends and acquaintances. If employees know that their friends will receive due consideration, they tend to refer them to the company for employment. In general, employees tend to recommend better-qualified candidates because such candidates are a reflection on the workers themselves.

• **Industry contacts.** Other fleet supervisors can be another dependable source of applicants. Trade association

meetings are good places for managers to meet their peers and let others know they are looking for good candidates.

• **Other sources.** Driving schools, vocational schools, and other similar places are additional sources of recruitment. Many schools promote "career days" during which company representatives and students can meet to discuss employment opportunities.

Step 2—Application Form

The employment application form is usually the hiring officer's most complete source of information about the applicant. It serves as a quick means of selecting candidates who appear to be qualified and of eliminating unsuitable candidates.

The hiring officer should choose or develop an application form best suited to the company's needs. The form should take into consideration the type and size of the operation, the specialized requirements of the job, the fair-hiring laws of the state and the federal government, and any regulatory agency requirements. The final application form might be a preprinted general form, a special company form, a regulatory agency form, or a combination of these.

Regulatory agency forms. Motor fleets that are under the jurisdiction of the *Federal Motor Carrier Safety Regulations* should be sure their driver employment forms comply with the regulations. The Department of Transportation's (DOT) physical, medical, and other minimum qualification standards differ from those required by most motor fleets.

General forms. Preprinted employment application forms can be purchased from trade associations such as the American Trucking Associations or through transportation form publishers such as J.J. Keller & Associates. A good example of a preprinted application is shown in Figure 8–2.

Company forms. If a company uses an individualized application form, management should develop it carefully to conform to all pertinent regulations and to reflect the needs of the company. In addition, the hiring officer should have the form revised frequently to be sure it contains only those facts pertinent to the particular jobs available in the firm. No questions or blanks should be permitted on the form unless they are justified. The hiring officer can apply the following test to each item:

• Why do I need this information?

• Am I likely to get a correct and honest answer from the applicant?

• From the information likely to be given, what will I be able to tell about the applicant's ability to perform the job for which he or she is being considered?

(*Text continues on page 97.*)

APPLICATION FOR EMPLOYMENT

Company _____

Address _____

City _____ State _____ Zip _____

(answer all questions - please print)

In compliance with Federal and State equal employment opportunity laws, qualified applicants are considered for all positions without regard to race, color, religion, sex, national origin, age, marital status, or non-job related disability.

Date of application _____

Position(s) Applied for _____

Name _____ Social Security No. _____
       Last   First   Middle

Address _____
        Street   City

_____ Phone _____
     State   Zip

ADDRESS FOR PAST THREE YEARS

| Street | City | State & Zip Code | How Long? _____ |
| Street | City | State & Zip Code | How Long? _____ |

Do you have the legal right to work in the United States? _____

Are you over the age of 18? _____ If no, can you provide proof of age? _____

Have you worked for this company before? _____ Where? _____

Dates: From _____ To _____ Rate of Pay _____ Position _____

Reason for leaving _____

Are you now employed? _____ If not, how long since leaving last employment? _____

Who referred you? _____ Rate of pay expected _____

Is there any reason you might be unable to perform the functions of the job for which you have applied [as described in the attached job description]?

_____

If yes, explain if you wish. _____

_____

_____

_____

_____

_____

_____

© Copyright 1992 & Published By:
J. J. KELLER & ASSOCIATES, INC.
3003 W. Breezewood Lane – P.O. Box 368
Neenah, Wisconsin 54957-0368
(800) 327-6868

15F-A (Rev. 5/94)

Figure 8–2. Sample Application for Employment. Courtesy J.J.Keller & Associates, Inc.

EMPLOYMENT HISTORY

Provide employment information for the past 3 years. Attach a sheet if more space if needed.

EMPLOYER	DATES	POSITION HELD
NAME	FROM	
ADDRESS	MO. YR.	
CITY STATE ZIP	TO	REASON FOR LEAVING
PHONE NUMBER	MO. YR.	

EMPLOYER	DATES	POSITION HELD
NAME	FROM	
ADDRESS	MO. YR.	
CITY STATE ZIP	TO	REASON FOR LEAVING
PHONE NUMBER	MO. YR.	

EMPLOYER	DATES	POSITION HELD
NAME	FROM	
ADDRESS	MO. YR.	
CITY STATE ZIP	TO	REASON FOR LEAVING
PHONE NUMBER	MO. YR.	

EMPLOYER	DATES	POSITION HELD
NAME	FROM	
ADDRESS	MO. YR.	
CITY STATE ZIP	TO	REASON FOR LEAVING
PHONE NUMBER	MO. YR.	

MILITARY STATUS

HAVE YOU SERVED IN THE U.S. ARMED FORCES? _____ BRANCH _____

EDUCATION

CIRCLE HIGHEST GRADE COMPLETED: 1 2 3 4 5 6 7 8   HIGH SCHOOL: 1 2 3 4   COLLEGE: 1 2 3 4

LAST SCHOOL ATTENDED _____

                (NAME)   (CITY)

EXPERIENCE AND QUALIFICATIONS – DRIVER

	STATE	LICENSE NO.	TYPE	EXPIRATION DATE
DRIVER				
LICENSES				

A.   Have you ever been denied a license, permit or privilege to operate a motor vehicle?   YES _____ NO _____

B.   Has any license, permit or privilege ever been suspended or revoked?   YES _____ NO _____

    IF THE ANSWER TO EITHER A OR B IS YES, ATTACH STATEMENT GIVING DETAILS

DRIVING EXPERIENCE

CLASS OF EQUIPMENT	TYPE OF EQUIPMENT (VAN, TANK, FLAT, ETC.)	DATES		APPROX. NO. OF MILES (TOTAL)
		FROM	TO	
STRAIGHT TRUCK _____				
TRACTOR AND SEMI-TRAILER _____				
TRACTOR - TWO TRAILERS _____				
OTHER _____				

LIST STATES OPERATED IN FOR LAST FIVE YEARS _____

_____

SHOW SPECIAL COURSES OR TRAINING THAT WILL HELP YOU AS A DRIVER: _____

WHICH SAFE DRIVING AWARDS DO YOU HOLD AND FROM WHOM? _____

PAGE 2 15F-A (Rev. 5/94)

Figure 8–2. (*continued*)

ACCIDENT RECORD FOR PAST 3 YEARS OR MORE (ATTACH SHEET IF MORE SPACE IS NEEDED)

DATES	NATURE OF ACCIDENT (HEAD-ON, REAR-END, UPSET, ETC.)	FATALITIES	INJURIES
LAST ACCIDENT _____			
NEXT PREVIOUS _____			
NEXT PREVIOUS _____			

TRAFFIC CONVICTIONS AND FORFEITURES FOR THE PAST 3 YEARS (OTHER THAN PARKING VIOLATIONS)

LOCATION	DATE	CHARGE	PENALTY

(ATTACH SHEET IF MORE SPACE IS NEEDED)

EXPERIENCE AND QUALIFICATIONS - PLATFORM

LIST TYPES OF PLATFORM EXPERIENCE AND YEARS OF EACH _____

LIST PLATFORM EQUIPMENT YOU CAN OPERATE (LIFT TRUCK, ETC) _____

SHOW COURSES OR TRAINING IN PLATFORM WORK _____

EXPERIENCE AND QUALIFICATIONS - MAINTENANCE

LIST TYPES OF MAINTENANCE EXPERIENCE AND YEARS OF EACH _____

SHOW EQUIPMENT YOU CAN OPERATE	CHECK	YEARS OF EXPERIENCE	EQUIPMENT	CHECK	YEARS OF EXPERIENCE
Woodworking Equipment			Electric Welder		
Sheet Metal Equipment			Oxyacetylene Welder		
Clutch Rebuilding			Paint Spray Gun		
Differential Rebuilding			Wheel & Tire Balancing Machine		
Transmission Rebuilding			Tire Recapping Mold		
Body Work			Engine Dynamometer		
Frame & Axle Straightening Equipment			Chassis Dynamometer		
Electrical & Ignition Repair			Magnetic Crack Tester		
Engine Rebuilding Equipment			Vacuum & Air Brakes		
Diesel Injection Equipment			Other:		

LIST COURSES AND TRAINING IN MAINTENANCE WORK _____

EXPERIENCE AND QUALIFICATIONS - CLERICAL

INDICATE TRAINING AND SHOW EXPERIENCE IN THE FOLLOWING:

*INDICATE WORDS PER MINUTE	TRAINING (CHECK)	YEARS OF EXPERIENCE		TRAINING (CHECK)	YEARS OF EXPERIENCE
Typing *			Rates **		
Shorthand *			OS & D		
Billing			Interline		
TWX			Claims		
PBX			Cashier		
Key Punch Operator			Accounting		
Calculator			Dispatcher		
Dictating Machine Transcriber			Tabulator		
Bookkeeping Machine			Mimeograph		
Adding Machine			** Indicate tariffs with which you		
Other:			have worked		

LIST COURSES AND TRAINING FOR OFFICE WORK _____

Figure 8–2. *(continued)*

EXPERIENCE AND QUALIFICATIONS – OTHER

SHOW ANY TRUCKING, TRANSPORTATION OR OTHER EXPERIENCE THAT MAY HELP IN YOUR WORK FOR THIS COMPANY

_____

_____

LIST COURSES AND TRAINING OTHER THAN SHOWN ELSEWHERE IN THIS APPLICATION

_____

_____

LIST SPECIAL EQUIPMENT OR TECHNICAL MATERIALS YOU CAN WORK WITH (OTHER THAN THOSE ALREADY SHOWN)

_____

_____

TO BE READ AND SIGNED BY APPLICANT

This certifies that this application was completed by me, and that all entries on it and information in it are true and complete to the best of my knowledge.

I authorize you to make such investigations and inquiries of my personal, employment, financial or medical history and other related matters as may be necessary in arriving at an employment decision. (Generally, inquiries regarding medical history will be made only if and after a conditional offer of employment has been extended.) I hereby release employers, schools, health care providers and other persons from all liability in responding to inquiries and releasing information in connection with my application.

In the event of employment, I understand that false or misleading information given in my application or interview(s) may result in discharge. I understand, also, that I am required to abide by all rules and regulations of the Company.

_____   _____
Date   Applicant's Signature

PROCESS RECORD

APPLICANT HIRED _____ REJECTED _____

DATE EMPLOYED _____ POINT EMPLOYED _____

DEPARTMENT _____ CLASSIFICATION _____

THIS SECTION TO BE FILLED IN BY RESPONSIBLE
OFFICER OR COMPANY REPRESENTATIVE

	SUPERIOR	GOOD	FAIR	BELOW AVERAGE	POOR	WRITTEN RECORD ON FILE
1. APPLICATION						
2. INTERVIEW						
3. PAST EMPLOYMENT						
4. WRITTEN EXAM						
5. ROAD TEST						
6. CRIMINAL AND TRAFFIC CONVICTIONS						

SIGNATURE OF INTERVIEWING OFFICER _____

TRANSFERS

FROM: _____ TO: _____   FROM: _____ TO: _____
DATE: _____   DATE: _____
REASON FOR TRANSFER _____   REASON FOR TRANSFER _____

FROM: _____ TO: _____   FROM: _____ TO: _____
DATE: _____   DATE: _____
REASON FOR TRANSFER _____   REASON FOR TRANSFER _____

TERMINATION OF EMPLOYMENT

DATE TERMINATED _____ DEPARTMENT RELEASED FROM _____

DISMISSED _____ VOLUNTARILY QUIT _____ OTHER _____

TERMINATION REPORT PLACED IN FILE _____ SUPERVISOR _____

PAGE 4 15F-A (Rev. 5/94)

Figure 8–2. (*continued*)

In some cases, certain background information about the applicant will be useful to the personnel department only if the applicant makes it through the selection process and ends up on the payroll. Therefore, questions eliciting such background details should not be included on the application form. This information can be provided later to the personnel office on a special form designed for this purpose.

No matter who develops the application form, there are strong fair-hiring laws (discussed in the previous section) that management must carefully consider when creating it. In addition, management should be equally careful in drawing up the criteria for rejecting an applicant. This is an area where the hiring officer must get qualified help. Even innocent, well-intentioned actions can lead to expensive fines and, occasionally, may force a company into hiring a poor driver.

After candidates have filled out the forms, the hiring officer should carefully evaluate them to determine which applicants appear most promising. The officer should ask those people to come in for the next step in the selection procedure. Those who are eliminated in the first round deserve to be notified promptly. Of course, this step of the selection process must be in compliance with all applicable provisions of the Fair Employment Practices Act and the Americans with Disabilities Act.

Step 3—Driver, CDL, and Company-Administered Tests

On October 26, 1986, Congress passed the Commercial Motor Vehicle Safety Act of 1986. Their action was prompted by the diversity of state motor vehicle safety laws and the frequency of truck-related fatalities on the highways. Similar to the impact OSHA has had on the manufacturing sector, the Act changed the way the commercial transportation industry did business. The Act covers all aspects of safety for the transportation of passengers and commodities. The provisions range from the training and licensing of drivers to the actions required in the event of a motor vehicle accident.

The first effect of the Act was to change the licensing requirements. All commercial drivers in the United States were required to change their current license to the Commercial Drivers License (CDL) by April 1, 1992. In order to qualify for the CDL, commercial drivers had to pass a written test and three skills tests, all related to the type of vehicle to be driven.

Before discussing the various tests, it is appropriate to define which drivers need the CDL. As specified in the Act, drivers of a commercial motor vehicle (CMV) or combination of motor vehicles used in commerce to transport passengers or property must obtain a CDL if the CMV:

- has a gross combination weight rating of 26,001 or more pounds inclusive of a towed unit with a gross vehicle weight rating of more than 10,000 pounds; or

- has a gross vehicle weight rating of 26,001 or more pounds; or

- is designed to transport 16 or more passengers, including the driver; or

- is of any size and is used in the transportation of materials found to be hazardous and which require the motor vehicle to be placarded under the Hazardous Materials Regulations (49 *CFR* Part 172, Subpart F).

All applicants must take a general knowledge test. Depending on the type of vehicle used, the driver may need to take additional tests, which include the following:

- Passenger Transport Test, for bus drivers
- Air Brakes Test, for vehicles so equipped
- Combination Vehicles Test
- Hazardous Materials Test, if hauling hazardous material or waste
- Tanker Test, if hauling bulk liquids
- Doubles/Triples Test, if pulling doubles or triples

When drivers pass the knowledge tests, they can then take the skills tests. These tests include the pre-trip inspection test, the basic control skills test, the safe driving skills test, and the air brake skills test (which encompasses the pre-trip inspection skills evaluation).

The basic vehicle control skills test is essentially an obstacle course that the driver must negotiate with an established minimum of corrections and errors.

The safe driving skills test gives an examiner the opportunity to evaluate (road test) a driver's ability to control the vehicle in actual driving situations. The driver is told to negotiate a predetermined course that includes turns at intersections and driving on grades, curves, over railway crossings, and in highway situations. The examiner watches for proper signaling, speed control, and ability to position the motor vehicle correctly when changing lanes or turning.

Before the driver takes the vehicle on the road, the examiner asks him or her to demonstrate the skills necessary to inspect the vehicle and check the air brakes. Drivers must be able to:

- locate and verbally identify air brake controls and monitoring devices
- evaluate the condition of the motor vehicle's brake system and make proper adjustments
- determine that all air-system connections between motor vehicle components have been properly made and secured
- inspect the low-pressure warning device(s) to ensure they will activate in emergency situations
- ascertain, with the engine running, that the system maintains an adequate supply of compressed air
- determine that required minimum air-pressure build-up time is within acceptable limits and that required

alarms and emergency devices automatically deactivate at the proper pressure level

- operate the brake system to check for proper performance

Although many companies use the employment application as a kind of written test, for some driving jobs it is valuable to give applicants a general knowledge test (either oral or written) covering trucking terms and perhaps how to fill out DOT log books. Drivers who work with numbers might be given a validated clerical skills test. Drivers requiring a CDL will be tested as part of the licensing process.

Step 4—The Employment Interview

The employment interview between applicant and hiring officer is normally the most decisive step, although not the final one, in the selection procedure. At this point, the hiring officer makes a preliminary decision whether to hire the applicant, barring any disqualifying information.

Prior to the interview, the hiring officer looks over the information on the employment application form and reviews any test scores achieved by the applicant in the testing program. The officer tries to form an overall impression of the applicant's total qualifications in terms of the job requirements. He or she estimates the applicant's strong and weak points and decides what questions to pursue in the upcoming interview regarding the applicant's background.

The setting for the interview should provide privacy. No other person should be in the room with the interviewer and the applicant. The room should be quiet and free of distractions throughout the interview. The interviewer's manner should be friendly and informal.

It should be remembered that an interview is a conversation with a purpose. The interviewer should try to accomplish the following:

- Verify or expand on information shown on the application blank. It is especially important to fill in gaps in the employment time record and to reduce entries to factual data.

- Be able to form an opinion about the applicant's personality, appearance, attitude toward employment, and attitude toward safe driving.

- Give the applicant an idea of what the job involves and what working for the company would be like.

The interviewer should remember that the employment interview has many weaknesses as an objective device for measuring the potential capabilities of an applicant. Studies have shown that interviewers are frequently influenced by their prejudices and biases for or against an applicant. Equally competent interviewers frequently disagree about their appraisal of the same applicant. The interview often results in obtaining inaccurate information about the applicant.

In spite of its weaknesses, the interview remains a primary tool of the employee selection process. The previous selection steps are designed to develop information on which the interviewer can make a final decision regarding the applicant's suitability for the job. Therefore, the interviewer should approach the task with objectivity, try to form an unbiased appraisal of the applicant's abilities, and keep focused on the requirements of the job. The interviewer is not a politician handing out patronage jobs to friends but more like a purchasing agent bent on finding quality material for the enterprise.

The interview itself represents a complex social encounter. The conscientious personnel officer should study all the published literature on the subject and strive to put the best suggestions and guidelines into practice. Successful interviewing is a difficult art to master; proficiency can be attained only through conscious study and practice.

After all interviews have been completed, the hiring officer makes a further appraisal of the candidates. The officer notifies the interviewees who have not been selected. The next step for the remaining candidates is to check references.

The interviewer must be very careful not to mislead an applicant at this point. Candidates who believe that the job is secured and that other steps are mere formalities may leave their current position, or at the very least, have very high hopes. Candidates should be told that even though they are still in the running, other applicants are being considered as well.

Step 5—Checking References

Thus far in the selection procedure, the hiring officer has pretty much relied on what the applicant has said and what objective tests have revealed. Most of what the applicant has said can be taken at face value; but it is only human to exaggerate good points and minimize or conceal anything that might jeopardize getting the job. It is therefore critical for the hiring officer to consult other people who have known the applicant in the past and who can provide details about the person's professional abilities and general character.

The most important source of this information is previous employers. These sources can provide information regarding the applicant's length of employment, type of work performed, number of accidents, and general character. The applicant should be asked to provide names and addresses of three past employers or just the previous employer if the person has worked at the same company for ten years or more. Some fleet supervisors say five years.

EMPLOYMENT INQUIRY

Name of Applicant: _____
Previous Employer: _____
Former Supervisor: _____ Telephone: _____

_____ has applied for employment with our firm.
May we please confidentially verify some of the information that has been given to us?

1. Dates of employment with your company?
   From _____ to _____
2. What type of work was performed? _____
3. Were there any lost-time injuries while on the job? _____ Yes _____ No _____
   How many? _____
4. Was this employee involved in any traffic accidents? _____ Yes _____ No _____
   How many? _____ If yes, were any considered preventable?_____
5. Did this employee get along well with supervisors? _____
6. Was this employee considered to be trustworthy? _____ Honest? _____ Punctual? _____
   Steady? _____
7. Why did this employee leave your company? _____
8. Would you rehire? Yes _____ No _____ If not, why not? _____
   _____

COMMENT:
_____
_____

Date of Inquiry _____ By _____

Figure 8–3. This Employment Inquiry checklist is easy to use and file.

There are three methods of checking with past employers: the telephone check, the form letter, and the personal visit.

The telephone check. This call should be made by the interviewer, who uses a printed form both as a checklist to make sure all pertinent information is requested and as a form on which to record the information. The call should be made, if possible, to the immediate supervisor of the driver, since this person will sometimes provide more information than will a personnel officer. An example of an Employment Inquiry checklist is shown in Figure 8–3.

Quick response is the primary advantage of this method of checking references. The disadvantage is that previous employers may be reluctant to provide information over the telephone. To double-check a caller, some companies will ask for a phone number and call back only after checking the source.

The form letter. This method is perhaps the most frequently used. Usually, the hiring officer sends out a printed form and a stamped self-addressed envelope for the convenience of the person giving the reference. The advantage of this method is that it is a routine clerical operation that provides a written report from the previous employer. The disadvantage is that the previous employer may be reluctant to make any signed report about a former employee, especially if the report contains derogatory information. A second disadvantage is that letters are slow—the personnel staff may not be able or willing to answer written reference checks quickly. An example of the form letter reference check is shown in Figure 8–4.

A personal visit. Perhaps the most reliable method is a personal visit to the previous employer to discuss an applicant's work history. Previous employers will talk about an applicant much more frankly in a personal interview than over the phone or in writing. The disadvantages are the time and cost involved and the fact that it is not possible to do personal visits when hiring a large number of drivers or when long distances are involved.

Professional agencies exist that will conduct personal investigation for a fee. Such investigations usually include checking with the police department, credit agencies, and neighbors and acquaintances of the person investigated.

Additional checks. In addition to reference checks, the hiring officer should always review the applicant's

---

INQUIRY TO PAST EMPLOYERS

FROM - Prospective Employer
Company _____
Individual _____
Street _____
City _____ State ____ Zip _____

TO - Previous Employer
Company _____
Name _____
Street _____
City _____ State ____ Zip _____

Personnel Manager:

    The person named below has applied to this company for employment. Your firm is listed by the applicant as a past employer. Kindly reply to this inquiry respecting this applicant. As you will note from the waiver stated below, **the applicant has waived any claim of liability against your company (and its agents) for information submitted in response to this inquiry.**

    For your convenience in replying by return mail, we have enclosed a stamped, self-addressed envelope.

Very Truly Yours,

Name of applicant: _____
Social Security No. _____
Job applied for: _____

---

1. This applicant lists dates of employment with your firm from: _____ to: _____ Is this correct? Yes ☐; No ☐
   If no, please explain: _____
2. What kind(s) of work did he/she do? Driver ☐ (type of vehicle _____); Dock ☐; Office ☐; Shop ☐; Other
   (Specify) _____
3. If employed as a driver, please indicate type of equipment driven. Tractor trailer ☐; Straight truck ☐; Twin-Trailers ☐; Bus ☐;
   Other (Specify) _____
4. Number of reportable accidents _____; number of accidents in which applicant was ticketed _____; number of accidents in
   which the applicant was at fault _____ (please explain) _____; Date of each accident _____
5. To your knowledge, was this person's chauffeur/operator's license suspended while in your employ? _____ If so, please explain:
   _____
6. (Respond only if checked*) [ ] Was this person bonded while with your company? _____ If so, were there any circumstances
   that were reported to the bonding company?
   * Prospective employer—check this question only if bonding is required for this position.
7. Is there anything in the applicant's history that could suggest he or she may not be trusted to handle company funds? _____
8. Did the applicant pose either repeated and/or severe disciplinary problems? Yes ☐; No ☐; If so, please explain: _____
   _____
9. Why did this employee leave your company? Resigned ☐; Discharged ☐; Laid off ☐.
10. Would you re-employ this person? Yes ☐; No ☐ Please explain: _____

11. Remarks: _____

By: _____ Date: _____
(Signature of person supplying information)

(Detach here for your files)

WAIVER

_____   _____
(Former employer)   (Date)

    I hereby authorize you to release all information concerning my employment, including oral assessments of my job performance, ability, and fitness, to each and every company (or their authorized agents) which may request such information in connection with my application for employment with said company. I hereby release you from any and all liability of any type as a result of providing the above mentioned information to the above mentioned person.

_____   _____
(Applicant's signature)   (Witness's signature)

Figure 8–4. This sample Inquiry to Past Employers can be used to check the applicants' references by mail. Reprinted with permission from the American Trucking Associations, Inc. ("ATA"). For more information or to order a copy of the Inquiry to Past Employers, call ATA's toll free telephone number (800-ATA-LINE) and ask for Form #C0760.

State Department of Motor Vehicles record. This record provides vital information on traffic accidents, convictions, and injuries. Check each state where the applicant has lived, worked, or been licensed in the past five years. Electronic computer-to-computer checks can be made, as well as checks by mail. In some states, it may be possible to make a personal call to the department.

Liability release form. To protect the company against any legal liability resulting from personnel investigation activities, all applicants should first sign a release. The document should contain the following statement.

> I hereby release the _____ company or any agency it may designate or any persons the _____ company or agency may contact in the course of its investigation from any liability which may result from the conduct of such investigation or from the result of the investigation.

The results of these reference checks are so important that it is very risky to start an applicant on the job before they are received. In practice, the interviewer usually makes telephone checks, relying on a letter of personal reference only as a last resort. Applicants cannot be kept "on the hook" until a previous employer mails in a written reference. On the other hand, putting the driver to work before references are checked is foolhardy and can put the company at risk for expensive accidents.

Step 6—Physical Examination

Motor carrier safety regulations for bus and truck operators (a) require a physical examination for all new drivers and (b) provide that motor carriers must have on file a certificate showing each driver to be physically qualified. In addition, these regulations require that the driver carry on his or her person evidence of such physical fitness.

Conducting the physical examination. All applicants for driver positions should be examined by a qualified physician as a part of the employment procedure. Figure 8–5 shows a certificate that drivers can carry as proof of their physical fitness to drive.

The *Federal Motor Carrier Safety Regulations* set minimum physical fitness requirements for drivers to operate in interstate commerce. Most fleet operators who are serious about safety establish physical requirements that are much more stringent than the ones set in the regulations.

Physicians selected to conduct the physical examination should be familiar with the requirements of the job for which the applicant is being considered. In larger cities, some physicians specialize in industrial practice. As a result, they are familiar with the DOT regulations and requirements, as well as with the attitudes of state agencies who administer workers' compensation laws. Such physicians can render valuable assistance to motor carriers in establishing standards, conducting examinations, handling workers' compensation cases, and maintaining the physical well-being of all drivers.

The Americans with Disabilities Act (ADA) will not force a company to hire anyone without a CDL to drive a commercial vehicle. If the decision not to hire a driver with a CDL is based on other physical requirements of the job, the human resources ADA specialist should be consulted. This is especially true if the carrier exercises the right to require an additional physical examination.

Conducting alcohol and drug testing. Besides the traditional physical examination, alcohol and drug testing of employees in safety-sensitive positions in the aviation, motor carrier, railroad, and mass transit industries is now required. The Federal Highway Administration (FHWA) has issued a rule that all drivers who are required to have a commercial driver's license be tested. Drivers are prohibited from taking part in safety-sensitive tasks under the following circumstances:

- while having a breath alcohol level of 0.04%
- while using alcohol
- within four hours of using alcohol

They also cannot refuse to submit to an alcohol test, nor can they consume alcohol within eight hours after an accident or until tested. The required tests include the following:

- preemployment—conducted before performing safety-sensitive functions for the first time (drug testing *only*)
- postaccident—conducted after accidents on drivers whose performance could have contributed to the accident
- reasonable suspicion—conducted when a trained supervisor observes behavior characteristic of alcohol misuse
- random—conducted on a random unannounced basis before, during, and after performance of safety-sensitive tasks
- return to duty and follow-up—conducted on an individual who violated prohibited alcohol conduct standards. This procedure includes six tests in first twelve months after the employee's return to work.

The alcohol tests will be conducted using evidential breath testing (EBT) devices approved by the National Highway Transportation Safety Association (NHTSA). If a test shows a breath alcohol level (BAL) above 0.02%, a confirmation test must be conducted on an EBT that prints out the results, date, time, a sequential test number, and the name and serial number of the device. The second test determines what actions must be taken.

A BAL level above 0.02% requires that the driver be prohibited from driving for 24 hours. If a driver's appearance and behavior suggest alcohol misuse but a test cannot

MEDICAL EXAMINER'S CERTIFICATE

I certify that I have examined

_____
(Driver's name (Print))

In accordance with the Federal Motor Carrier Safety Regulations (49 CFR 391.41 through 391.49) and with knowledge of his/her duties, I find him/her qualified under the regulations. Expiration date of certificate: _____

Qualified only when wearing; ❑ Corrective lenses ❑ Hearing aid
❑ Medically unqualified unless accompanied by a _____ waiver
❑ Medically unqualified unless driving within an exempt intracity zone
A completed examination form for this person is on file in my office.

_____
(Area Code/Phone No.)   (License/Certificate No.)   (State)

_____
(Medical Examiner: (Print Name and Title))   (Signature)

_____
(Signature of Driver)

_____
(Address of Driver)

Form C0750   4 / 94   Printed by American Trucking Assns.

Figure 8–5. This sample Medical Examiner's Certificate satisfies the requirement that drivers carry evidence of their physical fitness to drive. Reprinted with permission from the American Trucking Associations, Inc. ("ATA"). For more information or to order a copy of the Medical Examiner's Certificate, call ATA's toll free telephone number (800-ATA-LINE) and ask for Form # C0750.

be conducted, the driver must be barred from driving for 24 hours. If the employer decides to return the driver to safety-sensitive work, the employer must ensure that the driver

- has been evaluated by a substance abuse professional,
- has complied with any recommended treatment,
- has taken a return-to-work test with negative results, and
- is subject to unannounced follow-up tests.

A violation of these employer-based testing rules will not affect the driver's CDL record.

It is the employer's obligation to provide drivers with information about alcohol misuse, the employer's policy, the testing requirements, and how and where drivers can get help for alcohol abuse. Supervisors of these drivers should be trained to recognize alcohol abuse. The supervisors must attend at least one hour of training to help them identify the symptoms of alcohol misuse and the indicators used as a basis for recommending reasonable suspicion testing. The FHWA will conduct periodic audits of a firm for compliance, so it is important that fleet safety professionals conduct their own compliance audit.

The records of the testing and treatment of employees for alcohol misuse are confidential. They should be stored in a file away from their regular personnel or medical file. This information may be released only to the employer and substance abuse professionals. If the employee initiates a grievance, hearing, or lawsuit, the records may be turned over to the decision maker.

Drug testing is required for the same events as alcohol testing. A change from the 1988 rules requires a "split" test. The test sample is divided into two equal samples.

The primary sample is tested by a lab approved by the Department of Health and Human Services (DHHS). If the analysis of the primary specimen confirms the presence of illegal, controlled substances, the driver has 72 hours to request the split specimen be sent to another DHHS-certified lab for a second opinion.

The samples are analyzed for the following drugs:

- marijuana (THC metabolites)
- cocaine
- amphetamines
- opiates (including heroin)
- phencyclidine (PCP)

A confirmation test is conducted using gas chromatography/mass spectrometry (GC/MS) if the initial screening test is positive. The positive results are reviewed by a Medical Review Officer (MRO). The MRO will contact the driver to determine if there was some legitimate medical use of the drug before reporting to the employer. The positive result will have the same effect on the driver's work status as the alcohol violation.

One difference between tests for alcohol and for drugs is the frequency of random testing. Alcohol rules require that 25% of drivers be tested in a calendar year while drug rules require 50% of the workers be tested. Both rules have provisions that adjust that percentage based on the positive rate for the industry.

Because the rules for drug and alcohol testing change frequently, a company should purchase a compliance software package with frequent updates. The National Safety Council's RegScan MCS (Motor Carrier Safety) is one such program, with eleven monthly updates each year. The FHWA Electronic Bulletin Board Service (FEBBS) is also useful. The person coordinating this program must communicate changes in rules throughout the organization as they occur.

Once a company receives the results of a physical examination—or any required alcohol and drug tests—and the applicant has been found fit to handle the job, a road and skill test should be given.

Step 7—Road and Skill Test

Road and skill tests are used to qualify an applicant as a safe, professional driver. The safety director, or other hiring officer, is present as an observer while the applicant demonstrates the ability to operate the vehicle safely. The test may be conducted on a private driving course under simulated conditions or on a public road in actual traffic.

Michigan State University has developed the Driver Performance Measurement Test. This test can help assess safe driving ability during selection by pointing out the precise unsafe habits likely to lead to later accidents. Information on the test can be obtained from Michigan

State University, Lifelong Education Highway Traffic Safety Programs, telephone (517) 355–3270.

The system requires the preparation of a thoroughly calibrated test course on public roads. As many as fifty traffic situations may be charted, and the correct/incorrect driving procedures determined for each. After the course is validated, and companies have trained and certified their own observers, the course can be used by all nearby companies to test drivers. Although the test course obviously requires a lot of organization and test time, it does give a standardized measure of driving performance. Any company hiring large numbers of drivers in one area should investigate the Driver Performance Measurement Test.

Some companies maintain a truck roadeo to measure drivers' skills. This type of course may be important for a city driver who, for instance, may be backing into tight alleys and loading docks from the first day on the job. Information on truck driver championship courses can be obtained from the Safety Department, American Trucking Associations, 2200 Mill Road, Alexandria, VA 22314–4677.

Information on bus competitions can be obtained from the American Public Transit Association, 1201 New York Avenue, NW, Washington, DC 2005 and the National School Transportation Association, PO Box 2639, Springfield, VA 22452. Skill course diagrams, tests, and obstacle specifications can be secured from ATA or the National Private Truck Council.

In some trucking operations, job applicants may be tested for skill in nondriving tasks. Experienced tank truck driver applicants may be asked to hook up hoses to pumps. A driver claiming experience with "doubles" trucks may be required to hook up a set of trailers, thus demonstrating knowledge of procedures as well as driving skill.

Step 8—Acceptance Interview

An applicant who passes the previous seven steps in the selection process should be called in and told that he or she is either being hired or being placed on a waiting list. The acceptance interview should reinforce the applicant's enthusiasm for the job. It is important that the newly hired employee be made to feel that although company employment standards are rigorous, the person has attributes which the company sincerely wants. Management should welcome the new employee into the company as a valued new member, provide further orientation, explain what training will be given, and mention when and where the employee should report for work. Wages and working conditions also should be specified at this time.

LEGAL AND SOCIAL RESTRICTIONS

The motor transportation fleet is a constructive social and economic force in the community in which it operates—not only because of the transportation service it renders, but also because of the jobs it provides. Placing a person on the payroll has social and economic significance to the individual, to the fleet, and to the community.

In this context, today's employers are no longer as free to hire whomever they wish. Laws throughout our nation forbid discrimination against job applicants. Society often takes the view that if employers wish to tap the local labor market, they must do so with due regard for every applicant's right to fair consideration for the job.

These are not unreasonable restrictions. They should certainly not force the employer to hire unqualified workers. Management is not doing applicants any favors by hiring them for positions they are not qualified to handle. This policy can result in accidents, possible injuries, and substandard work. The hiring officer has a moral obligation to the applicant, to the company, and to the community to perform the job well by selecting highly qualified, safe drivers.

CHAPTER
9

Driver Training

One of the most important ingredients of efficient and profitable transportation services is safe driving skills. A diesel tractor is a frozen asset until a driver gets behind the wheel, starts the engine, and puts the vehicle to work.

The degree of skill with which this vehicle is maintained, operated, and managed will affect the amount and quality of service it provides, its service life span, and the number of traffic accidents in which it is involved. These are incentives for management to take great pains to see that drivers are skilled in driving safely.

Management should use the selection program described in the previous chapters to hire drivers who are capable of meeting management's standards. A good training program will bring drivers' skills up to this level, and good supervision of the drivers (discussed in subsequent chapters) can further improve their performance.

BENEFITS OF TRAINING

To what extent is training related to safe driving? The operation of a motor vehicle may seem to be a fairly common skill. However, safety experts have long known that safe driving is far from being a simple skill. The ability to make wise traffic decisions quickly should be acquired through planned training, not picked up haphazardly.

The professional driver's skill has an added economic dimension. Management cannot take for granted the quality of previous training the driver may have had. The only way to ensure top driving skills is to train each new employee. Training gives a driver the knowledge to do the job, the skill to do it properly, an appreciation for the job's importance, and an understanding of the need to do it safely.

The money, time, and effort that training costs will be more than offset by the following benefits:

• **Reduction in accidents.** The number of accidents and accident-related costs will be greatly reduced. The trained driver will know how to act safely and what situations to avoid.

• **Reduced maintenance costs.** The driver who knows a vehicle's mechanical limitations and tries to conserve the vehicle will develop good operating habits, take better care of the vehicle, and cooperate more fully with the maintenance department.

• **Reduced absenteeism and labor turnover.** Training helps a driver develop a better understanding of both job and fleet problems and increases the person's job satisfaction.

• **Reduced supervisory burden.** Training establishes a standard of performance and a basis for effective corrective action by supervision when needed. Well-trained drivers usually require less supervision because they understand these standards clearly and know how to meet them without continued reminders from the supervisor.

• **Improved public relations.** The driver represents the company in daily contacts with customers and other users of the highway. Good training reflects credit not only on the driver but also on the company.

DEVELOPMENT OF A TRAINING PROGRAM

Because there are many valid approaches to training, the detailed development of the fleet training program is highly individualized. Factors to be considered include the philosophy of fleet management, personalities involved in driver training, the function of the fleet, the time allotted to training, and labor/management relations.

Developing a training program is much like writing a speech. Each person must write his or her own but can use material from many sources. The program must cover the subject thoroughly and in an interesting manner. Because the program will be presented over and over as new drivers are hired, it must be constantly revised in terms of audience reaction, trainee success on the job, and the changing needs of the fleet.

The following ideas should help build a good driver training program.

When to Train

Training should be thought of as a process of personal development that begins when the driver is hired and continues until retirement. The most effective time for extensive, systematic training is right after the driver is hired and before he or she is assigned to a vehicle.

How Long to Train

In designing a training program, the first issue to determine is how long training should last. Initial, refresher, remedial, and ongoing training should all be addressed.

Initial training. The amount of time devoted to initial training will depend on the selection program, the type of person hired, his or her background, and the amount of usable training and experience a driver brings to the job.

The only practical gauge is that initial training time should be adequate to bring the knowledge and skill of the new driver up to the level needed to perform the job properly.

Refresher training. This material usually consists of one or two days of classroom instruction in which initial training material is reviewed or updated material is presented to familiarize drivers with new equipment, operating problems, or regulations. Refresher training is given annually or as needed.

One large city bus company recommends a special type of refresher training 90 days after initial training. The theory is that new trainees accept material without much question because many of them have no actual experience driving a bus. But after 90 days on the job, they have faced situations not fully covered in training and have many questions. This refresher course lasts one day and is devoted mainly to discussion.

Remedial training. Designed for drivers who have had a certain number of accidents, remedial courses should focus on the types of accidents the repeaters have had and should feature the discussion technique. If the instructor describes one class member's accident and lets the other members discuss how it could have been prevented, everyone learns a lesson from it. Remedial training has been shown to improve the performance of accident repeaters.

Ongoing training. Education should go on day after day to expose drivers continuously to safety information and ideas. In addition to classwork, this type of education uses safety posters, dash cards, bulletin boards, safety booklets, and driver letters.

Where to Train

Another issue in designing a training program is where it will be conducted. A special training room, behind the wheel, and the safety supervisor's office are all useful locations.

Special training room. The most effective training is done in a specially designed training room, which every fleet should have. If a separate room is not feasible, a suitable place can be adapted for training purposes. The training room should be soundproof, well-lighted, ventilated, and equipped with tables and comfortable chairs. If trainees are uncomfortable, the environment will not be conducive to learning, and training efforts will be wasted.

The training room should have a chalkboard, a magnetic board for showing traffic situations, model vehicles (these can be 2- by 6-inch slightly pointed 1/4-inch boards with concealed magnets), and other aids to training.

Care taken in the layout, design, decoration, and equipment of the training room will pay off in better-trained drivers. The room can also be used for other employee training, committee meetings, and management conferences. In fact, the training room can be a communications center for the entire organization. The costs of setting up and maintaining the training room can be jointly budgeted from the safety, sales, mechanical maintenance, and other departments.

Behind-the-wheel training. Only by riding with the driver can the supervisor observe the person's driving habits and responses to different traffic situations. The usual pattern is for the trainee to drive the vehicle over a prescribed course on public roads while accompanied by the supervisor. (Figure C–1 in Appendix C, Skill Drills and Test Courses, shows a test course layout.) The supervisor should not point out errors during the test; after the test drive, any driving errors and correct methods should be discussed.

A special type of behind-the-wheel training is "commentary driving." Here the supervisor also rides with the driver, but the driver describes what he or she sees in the traffic situation ahead and how to adjust to it.

The commentary might go like this: "The sign says 35 miles an hour. I'm well under that speed. There's an unregulated intersection ahead. A blue station wagon is pulling into the intersection. I think it's going to stop. Now I see it isn't, so I'm reducing my speed. It is now clear of the intersection and I can resume speed. My turn is up ahead. I see no vehicles following in my rear-view mirror, but I'm putting on my right turn signal anyway. I'm edging over to the curb lane, slowing down to make the turn. . . ."

Commentary driving allows the supervisor to gauge how much a driver notices in any traffic situation. It also teaches the driver how to use eye movement more effectively and note all the elements that enter into any driving situation.

Another place for training is on a closed test course in a vacant parking lot or driving range. In this situation, the driver can practice driving under close clearances and in tight quarters. Because trainees are shown how to maneuver their vehicles between barrels, flags, wooden horses, and pavement marks, these sessions are sometimes called skill drills (see Appendix C, Skill Drills and Test Courses). Drivers should be permitted to practice on the test course until they become proficient. Skill drills are also used as a basis for driving contests.

The safety supervisor's office. The supervisor's office is the best place for the safety director and a driver to discuss an accident when determining whether it was preventable. This session should be regarded as an excellent training opportunity and not as a disciplinary action.

Appendix B, Safety Meetings for Commercial Drivers, gives details of training meetings.

Continuous Training

Although there are special times and places for training, it can be effectively carried on at any time and almost any place. Good trainers know when and where to take advantage of training opportunities as they arise.

COMPONENTS OF TRAINING

The most important part of a training program is its subject matter. Because training is useful only when it fills a need, the subject matter should cover what drivers need to know to do their jobs well. Before assembling any training material, the instructor should outline what skills and information trainees need to learn, then use the following categories to rank these topics:

1. Vital subject matter is absolutely essential to success on the job.

2. Important subject matter provides a basis for understanding the job.

3. Helpful material relates to the job and gives a broader base of understanding on which to build performance.

4. Incidental material is nice to know but not necessary to job performance.

It is not always easy to decide what training material falls into which category. In making the final selection, trainers should use their own judgment. The training material outline, methods, and training aids make up a training session plan (see Appendix B, Safety Meetings for Commercial Drivers).

The amount of time devoted to each area is also a matter of individual determination. The trainer will have to assemble the details of each subject from the literature on that topic.

The following subject areas are discussed further in this section. Much of this material is covered in the Council's Driver Improvement Program.

1. scope of the traffic accident problem
2. traffic regulations
3. hazardous materials
4. causes of traffic accidents
5. personal traits affecting driving
6. defensive driving
7. preventability
8. two-vehicle collision prevention
9. backing accident prevention
10. stopping distance demonstration
11. the driver and the vehicle
12. basic driving maneuvers
13. driving in traffic
14. task-specific training
15. procedures in case of accident
16. handling passengers and freight
17. company safety program

Scope of the Traffic Accident Problem

Describe the national traffic accident problem: the number of fatal accidents and the number of property damage accidents and their costs. Show both direct and indirect costs of traffic accidents to the company. Explain how rates are determined and how company rates compare with those of other fleets and the industry in general. Show how the direct and indirect costs of accidents reduce the company's profits, affecting its ability to stay in business and provide top wages, benefits, and bonus programs to its employees.

Describe the cost of accidents to the driver: possible injury or death and loss of earnings if the driver is hospitalized or disabled for an extended period.

Describe how safe driving contributes to community safety by reducing the number of accidents and setting a good example for other drivers. Show how it contributes to the health of the company by reducing costs, improving efficiency of service to customers, and creating a favorable impression on the general public. Connect safe driving with employee welfare: it ensures job security and continuity of earning power.

Stress that the company has high standards of performance in everything it does, including safe driving. Remind drivers that the company expects not just average safe driving performance but award-winning safety performance because it knows that this is possible. Read and discuss the company's written safety policy (see Chapter 2, Elements of a Fleet Safety Program).

Be sure that the material motivates drivers to develop and maintain safe driving skills.

Traffic Regulations

Discuss state and municipal traffic laws and ordinances with drivers. If the fleet operates in interstate commerce, teach the *Federal Motor Carrier Safety Regulations* that affect drivers and distribute copies of these regulations.

Most drivers do not believe they need a refresher on the rules. To show them the value of a refresher, conduct an exercise that is sure to turn into a free-for-all argument. Ask them to discuss the proper location of warning devices on a two-lane highway. In the unlikely event that all of the drivers in the session agree on the proper placement, try quizzing them on the placement for a divided highway. When the dust settles, it will be painfully obvious that a refresher is exactly what is needed. A visual aid showing the proper placement will help reinforce the learning (Figure 9–1).

Review traffic signs and correct use of hand and automatic signals. Stress that the company—as well as the law—expects all drivers to observe all traffic rules. Explain the company's attitude if a driver is arrested or cited for a traffic violation.

This training should not only give knowledge of traffic rules and regulations, but also develop understanding and respect for them.

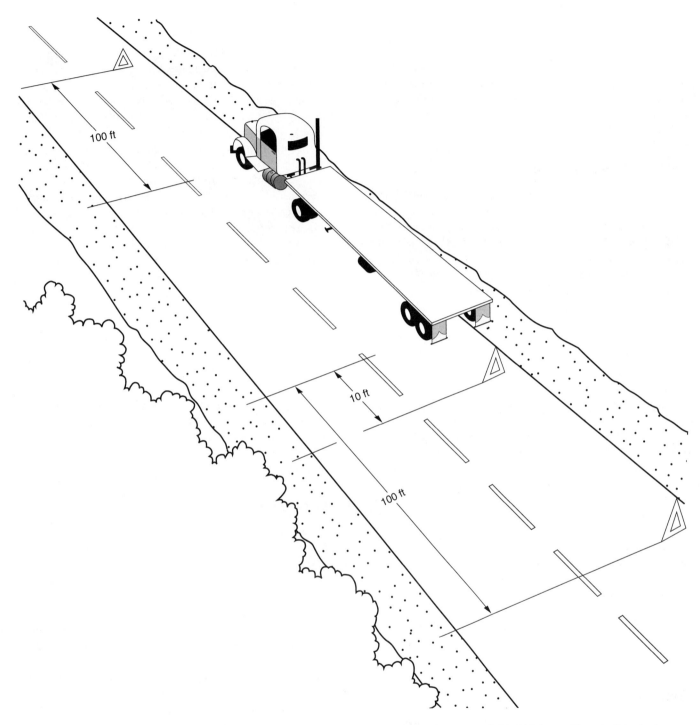

Figure 9–1. Emergency warning devices should be placed as shown on a two-lane or undivided highway. Permissible devices include triangles, DOT-over-DOTs, electrical emergency lanterns, torches, or (during daylight hours only) 2 red flags in lieu of the 2 triangles at the rear of the vehicle.

Hazardous Materials

Training for employees who transport hazardous materials is required within 90 days of employment, with recurrent training to be done semiannually. This is the minimum that must be documented in the training records. The records must contain the trainee's name, date of last training, location of the training materials used, name and address of trainer, and certification of training and testing.

If the driver is also trained as a first responder in the event of a spill, make sure the training is coordinated to avoid unnecessary duplication. The training should also be task-specific to reduce a driver's level of potential exposure.

The most common OSHA citation in fiscal 1993 was failure to have a written hazard communication program. The third most frequent was failure to train, and the fifth most frequent was inadequate or missing Material Safety Data Sheets (MSDS).

Causes of Traffic Accidents

Stress the key idea that vehicle accidents do not happen by chance. Most of the factors that cause them can be controlled or compensated for by the driver. These factors include the driver's physical, mental, and emotional condition; the vehicle's mechanical condition; and the acts of pedestrians and drivers of other vehicles. Discuss such other accident factors as road surface, weather, and light conditions.

Stress that the trainee is expected to be alert to all these factors, recognize how they can contribute to accidents, and take the proper precautions to avoid an accident. This lesson should convince trainees that accidents are preventable.

Personal Traits Affecting Driving

To enhance trainees' respect for the relationship of good health habits to safe driving, describe how the physical, mental, and emotional well-being of a driver affects safe driving.

For example, a number of psychophysical testing devices are available to measure how trainees perform according to several personal traits. Compensating habits can be taught if needed. For instance, if the trainee has narrow peripheral vision, he or she can compensate by turning the head from side to side to observe traffic conditions. Several psychophysical devices may be purchased from the American Automobile Association through any affiliate office.

Remind trainees how important it is to keep in good physical condition, avoid extreme fatigue, avoid drugs or medications that might impair driving ability, and manage stress and other distractions.

Defensive Driving

An entire unit of instruction should be devoted to one of the most important safe driving concepts: defensive driving.

Defensive driving means the driver must have both the desire and the ability to control accident-producing situations. Defensive drivers accept responsibility for avoiding accidents rather than passively surrendering to an adverse situation. They have a positive attitude; they expect to prevent accidents by taking the initiative.

But attitude alone is not enough. The defensive driver must also demonstrate alertness, foresight, knowledge, judgment, and skill. All of these qualities can be developed in the training program and further improved by experience.

The National Safety Council's Defensive Driving Courses teach driving techniques that can save lives, time, and money in spite of conditions and the actions of others.

To address a company's safety needs for specific vehicles, a variety of driver improvement programs have been developed. The Council currently offers Defensive Driving Courses for cars, vans, emergency vehicles, school and transit buses, and medium-to-large trucks. These ready-to-use programs are available for a fraction of the costs a carrier would incur developing its own. Check the National Safety Council catalog for courses related to specific types of vehicles.

For instance, a large fleet found a direct correlation between their use of the National Safety Council's Defensive Driving Course and reduced accident frequency. The fleet's semiannual use of the program provides a refresher course to drivers on collision prevention techniques. The firm also tailored its accident reporting format to match the topics covered in each section of the course. This cross-correlation allows in-house instructors to refer to specific company incidents as they teach the course. Using actual company statistics helps drivers understand the importance and usefulness of the material.

This type of program could also be used in conjunction with an off-the-job safety program (see Chapter 15, Off-the-Job Safety Programs). Some organizations offer this training to family members for a small fee to cover expenses or at no charge as an employee benefit.

Preventability

Closely allied to defensive driving are the terms "preventable" and "nonpreventable," which measure the defensive driving skill exercised by a driver in a given accident. If the driver did everything that reasonably could have been done to prevent the accident and it still happened, then it is graded nonpreventable. If the driver did not do everything reasonable, the accident is considered preventable. Tell trainees the ground rules under which the accident will be judged and how to appeal an adverse decision.

The concepts of defensive driving and accident preventability dovetail to make possible a third important idea: the standard of safe driving performance is driving without being involved in any preventable accidents. This standard must be thoroughly understood by top management, supervisors, and drivers. The National Safety Council's *Guide to Determining Motor Vehicle Accident Preventability* explains the concept and gives examples. On-site training courses on preventability are also available from the Council.

These three ideas are sometimes difficult for drivers to comprehend at first. But they are so essential to the development of professional safe driving attitudes and skills that trainers should allot time to explain them clearly. Once the rules are understood, drivers will acquire a new respect for safe driving ability, be more receptive to safety information, and develop a personal concern for their own safety records.

Two-Vehicle Collision Prevention

Another unit of training should be devoted to demonstrating how two vehicles can collide from each of six positions, and what defensive measures apply in each situation. Even normal traffic can offer such varied and complex problems that unless these situations are grouped, the training program can become an exhaustive list of do's and don'ts that drivers find impossible to remember.

There are only six positions in which one vehicle can collide with another. One vehicle can be (1) ahead of the other vehicle, (2) behind it, (3) approaching it from an angle, (4) approaching from the opposite direction, (5) passing it, or (6) being passed by it.

Backing Accident Prevention

Because backing accidents occur frequently, this subject belongs in the driver training program. Even though this type of accident is usually minor, the cumulative costs mount up. Sometimes a backing accident can even have serious results.

Drivers should be taught to avoid backing whenever possible. Backing around corners or out of driveways or alleys is especially dangerous. If there is a choice, backing out of traffic is safer than backing into traffic.

Some utilities require drivers to place a traffic cone behind their parked vehicles when backing will be required following any utility work. This is easy to audit, and drivers are forced to survey the scene behind their vehicle when they retrieve the cone, prior to backing.

Stopping Distance Demonstration

Most drivers firmly believe it is a mark of driving skill to be able to stop their vehicle on a dime. This misconception is hard to refute without convincing proof. The brake detonator dramatically demonstrates the distance it takes to stop their vehicle.

The device, equipped with two firing chambers for laying chalk marks onto the pavement, is attached to the vehicle's front bumper. The instructor fires the first charge when the vehicle attains a predetermined speed. This makes a mark on the pavement and signals the driver to apply the brakes and stop the vehicle in the shortest possible distance. When the brakes take hold, the second charge is fired and makes a second mark on the pavement. When the vehicle finally stops, the driver and instructor get out and mark the point on the pavement that is even with the front bumper.

There are now three marks on the pavement: (1) the point where the instructor fired the first charge and signaled the driver to stop; (2) the point where the vehicle's brakes began to take hold; and (3) the point where the vehicle stopped. The distance between the first and second marks is the reaction distance. It shows how far the vehicle traveled while the driver was responding to the signal and getting a foot on the brake pedal.

The distance between the second and third marks, known as the braking distance, tells how far it took the brakes to stop the vehicle. The two measurements represent total stopping distance required in every stop a driver makes at that speed. Tests can be run at different speeds. Brake detonators can be purchased from the American Automobile Association through any affiliate office.

When time does not permit testing all drivers, volunteers are selected while the rest of the training class observes. Even observers become convinced that they cannot stop on a dime.

This demonstration teaches drivers that they must maintain a safe distance from other vehicles in front of them, be alert for sudden stops, and start braking as soon as they anticipate that they may have to stop.

The Driver and the Vehicle

Each driver should know the mechanical principles of the gasoline or diesel engine, the power transmission train, the braking system, the electrical system, and other components of the vehicle. Even drivers with many years' experience can profit from a review of these subjects.

When new vehicles are added to the fleet, go over the differences in new equipment. Drivers should also be familiar with a new vehicle's quirks before they take it on a run. Encourage drivers to give their opinions on the handling qualities and running economics of new (and existing) fleet vehicles.

Of course, drivers are not expected to be trained mechanics, but they should know enough about the vehicle to recognize and describe mechanical defects when they arise and to avoid abusing the vehicle. Drivers should be able to tell when mechanical troubles are serious enough to warrant assistance.

This training unit should include practice drills in the step-by-step procedure for making a pre-trip inspection and inspections en route (see Chapter 12, Fleet Purchase and Maintenance).

Basic Driving Maneuvers

The basic driving maneuvers are starting the engine, shifting gears, steering and stopping the vehicle, backing, turning, and parking. The correct methods must be mastered so driving is smooth, safe, and efficient. If the vehicle has several forward gears, training should also cover double clutching when gearing up or down.

The instructor should demonstrate to each trainee the correct way to perform these tasks and then ask the trainee to do it. The instructor should correct any errors, make suggestions, and then allow the trainee to practice until the performance is correct and easy.

Trainees must understand that they are considered skilled only when they can perform these maneuvers the right way every time.

Driving in Traffic

Allot time for trainees to test drive the type of vehicle to which they will be assigned. The best time is near the end of the training program, after they have had the benefit of classroom instruction and have been checked out on the basic driving maneuvers.

The test drive should be conducted under the supervision of a driver trainer. The route selected should include a variety of traffic situations: controlled and uncontrolled intersections, residential and congested areas, narrow streets and freeways, railroad crossings, and dock areas.

The same route should be used for each test drive so the instructor can become familiar with the situations that cause trainees the most trouble and best test their skill. This also enables the instructor to better help the trainees and be more consistent in grading.

The test drive builds trainees' confidence in their ability to handle a vehicle properly and safely. The test also lets the instructor observe trainees under actual road conditions and decide whether each driver is sufficiently trained.

Trainees who pass the test may be assigned to a regular run, with or without an instructor. In bus operations, a new driver is often placed on a regular run with an experienced operator riding along for several days as a final check on competence and to be sure the driver knows the routes.

If a trainee fails the test, a decision must be made: additional training or practice, assignment to a nondriving job, or termination.

Task-Specific Training

The types of service drivers perform have specific hazards and preventive measures. In addition to being trained for a specific type of vehicle, drivers should be trained for a specific type of service. School buses are an example. Specific elements include:

- Boarding procedure

  Driver to motion child across street

  Bus to remain stationary until students are seated
- Deboarding procedure

  Driver to stop bus where it can be seen

  Driver to leave door closed until traffic stops

- Driver to inspect equipment

  Emergency door function

  Push-out windows

  Emergency equipment
- Driver to train children in proper passenger procedures
- Driver to be trained in assertiveness for student control

Specially modified equipment, coupled with the type of service, poses hazards that drivers should learn to recognize. Limousine drivers are faced with a long-wheelbase vehicle combined with tinted windows that limit side vision. The visibility problem of the small back window is compounded by the frequent need to haul luggage with the trunk deck up. If the trunk is full, a customer-oriented driver will stack overflow luggage in the front seat, blocking even more of the view.

Then the driver is faced with pressure from the client to speed or break other traffic laws, as well as self-induced pressure to speed and work long hours to meet expenses and, for owner/operators, to pay the note on the vehicle. Explain to drivers the fleet manager's expectations for driver performance; this is the only way to encourage their compliance with company policies and traffic regulations.

Procedures in Case of Accident

Although training is designed to keep drivers out of accidents, they should also be taught the correct procedures to follow if they are involved in an accident with a company vehicle. Review the accident procedures discussed in Chapters 4, Motor Fleet Accident Data, and 5, Accident Investigation.

To give trainees practice in completing the company accident report form, present case histories of actual accidents. Have them use this information to fill out a practice accident report form.

Trainees should be taught to make out a report for every accident, no matter how minor it may seem. They can learn a great deal about accident prevention from even a minor accident. Good accident reporting is essential to the success of any safety program.

Handling Passengers and Freight

Drivers of passenger-carrying vehicles should be taught how to prevent passenger accidents. This includes positioning the vehicle for safe boarding and alighting of passengers, driving smoothly and slowing down gradually to avoid onboard falls, and looking for and removing tripping and slipping hazards aboard the vehicle. If a passenger is hurt, medical assistance should be sought, and the police should be informed of the injuries.

Drivers of freight-carrying vehicles should be taught all regulations that apply to loading or transporting cargo.

Loads should be braced so that a sudden stop will not send freight flying toward the driver.

If an accident scatters cargo about, it is important to:

- Minimize damage to other vehicles (because of broken glass, spilled liquids, scattered boxes in the road).

- Notify police of especially dangerous cargo. People in the area and other motorists should be warned. DOT regulations require any vehicle carrying hazardous materials to carry a shipping document describing the load and its hazard. If the quantity or hazard is great enough, the vehicle must carry a hazard placard on all four sides. Fire-fighting instructions must also be posted when the cargo is especially hazardous. The driver should receive special HAZMAT training.

- Take steps to prevent (or minimize) theft of or additional damage to cargo, such as covering the cargo with tarps to prevent damage from exposure and posting a guard at the accident site if necessary.

Company Safety Program

Because all drivers will be in daily contact with the safety program, they should develop an understanding and cooperative attitude toward it. Time devoted to explaining the program will pay dividends.

Trainees should know why the safety program is necessary, its main elements, what safe driver awards or bonuses are offered, the rules for earning them, what fleet contests the company has entered, and the rules governing them.

TRAINING METHODS

Teaching is more than exposing the trainee to information: the trainee must exert mental effort to learn. The process is like playing ball. The instructor throws a pitch, but the learner must catch the ball. Responsibility for success of the exchange, however, always belongs to the instructor. The teacher must motivate trainees to learn by making presentations clear, interesting, memorable, and of personal value to them.

Instructor and Trainee Roles

New trainees have a natural motivation to learn when embarking on an important venture—a new job. But they may have certain barriers to learning that the instructor must anticipate. For example, the trainees may feel that they already know the subject, that the instructor is exaggerating the importance of the subject matter, or that the material is too difficult to understand.

The good instructor is sensitive to these attitudes and develops ways to overcome them. The object is to present the material effectively and to encourage trainees to learn. The instructor must be like a salesperson, full of energy and enthusiasm for the subject, to persuade the trainee to buy into the program.

Just as every good leader is also a teacher, every instructor is a leader. Instructors should exemplify the qualities they seek to transfer to trainees. Instructors must demonstrate pride in themselves, their job, and their company. Neatness, fairness, and friendliness are also important qualities to model.

Developing and Presenting the Materials

After deciding what material to present, the instructor must organize each lesson and establish the class time and the material to be covered. A good span of class time is 50 minutes, with a 10-minute break between sessions. The amount of material to be covered in a given session is based on how much trainees can comprehend at one time. Four or five main points are about all the average trainee can learn in one lesson. Trying to crowd in more material usually results in less learning rather than more.

The lecture method. In the lecture method, the instructor stands before the class and explains the material. This is the most commonly used teaching method because the instructor can cover a great deal of material in a short time. The danger is that lectures can become monotonous and boring.

The instructor can make the lecture interesting by keeping to a few basic points, selecting good examples and anecdotes, using audiovisuals, asking rhetorical questions, changing the pitch and speed of the delivery, making clear transitions from one main point to the next, and summarizing the material at the end of the lecture.

Demonstration. This approach is usually combined with other methods. The instructor displays a physical object to the class and shows how or why it works.

Discussion. The discussion method lets class members participate by answering questions, relating their own experiences, or thinking through a problem under the instructor's guidance. Although this is a slower method of covering a subject, it keeps the trainees' interest, provides a more vivid learning experience, and fosters a spirit of unity in the group. A short discussion period makes a good end to a training lecture or demonstration.

Practice. Trainees must practice what they learn. The instructor first explains how the job is done—for example, how a tractor is hooked up to a trailer—and demonstrates it. Then a trainee tries it, with the instructor correcting the performance when necessary. The trainee repeats the correct procedure and practices until the right way becomes a habit.

Examination. This is actually another teaching method. Whether oral, written, or performance type, tests allow trainees to show what they have learned and what they still need to study. They let the instructor evaluate trainees' progress and give the trainees a sense of accomplishment. Examination results can be kept confidential or posted, whichever seems more effective.

Testing is a form of reinforcement or review that intensifies the learning process; it should be used throughout the training program. Even a question put to a trainee during a lecture is a type of test.

Reading. Reading plays an important part in both shortening and enriching the training program. Reading is usually done after course hours and on the trainees' own time. To make sure trainees have read and understood the material, reading assignments should be followed up by classroom discussion and/or written examination.

Training Aids

Because it is not always possible for instructors to express ideas vividly or quickly enough by the spoken word alone, they can use audiovisuals to supplement the lecture. In a discussion of accident costs, for example, figures written on the chalkboard will help trainees appreciate the dollar amounts involved. Graphs or bar charts can be used to show quantitative relationships. Diagrams can save precious minutes of explanation, and even key words or points written on the chalkboard help trainees remember the ideas presented.

Many visual aids are available, and it is important to learn how to use each effectively. Instructors must remember that training aids are aids only. They should never be used just because they are available, but rather because they contribute to the instructor's training objective. Whatever aids are chosen, check to make sure they are available and set up before class begins. A missing chalkboard or projector will sabotage the best presentation.

Chalkboard. One of the first and still most widely used visuals is the chalkboard. It can be used to show key words, phrases, or points in the lecture. It can be used for diagrams, graphs, and sketches that will increase trainees' understanding. Whether writing is placed on the chalkboard before class or as the instructor talks, it must be large enough for all to see clearly. The instructor should stand at the side of the chalkboard and face the class as much as possible. Colored chalk can add further interest to the presentation.

Flip chart. The flip chart is similar to the chalkboard, but its successive pages accommodate far more material than does a single chalkboard. If the chart will be used over and over again, it's worth the time to make each page as attractive and informative as possible. Words can

be carefully lettered (Figure 9–2), diagrams drawn to scale, sketches painstakingly drawn, and colored inks used to add interest and readability to the chart. Each successive page should help to develop the lesson.

Sometimes blank flip charts are used and the instructor writes on them with a marking pen while lecturing. This can be dramatic, but since the pages cannot be erased, they must be discarded after each lesson. This can be an asset, however, since old pages serve as a record.

Magnetic white board. The magnetic white board combines features of the chalkboard and a display board. Because the material to be magnetically attached to the board can be reused, time can be taken to create work with professional visual impact. With a laser printer and proper software, anyone can produce quality presentation materials.

Key words can be printed on strips of cardboard, then applied to the white board as the points are being made. With double-stick tape, magnetic materials can be applied to photographs, newspaper articles, shapes, or sample forms.

The instructor can use a magnetic overlay to explain correct driving maneuvers, reconstruct accidents for class discussion, or reenact an accident when counseling the driver involved to determine its preventability. The National Safety Council offers a magnetic intersection overlay that can be used with vehicle shapes to discuss various traffic conditions and proper defensive driving techniques.

Accident demonstration board. Miniature vehicles and demonstration boards can also be used for portraying accidents. An instructor can make an excellent vertical demonstration board at little cost by thumbtacking different-colored pieces of felt on drywall or pressboard. The felt pieces can be sized to indicate curb lines, view obstructions, signal lights, and buildings. Miniature vehicles (obtained at toy stores) are fitted with pins for moving about on the board.

Several types of vertical demonstration boards on the market use a simple adhesive process to hold materials to the board. Diagrams can be shifted and illustrations moved about easily.

Demonstration mockups. Talks given in conjunction with demonstrations using actual equipment (or a model) hold trainees' interest. For example, an actual setup or model of the vehicle's braking system—showing the master cylinder, brake lines, brake cylinders, shoes, and drums—can show students how the brakes operate. Other subjects particularly adaptable to demonstrations are ignition, cooling system, headlights, tires, electrical equipment, and carburetion. Demonstrators should be experts in their fields.

Showing a cutaway of a seat-belt mechanism or air bag module might help drivers appreciate how they work. The best demonstration of seat belts is a ride on the seat-belt Convincer™, a ramp with a car seat attached. The jolt at the bottom converts many daredevils to seat-belt users. Antilock

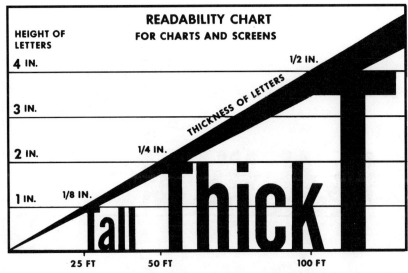

Figure 9–2. For easy viewing of nonprojected and projected visuals, make letters and symbols large enough for the most distant viewer.

brakes are difficult to demonstrate, but videos showing their effectiveness are available from auto manufacturers and insurance companies.

Abused equipment. Actual tires can be displayed to show the results of climbing curbs when making turns or the amount of rubber an excessively fast stop can wear off a tire. Worn mechanical parts can show the results of careless operation. Actual replacement cost figures are also effective communicators.

Driver testing equipment. Although no definite relationship has been established between psychological and physiological accident proneness, drivers do like to compete for honors in demonstrating their ability to operate equipment. Tests of their responses may be conducted as part of the safety meeting program. Some insurance companies and automobile clubs have testing equipment and are glad to cooperate in giving tests.

The educational value of these tests lies in explaining how trainees can compensate to offset the deficiencies revealed. These tests should be given with extreme care by trained examiners; otherwise, they can create as many problems as they may solve.

Slides. The slide projector is another valuable method of showing visual aids. The instructor can take color slides of vehicles, traffic situations, accidents, damaged equipment, unsafe practices, and many other scenes to show the class.

Some trainers take slides of bad driving practices as they occur, then stage the proper practices to contrast with the incorrect ones. This approach has an excellent effect on drivers. The cost of equipment is reasonable, and good pictures can be produced with a little practice.

When homemade slides are used, the safety department should prepare a short talk discussing the practices shown and emphasizing the correct methods.

Slide projectors integrated with cassette tape decks can be used to make sound and slide presentations to be shown at different company locations. The message will always be the same because the narration is taped. These projectors are not too expensive.

The slide projector can also be used like a giant flip chart. Pages of a flip chart, company report forms, graphs, and many other subjects can be photographed for projection to the class.

Many video programs are also available for training. They are useful in clarifying technical discussions, and their combined visual and spoken message make a lasting impression on employees.

Overhead projectors. The main difference between overhead projectors and slide projectors is that the transparencies used for projection can be prepared with materials available in most offices. Printed or typed materials can be run through a dry-process photocopier and transferred to the clear acetate sheets. Pictures and charts can be drawn on the 8½- by 11-inch transparencies with black or colored marking pens.

The overhead projector can be used in a fully illuminated room. This allows the instructor to emphasize critical points during a lecture or demonstration training session, and everyone will be able to see both the transparencies and the demonstration (Figure 9–3).

Film/video. Driver training movies can make an important contribution to the training program. Even a

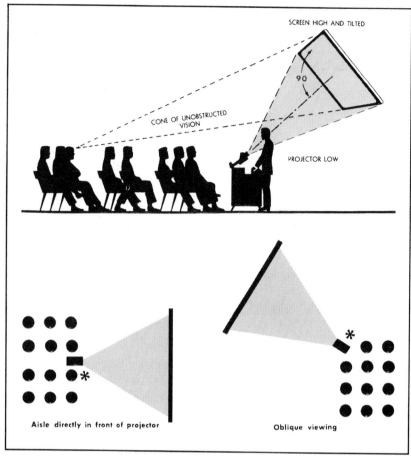

Figure 9–3. When instructing large groups, tilt the overhead screen (shown at top) or place it toward the corner of the room (lower right). Both placements reduce the possibility of the instructor and equipment blocking the vision of some viewers, as might be the case when the projector is located in front of the group.

film or video that makes a limited number of points focuses attention on the problem and promotes discussion or further instruction.

Because a driver training film/video usually runs only 10 or 20 minutes, it cannot carry a very heavy training load by itself. To make a film-based training session effective, the instructor should describe the film, tell why it is being shown, and direct trainees' attention to certain points before showing it. After the screening, review and discuss the main points and apply them to particular problems. A quiz can further reinforce the lesson. The quiz can be discussed at the end of class or at the beginning of the next class.

The instructor should review a film or video before showing it in a training session. It's best if the vehicles and scenes depicted are very similar to those encountered by your drivers. Drivers of vans, for instance, tend to ignore training materials aimed at tractor-trailer drivers, and vice versa. Both groups often reject materials directed at passenger car drivers.

However, that does not mean the trainer must pass up a good film because it does not deal with the specific operations of the fleet. The instructor can explain that although the presentation features passenger cars, it contains many valid points for truck drivers. Then enumerate these points.

Tape recorders/video camcorders. Recorders can add variety, interest, and emphasis to a training program. Trainees can listen to the actual commentary of a driver during a trip or play back a counseling interview in which the preventability of an accident was determined. The resourceful instructor will think of many other ways the recorder or camcorder can be used as an effective training aid.

Interactive laser disk. By using a personal computer equipped with a CD-ROM, a trainer can present material at the level best suited to each individual. The computer system presents information to the driver, then asks a question on the material. If the driver's response demonstrates a lack of knowledge about, say, tire care, the program will automatically present the segment on tires. If the driver answers correctly, the program moves on to the next subject.

Interactive training recognizes that different trainees are at different levels of understanding and competence. Because the training is private, drivers will not be afraid to ask the computer a question that might have drawn a laugh in an open training session. Some systems have glossaries of terms and self-directed branching to related topics of interest. The cost is reasonable—and short of one-on-one contact, there is no better way to individualize training.

Additional Help

Remember that any training program must be designed to fit the training needs of students, not the training aids available. Ask "What is the trainee expected to do as a result of this training?" and "What behavioral change is expected?" Then decide on (a) the method of instruction, (b) the training aids to use, and (c) how inclusive to make the program.

The point is to fit the subject to the audience, so evaluate the advantages and disadvantages of all types of audiovisuals before deciding which ones to use. The National Safety Council publishes *Occupational Safety and Health Data Sheets* to help select the best aids. Call the Council to request the latest Index of available Data Sheets.

CHAPTER
10

Driver
Supervision

WHAT IS DRIVER SUPERVISION?

HOW TO PREVENT ACCIDENTS
Check Traffic Rule Compliance
Check Vehicle Abuse
Set Good Schedules

REMEMBER PUBLIC RELATIONS

ENCOURAGE HIGH PERFORMANCE
Set Performance Standards High
Set a Good Example
Build a Sense of Participation
Foster Good Communications
Promote a Competitive Spirit
Motivate through Recognition

CHALLENGE OF DRIVER SUPERVISION

Supervision is not only the art of getting things done through people, it is the art of getting them done well.

Most driving jobs require two types of duties: those that relate to driving and those that don't. The two pose different supervisory problems. Some nondriving duties can be supervised by ordinary techniques used throughout industry. The special techniques for supervising the driving part of the job, however, are more complex.

WHAT IS DRIVER SUPERVISION?

Drivers are capable of committing any number of errors that can be costly to the company. The driver supervisor must know (a) what these errors are, (b) how they can be spotted, and (c) how to prevent them. The supervisor must enforce a high standard of performance that does not condone accidents that could reasonably be prevented. This chapter explains how to set such standards.

The driver supervisor is responsible for the quality of driver performance. In a small fleet, this person may be the fleet manager or owner. In a large common carrier fleet, several persons may share supervisory responsibility, sometimes with overlapping authority.

For example, the terminal manager is usually thought of as the driver's direct supervisor. But the dispatcher shares some of the supervisory load because the dispatcher both (a) assigns runs and vehicles to the driver and (b) makes sure these runs are completed on time and correctly.

The fleet safety director (who is responsible for overall safety performance) should work through the supervisor at the driver's home terminal. Additional supervision may be provided by a safety road patrol: supervisors, insurance companies, or contract services that can make on-the-spot observations of driving performance and report them back to company headquarters for follow-up. This road patrol may even be authorized to stop a vehicle and correct the driver or place the driver out of service.

Even the public can provide valuable feedback on driver behavior. The National Safety Council Driver Check[TM] is a combination of a driver management program and a decal bearing a toll-free number, 1–800–2ADVISE, a vehicle number, and the legend "HOW'S MY DRIVING?" When motorists observe unacceptable driving behavior, they call the toll-free number and report the facts. The facts are then reported to company management for discussion with the driver. This program guarantees at least a 10% reduction of accidents in the first year or the service is free.

But what about that ancient rule of supervision that a person cannot serve two masters? How can a driver please so many different people who all seem to have something to say about doing the job? Because these supervisory practices are created by the operating conditions of a motor transportation fleet, all supervisors should agree on how the driving job should be performed. Written guidelines on specific driving techniques are an excellent way to achieve unity on judging driving performance.

Most safety programs ultimately depend on the immediate supervisor to get results. If this person undercuts safety through words or actions, little can be achieved. However, a strong safety director may get results from even a reluctant supervisor through the judicious use of pressure. It is best to have a motivated manager actively promoting the program, but at times the safety director must settle for less.

HOW TO PREVENT ACCIDENTS

Because motor vehicle accidents can result in serious losses in terms of human life, bodily injury, and property damage, the primary responsibility of supervision is to prevent future accidents. The supervisor should learn certain techniques for spotting the kind of substandard performance that often results in accidents. For example:

- Personally observe the driver's performance.
- Check driver trainer reports, road patrol reports, arrest records, and comments from other drivers and employees.
- Review complaints from other drivers or pedestrians as a possible barometer of driving performance. Attitudes like belligerence or indifference can lead to an accident. The supervisor should try to find out why the driver's behavior has changed and seek to help solve the problem. Sometimes an emotionally troubled driver can be transferred to nondriving work.
- Be alert to personality and performance changes before they reach the incident stage by making frequent personal contacts with the drivers.

A fleet safety supervisor should watch for the following typical symptoms of accidents in the making:

- errors in performance of work
- changes in everyday behavior and manners
- changes in simple habits or routines
- near accidents

These events can fluctuate under different circumstances but reflect such mental and emotional states as long-standing resentments, high stress, fatigue, or a series of disappointments. Such feelings can lead to an accident.

This type of checking or observation does not mean that driver supervisors must be psychologists. However, recognizing that substandard performance often has a psychological base lets them be more understanding and effective in dealing with it.

Errors in work performance fall into a number of categories. This section discusses each main category, along with the specific errors that a supervisor should watch for. These errors may not be of equal importance to all fleets. Each driver supervisor should adapt the list to fit his or her operation.

Driving errors that often lead to accidents were compiled from a survey of more than 150 of the nation's top fleet safety directors. Those errors are listed in Figure 10–1. Knowing them is especially helpful in training drivers.

Check Traffic Rule Compliance

Because fleets must use public streets and highways, they have a special obligation always to operate within the law. Violation of traffic laws is never acceptable. Even a single violation may reflect badly on the company; repeated violations may result in revocation of its operating rights. A long record of noncompliance can damage the image of the entire industry and may lead to more restrictive legislation.

Fleets usually do not pay traffic fines incurred by drivers, nor do they put up bonds for them. A record of traffic violations is kept in the driver's personnel folder, and repeated violations are the basis for disciplinary action or discharge.

Drivers with a CDL have a legal obligation to notify their employer within 30 days of conviction for a traffic violation, even if it occurred in their personal vehicle. They must notify their licensing state within 30 days if the conviction occurred in another state. The employer must be notified immediately if the CDL is suspended, revoked, or canceled or if the driver is disqualified from driving.

The following are some of the most frequent driving errors that are also violations of traffic laws. Conviction for two or more of the starred items or traffic offenses in connection with fatal traffic accidents will result in a 60- to 120-day CDL driving disqualification.

- running errors
- excessive speed*
- speed too fast for conditions
- speed too slow for conditions
- following the vehicle ahead too closely*
- reckless driving*
- passing errors
- passing at illegal place
- passing at unsafe place
- unnecessary passing
- returning to lane too soon after passing
- intersection violations
- failure to yield right-of-way at unmarked intersections
- running red light
- coasting through stop sign

- failure to reduce speed for intersection
- failure to yield to oncoming traffic when turning left
- failure to yield right-of-way to pedestrians
- improper lane usage
- failure to select proper lane
- turning from wrong lane
- improper or erratic lane changes*
- failure to signal a lane change
- failure to make sure lane is clear before entering
- parking and stopping errors
- illegal stopping on street or roadway
- obstructing traffic
- double-parking
- failure to secure parked vehicle

The fleet's loss for traffic violations could far exceed the fines paid by the driver. The lost services of a trained driver during a conviction-related disqualification can cost a company thousands of dollars. The costs of lost goodwill and litigation for accidents with violations can soar. Drivers should be reminded of the penalties for the starred items above and those noted below to emphasize how important it is to always follow the rules. If convicted *while driving a commercial motor vehicle (CMV),* drivers will be disqualified and lose their privilege to drive for one year, three years, or life, depending on the offense.

Drivers will be disqualified or lose their driving privilege one year for any of the following offenses:

- driving under the influence of a controlled substance or alcohol (0.04% blood alcohol),
- leaving the scene of an accident, or
- using a CMV to commit a felony.

The penalty term is three years for:

- any of the one-year offenses while operating a CMV that is placarded for hazardous materials.

The penalty term is life for either of the following offenses:

- second offense of any of the one- or three-year offenses
- committing a felony involving the manufacture, distribution, or dispensing of controlled substances

Check Vehicle Abuse

From 10% to 25% of the typical fleet's annual maintenance cost is due to faulty operation or abuse of the vehicle by the driver. Such behavior stems from carelessness, lack of training, or inadequate supervisory control.

Not only do excessive repair bills suggest substandard driving performance, but they are directly related to the number of accidents. A "rough" driver has a high accident

DRIVING ERRORS THAT LEAD TO ACCIDENTS

Starting

- failure to first check clearances (front, rear, over-head)
- failure to signal when pulling out from curb
- failure to check for a break in traffic before moving

Speed control

- too fast for volume of traffic
- too fast for condition of road surface
- too fast for visibility (due to weather or road)
- too fast for amount of light (dusk/darkness)
- too fast for neighborhood or roadside environment
- too fast for street/highway layout and traffic signals
- too slow for stream of traffic

Lane usage

- failure to select proper lane
- failure to drive in middle of lane
- abrupt lane change
- failure to signal intent to change lanes
- weaving

Passing

- misjudging speed and nearness of oncoming vehicle
- failure to check to the rear before pulling out to pass
- overtaking and passing too slowly
- cutting in too quickly after passing
- failure to signal intention of passing
- unnecessary passing
- racing vehicle that is trying to pass driver
- passing in an intersection

Turning

- turning from wrong lane

- failure to let oncoming traffic clear before turning left
- failure to block area to right of vehicle on right turns
- running over curb on right turns
- abrupt turn on slippery road surface, causing a skid
- failure to signal intention to turn

Stopping

- failure to make smooth, gradual stop
- failure to signal stop
- failure to stop in time
- abrupt braking on slippery road surface, causing a skid

Parking

- parking in unsafe or illegal place
- parking with front or rear of vehicle protruding into traffic
- failure to secure unattended vehicle on hill
- failure to mark disabled vehicle properly

Specific signaling errors

- failure to signal
- signal too late
- wrong signal
- failure to use horn
- excessive or improper use of horn

Errors in clearance judgment

- following vehicle ahead too closely
- failure to check clearance to rear when backing
- failure to check right side clearance
- failure to check left side clearance
- failure to check top clearance
- failure to yield space in any traffic encroachment

Figure 10–1.   Drivers and driver supervisors should watch for and eliminate these driving errors that lead to accidents.

potential; a "smooth" driver is usually more alert and able to avoid accident hazards and respond to emergencies.

Rough operation—including fast starts, delayed braking, and sudden stops—can indicate a bad attitude toward authority that may eventually lead to an accident. It may also indicate driver inexperience. It is important to screen out driver applicants who are inept or have poor attitudes because these are usually irremediable faults. If, however, lack of training is the cause of rough operation, it can be corrected.

Freedom to abuse an expensive vehicle is not a fringe benefit of employment. The company has a right to expect that its drivers will respect company property and care for equipment put in their charge.

Driving abuses causing undue wear on vehicles include:

- engine (motor) abuse:

    lugging engine by using too high a gear while accelerating

    idling for several hours while sitting in truck stops, etc.

DRIVING ERRORS THAT LEAD TO ACCIDENTS (continued)

Errors in observation

- failure to see object or pedestrian in path of vehicle
- failure to watch traffic at rear of vehicle while moving
- failure to look to left and right of vehicle at locations where vehicles or pedestrians could enter path of vehicle
- failure to see vehicle or pedestrian approaching
- observation too late
- failure to anticipate parked vehicles pulling out

Lack of personal control

- inattention (any cause)
- distraction (any cause)

- driving while drowsy
- reacting emotionally to driving situations
- driving under the influence of alcohol or drugs
- driving while ill

Lack of knowledge and awareness of equipment, load, route

- failure to inspect equipment (before, during, after trip)
- unfamiliarity with equipment
- unfamiliarity with load
- unfamiliarity with route
- failure to secure doors or cargo

Figure 10–1. (*continued*)

- clutching errors:
  riding the clutch
  snapping the clutch
- errors in shifting gears:
  starting out in wrong gear
  accelerating rapidly from stops
  scraping and jerking the gears
  shifting gears into neutral and coasting downhill
  failure to double clutch if needed when changing gears
  lugging (operating in improper gear)
- errors in use of brakes:
  failure to fully release hand brake when moving
  abrupt stops
  delayed braking
  excessive brake applications
  running downhill in too high a gear
  failure to use parking brakes and other elements of brake systems
- errors in tire care:
  operating with flat or underinflated tires
  driving over curbs or objects or into potholes
  rubbing tires against curbs in parking
  letting air out of tires for a smoother ride
  spinning tires needlessly on ice or snow
  running with flat tires until a repair facility can be reached
- tampering with equipment:
  overriding governors

stopping up the fuel return line to get more power
tampering with trip recorder
abusing cab interior
tampering with electrical system
- lack of maintenance responsibility:
  driving unit even though it needs repairs
  failure to write up defects and repairs
  failure to inspect equipment properly before each trip
  inability to recognize signs of an en route problem

Set Good Schedules

The motor transportation fleet cannot conduct its business without schedules. However, a schedule is only a piece of paper until a driver and vehicle translate it into on-time transportation. Observance of schedules is therefore a prime ingredient of driving skill. A driver's failure to observe schedules is not only poor production but may also be a symptom of an underlying negative attitude toward the job or a personal problem that is interfering with efficiency. If the average driver can maintain the given schedule, then the supervisors should find out why a particular driver cannot.

The following driving errors can result in schedule delays:

- errors in departure procedure:
  reporting late for scheduled run
  spending excessive time preparing for departure
  pulling wrong trailer
  taking wrong freight bills
  stopping at home for personal business after departure

not getting enough rest before run and having to stop for sleep along road

- errors leading to delays en route:

  accidents

  arrest

  excessive or prolonged coffee stops

  excessive time at meal stops

  excessive time at scheduled stops

  excessive time at weigh stations

  failure to follow designated route

  failure to call in for instructions

  stops at unauthorized places

REMEMBER PUBLIC RELATIONS

When a vehicle is painted attractively and shows the company name, it becomes a traveling advertisement. Such ads purchased through regular advertising media would cost a great deal of money. But there is one difference: the advertising on the vehicle can be good or bad, favorable or unfavorable, depending on how the driver behaves toward other motorists and pedestrians. Driving with courtesy and consideration for the public is therefore an important part of the driving job. Courtesy can build public goodwill for the company and lead to increased business. The following list of discourteous driver behaviors can damage a company's public image:

- errors in speed control:

  exceeding speed limit and passing motorists who are abiding by the law

  speeding through towns and residential areas

  backing up traffic by driving too slowly

- errors in following:

  following passenger cars too closely

  tailgating

  following too closely at night without dimming lights

- errors in passing:

  passing unnecessarily

  cutting in too sharply after passing

  creating excessive splash and spray while passing

- errors in lane use:

  crowding center line

  straddling two lanes

  drifting across lane dividers

  weaving between lanes

  running two or three abreast on limited-access highways

  using wrong lane for speed or traffic flow

- errors that block traffic:

  blocking crosswalk

  double-parking in heavy traffic

  not pulling off to allow built-up traffic to pass

  failing to use designated truck lanes, especially on steep hills

  errors in noise and smoke abatement:

  excessive diesel smoke

  excessive engine noise or unnecessary use of noisy engine retarders

  unnecessary use of air horns

  racing engine to hurry pedestrians across intersection

  splashing pedestrians in sloppy weather

ENCOURAGE HIGH PERFORMANCE

So far, the negative aspects of supervision have been emphasized because the observation of performance involves finding and correcting faults. However, even though correction is an essential part of any supervisor's job, it is far from the most important part.

For high performance, management (through supervision) must offer drivers more than good wages and the fear of being disciplined or discharged. The true test of a supervisor's skill is the ability to create conditions under which drivers will maintain high standards. Here are some techniques a supervisor can use to motivate drivers.

Set Performance Standards High

Setting job standards high is one way to secure compliance. High standards are challenging; a driver feels a keen sense of pride and espirit de corps when meeting them. Mediocre standards—when they fail to inspire respect—are just as difficult to enforce as are high standards.

Set a Good Example

Driver supervisors must set a good example. They should radiate pride in the company, be dedicated to it, and never say or do anything that would suggest disloyalty to its officers and objectives.

Build a Sense of Participation

Give drivers a sense of participation in their company. Keep them informed of company plans. Let them know how they are meeting their objectives. Sharing information with workers makes them feel they are part of the company.

(*text continues on page 127*)

 **National Safety Council**

SAFE DRIVER AWARD PROGRAM

Annually, thousands of employers use the National Safety Council's Safe Driver Award Program to recognize their drivers across the United States and Canada. The Safe Driver Award is the accepted trademark of safe driving performance in business and industry. The Award lapel pins, wallet cards, and patches serve as a daily reminder that reinforces the accident avoidance skills and behaviors of all those who drive an organization vehicle as part of their daily work assignments.

For one driver or a thousand, this program is an excellent way, **each year**, for an employer to express gratitude to those who have made a positive **individual** contribution to the organization's safety record.

Who is eligible to participate in the Safe Driver Award Program?
Employees of organizations who drive an employer-owned or -leased vehicle as part of their regular daily assignment should be considered for a Safe Driver Award. Eligible organizations include:
* employer members of the National Safety Council
* school transportation members of the National Safety Council
* members of Chapters of the National Safety Council
* National Safety Council members subscribing to the Motor Fleet Safety Service

How do I participate in the Safe Driver Award Program?
The steps for participation in the Safe Driver Award Program include:
* identify all eligible drivers
* select a method to track each driver's record
* determine each driver's annual award date
* calculate all drivers' records and determine what awards have been earned
* choose the type of awards to be used: wallet card, lapel pin or patch
* complete the Safe Driver Award certification form
* mail or fax the certification form with an order to the National Safety Council

What information should be maintained to determine an employee's Safe Driver Award record?
The following records should be maintained for each employee:
* date award record initiated (date of hire, date employee began driving for the employer, or date the organization initially began tracking all driver's records)
* dates of preventable accidents
* dates and lengths of periods of nondriving time
* safe driving time accumulated from previous employers
* most recent National Safety Council award earned and date earned

There is no fee to enroll in the Safe Driver Award Program. Participants pay only for the awards they need and the price is based upon the total number of awards ordered and which type of award(s) are requested.

FOR MORE INFORMATION CONTACT MOTIVATION PROGRAMS AT 1-800-621-6339

Figure 10–2. More than seven million National Safety Council safe driver awards have been earned since the program began in 1930.

NATIONAL FLEET SAFETY CONTEST

The National Fleet Safety Contest is a competitive award program designed to promote safe driving. The program provides award recognition to fleets with the lowest rate of accidents per 1,000,000 miles driven within their division and group. The Contest is open to all National Safety Council members and members of co-sponsoring associations who have fleets in the United States or Canada.

Ten or more motor vehicles of a single type that operate as a single unit shall be considered a fleet for the Contest. A small fleet is a group of five to nine vehicles. There are participants in 16 divisions which classify the fleets by type of operation and vehicle. This classification allows comparisons to be made of similar fleets within an industry. The current Fleet Divisions are:

AUTOMOBILE TRANSPORTERS–DAIRY INDUSTRY

EMERGENCY AND MEDICAL RESPONSE–GAS INDUSTRY

GOVERNMENT–INTERCITY BUS–MAIL CONTRACTORS–MEAT PACKING

PASSENGER CAR–PETROLEUM–U.S. POSTAL SERVICE

SCHOOL BUS–SMALL FLEET–PUBLIC UTILITY–TRANSIT–TRUCK

Data are collected on a monthly basis from January 1 through December 31 each year. These data include the year-to-date miles driven, the year-to-date accidents experienced, and the number of vehicles in the fleet. From these data, an accident rate is developed and used as a means of comparison. Those fleets having the lowest accident rates are ranked at the top of their competitive group.

$$\text{Accident Frequency Rate} = \frac{\text{Number of Accidents x 1,000,000}}{\text{Vehicle Miles Driven}}$$

Contest Bulletins showing participant standings and accident rates are distributed quarterly. First, Second, and Third Place Awards are given annually within each group based upon final standings as published in the December Bulletins and as permitted by the National Fleet Safety Contest Rules.

Two noncompetitive awards can also be earned by participating fleets. A Perfect Record Award will be given to every fleet that completes the year without an accident. A Certificate of Achievement is given to each fleet that meets the criteria for a significant reduction of their current year accident rate as compared to their two prior years and their division.

FOR MORE INFORMATION CONTACT MOTIVATION PROGRAMS AT 1- 800/621-6339

Figure 10–3. This fact sheet explains the recognition and awards available to fleets through the National Fleet Safety Contest conducted by the National Safety Council.

This sense of participation is fostered when supervisors welcome suggestions for improving services or overcoming specific problems. Drivers often have good ideas that can save the company substantial amounts of money. Many companies have formal systems that require drivers to submit their suggestions on a special numbered form. Each suggestion is carefully considered by a committee, and the driver is told how it was received. In some cases, cash awards are made for ideas that are accepted.

Whether or not a suggestion program exists, a driver should get personal recognition for any idea used. If it is practical (and the driver agrees), the individual can be recognized publicly for his or her contribution to the company.

Foster Good Communications

Communication is vital to good human relations and scientific management because it is a two-way street: management keeps drivers informed, and drivers feel free to offer suggestions.

The most important message management can communicate to drivers is that their job is vital. This builds pride and job satisfaction and improves performance.

Promote a Competitive Spirit

To create additional job interest, appeal to drivers' competitive spirit. Safety contests between fleet divisions or with outside fleets (such as in the National Fleet Safety Contest) generate interest when drivers understand the rules and are kept informed of contest ratings. Company publications, special posters, contest scoreboards, bulletin board displays, and safety meetings all promote pride and enthusiasm. Contests can be successful for both large and small fleets.

Motivate through Recognition

Individual safe driving awards are a powerful incentive to improve driving performance. Because drivers generally do the same type of work and are usually covered by a uniform union contract (that spells out wages, work conditions, special assignments, and seniority), it is rare for an individual driver to receive recognition. Safe driver awards provide an opportunity for drivers to distinguish themselves.

The National Safety Council conducts the Safe Driver Award Program. The well-respected Council program, begun in 1930, has presented more than seven million awards (Figure 10–2). Another popular National Safety Council program among trucking companies is the Million Mile Club, which recognizes outstanding drivers with a million miles or 25,000 hours free of preventable accidents. Other associations, such as the American Trucking Associations, and insurance carriers also offer driver award programs.

The Council also provides award recognition to fleets with the lowest rate of accidents per 1,000,000 miles driven within their division and group (Figure 10–3).

Awards work best when the rules are explained to drivers and when decisions on accidents are consistently fair. Fleet management should take pains to present the awards in a dignified manner that reinforces their importance as symbols of achievement.

There is publicity value in safety awards. See Appendix A, Getting Publicity from Safe Driver Awards, for details.

CHALLENGE OF DRIVER SUPERVISION

Maintaining our society's high standard of living and its rate of technological change depends primarily on the mass production of goods and availability of services. This is not so much a matter of working harder as of working smarter. To organize their resources, business and industry depend on the millions of supervisors who are in direct charge of workers and whose skill in human relations increases production. Transportation is a vital resource for maintaining our living standards.

Motor fleets play a big part in meeting our nation's transportation needs. Efficient, cost-effective fleet operation demands driving that is as free as possible from errors that incur waste.

To achieve this level of excellence, the industry depends on its driver supervisors, whatever their title and wherever they serve. Driver supervision is a rewarding occupation, requiring a positive attitude and a determination to succeed.

Accident Review Committees

The two key factors in any safety incentive program are (a) a high standard of safety performance and (b) a method of recognizing all individuals who meet this performance standard.

If management is satisfied with mediocre standards of performance, it will get nothing better. Setting high standards is no harder than setting low standards. The same amount of supervisory time and effort is involved in either case. However, when standards are set high, an additional incentive is created—a challenge to each individual worker. The skilled workers have a chance to show their ability. Their example spurs the rest of the group to improve their performance—one of the primary objectives—which eventually shows up on the profit side of the profit-and-loss statement.

Nothing discourages or annoys a skilled driver more than lack of recognition after meeting the standards of safety performance prescribed by management. Positive recognition is one of the chief job satisfactions of the skilled driver. It does not matter greatly what form this positive recognition takes, only that it be given promptly and impartially whenever it is earned. Negative recognition, such as penalizing a driver for an unpreventable accident, is worse than overlooking a preventable accident. (See also Chapter 7, Employee Safety Program; Encouraging High Performance in Chapter 10, Driver Supervision; and Appendix A, Getting Publicity from Safe Driver Awards.)

SET HIGH PERFORMANCE STANDARDS

What defines a standard of safe driving performance? Perfect safety performance is operation of a car, bus, truck, or other commercial vehicle without any accidents at all, ever. Such a standard may be too high, yet some drivers meet it. Drivers may become involved in accidents over which they have no control and for which it would be unfair to penalize them. In most cases, however, it takes two drivers to create an accident. Usually one of the drivers has violated some defensive driving principle relating to alertness or safe speed. Either driver could have prevented the accident; therefore, both are at fault.

Here is a workable definition of standard safe driving performance: although we cannot reasonably penalize drivers for all accidents they might become involved in, we can educate them about preventable accidents. Our standard of safe driving performance is therefore the ability to drive without having preventable accidents.

PREVENTABLE ACCIDENTS

A preventable accident is defined in the rules of the National Safety Council's Safe Driver Award Plan as: "any accident involving a company vehicle which results in property damage and/or personal injury, regardless of who was injured, what property was damaged, to what extent, or where it occurred, in which the driver in question failed to exercise reasonable precaution to prevent the accident."

The key word in this definition is "reasonable." How this word is interpreted when applied to actual accident cases will determine how high the standard of safety performance is in any particular fleet. If it is interpreted too strictly, drivers will conclude that the company expects the impossible. They may give up trying to meet the desired standard of safety performance. On the other hand, if the word "reasonable" is interpreted loosely, driving errors are likely to be overlooked and uncorrected, and may lead to more accidents. The company safety record will fall far short of its potential effectiveness.

Classifying accidents as preventable or nonpreventable for purposes of safe driving records is one of the most important tasks the safety director is called upon to perform. Training in how to judge the preventability of accidents is available through the National Safety Council.

Clear-Cut Preventability

Most accidents are preventable. By attending company driver training programs and safety meetings, drivers learn what standard of defensive driving is required of them. When involved in a preventable accident, they can usually point out where they failed and how the accident could have been prevented. The goal is to educate drivers so that this same type of accident will not happen in the future. The safety director will have little difficulty explaining why such accidents are being classified "preventable" and why the driver is being judged by the rules of the company incentive or safe driver award program.

Borderline Cases

Some of the accidents in the average fleet, however, are not so clear-cut. Their classification presents a special problem. Whether or not the driver did everything "reasonable" to prevent the accident depends a great deal on personal opinion. These borderline cases are the "hot potatoes" in any accident report file. How they are handled can spell the difference between a superior safety record and a mediocre one.

Some safety directors think that deciding borderline cases poses no particular problem at all and that the decision should be made by the safety director or the person in charge of the safety program at the particular location. They point out that since the safety professional is best informed on the subject of accident prevention and responsible for the safety program, he or she is the only logical person to decide whether or not an accident could have been prevented.

Borderline accident cases are the most sensitive points in the whole safety program. Whether or not the driver could have prevented the accident is a matter of conjecture. Drivers will resent any arbitrary decision by management that suggests it was their fault. Remember that the goal is not to find fault but to educate and prevent.

Such an attitude is entirely justified and indicates that these drivers take pride in their safety records. Such pride is a valuable asset that must not be destroyed. When drivers no longer care how their accidents are classified, the safety program will have become a lost cause. Close cases, after they have been reviewed by an in-company accident review committee, can be appealed to the National Safety Council.

ACCIDENT REVIEW COMMITTEE

If we expect drivers to continue to take their safety records seriously, we must classify accidents in a manner that assures drivers their rights have been scrupulously protected. Deciding such cases solely on the basis of the facts solidifies the safety director's proper relationship with the drivers. The decision on borderline cases should reflect the weight of the entire organization's informed opinion. For these reasons, such cases should be decided by a formal accident review committee.

Deciding borderline cases by the committee method has the following advantages:

- The importance of the individual's safety record is emphasized.
- The help of all departments is enlisted in making the safety program successful.
- The safety director is protected from being the target of ill will from drivers who have accidents.
- Drivers are assured that all their rights are being protected.
- For the driver involved, it takes a great deal of the sting out of an adverse decision.
- The responsibility for the decision is removed from line supervision.

Committee Membership

Whether an accident could or could not have been prevented is not a matter to be decided by popular vote.

The committee's purpose is to decide borderline cases by the weight of informed opinion. The committee should represent all departments of the organization directly involved in the safety program—safety, transportation, and maintenance—as well as driving personnel. A decision from such a balanced group will satisfy the driver involved, and, if the individual members are carefully selected and trained, it will represent the best and most reasonable thinking of the entire organization.

For these reasons, the following persons should serve on the committee:

- One representative from the safety department, trained in the principles of accident prevention and safety supervision, to serve as chair. This person should be familiar with company safety rules, the content of the driver training program, and the rules of the safe driver award plan or incentive plan.
- One supervisory representative from the transportation department, familiar with operating rules pertaining to schedules, routes, speed limits, hours of work, and related subjects. This person can advise the committee when a driver claims that a conflict exists between operating rules and safe practices.
- One representative from the maintenance department, familiar with the mechanical aspects of company maintenance policy. This person can advise the committee when a driver claims that faulty equipment caused the accident.
- Two professional drivers, because drivers are thoroughly familiar with traffic conditions and with the everyday hazards of the job. If given the opportunity, they can often explain authoritatively how an accident could have been prevented.

It has been suggested that drivers should outnumber so-called management representatives on the committee. This implies that the accident review committee is an arena for labor-management controversy. Nothing could be further from the truth. The accident review committee is not a joint labor-management function. It is a supervisory tool that should be controlled by management to advance the accident prevention program. Management should never relinquish control to the point where the committee is no longer capable of producing decisions that sustain a high standard of safe driving performance.

The First Committee

Members of the first accident review committee should be selected with special care, because the way they perform their functions will set a pattern for future committees. The supervisory representative and the maintenance representative should be selected for their proven interest in furthering the accident prevention program. Drivers selected should have superior safety records and command the respect and confidence of their fellow drivers.

The chair should instruct the members of this first committee with great care, defining a preventable accident and the meaning of defensive driving. Usually, the committee should handle a practice case first; that is, the chair selects an accident report from the file, has the committee discuss it and come to a decision, then tells them how the accident was originally classified and why. When members are thoroughly familiar with the "defensive driving" approach toward accident prevention, they are ready to decide on actual cases.

Rotating Committee Membership

As much as possible, the chair should try to share the educational benefits of serving on an accident review committee by rotating its membership. Members who have served on the committee will take this experience back to their various departments. This process alone will in time build a high degree of safety-mindedness throughout the entire organization. However, only one new member should be taken onto the committee at a time. This allows the new member to absorb some of the experience of the senior members before another member is rotated.

COMMITTEE PROCEDURES

Three committee procedures are recommended:

- The name of the driver involved in the accident should not be revealed to committee members.
- The driver involved should not be called before the committee to discuss the accident. The accident report should represent the case.
- The committee's decision should be arrived at by secret ballot.

Presenting the Facts

As chair of the accident review committee, the safety representative presents the facts about each accident under review and guides the discussion.

The chair should refer to the accident by file number only. Introducing the driver's name would tend to bring personalities into the discussion. Members might be swayed by their prior knowledge of the person's driving habits and general conduct. By considering the accident without reference to names, the committee can be more objective.

The committee should not call the driver before it for questioning. The driver should have already written all he or she knows about the accident on the report. The facts are there (or should be). If called before the committee, the driver might argue, cloud the issue, and sway the judgment of the committee by "salesmanship" (or lack of it). It is unfair to that driver and to all other drivers.

The facts of each accident presented to members of the committee should come from the following sources:

- driver's report of the accident
- police investigation reports
- insurance company investigation reports
- facts based on an investigation by company representatives

- statements of witnesses
- diagrams, photographs, and any other available evidence

Guiding the Discussion

After presenting the facts, the chair should guide the discussion. The only question before the committee is "Could the driver have prevented this accident?"

The answer depends on the kind of defensive driving philosophy that has come to be accepted in the company. This in turn depends on how good a job the safety director has done in indoctrinating the entire organization in the principles of accident prevention.

But how far can any safe driver be expected to go in foreseeing and compensating for the driving errors of others? The standard must be high, but it must also be reasonable. It must be the product of the safety training program initiated and maintained by the safety director. It must reflect a meeting of minds of the line organization regarding what is reasonable and possible in the realm of accident prevention.

It is important to remember that when a particular accident is declared nonpreventable, a precedent has been set and the committee is obliged to render the same decision on similar accidents occurring under similar circumstances. Calling an accident nonpreventable absolves the driver of all blame. If too many accidents are admitted to this classification, however, the safety program will gradually lose its effectiveness. The chair should point this out and should also remind the committee members that judging the accident nonpreventable is in effect saying that if any one of them had been driving, he or she would have been unable to prevent the accident. This approach tends to remove the element of sympathy and make the decision more objective.

Voting by Secret Ballot

When satisfied that the members of the committee have mastered all the facts of the accident and have discussed it sufficiently, the chair should pass out slips of paper and ask for a vote. Members should write "preventable" or "nonpreventable" on the slips and pass them back to the chair.

The chair counts the ballots and casts a vote only in case of a tie. The majority decision is announced: either "preventable" or "nonpreventable." Experience has shown that when the committee is well briefed, the chair's vote will be necessary in less than 3% of the cases.

Telling the Driver

After the meeting, the chair should inform each driver in writing of the committee's decision and, if the accident was judged preventable, what the reasons were for classifying it so. Having followed the discussion, the chair will be familiar with the majority point of view and can summarize it for the driver.

A copy of the written decision should be given to the driver and another copy placed in his or her personnel file. Copies may be provided to other interested parties, such as the driver's immediate supervisor or union officials, depending on company policy.

It is usually advisable for the safety director or the driver's immediate supervisor to tell the driver the decision in a personal interview. This should be done immediately. This interview is an opportunity to discuss corrective measures with the driver and to relate the decision to the driver's overall accident record.

APPEAL PROCEDURES

Decisions about whether an accident was preventable should be made as close as possible to the lower management ranks. As stated earlier, most of a fleet's accidents are clear-cut cases and can be decided one way or another by the safety director, the driver's immediate supervisor, or the person directly in charge of safety at the particular location. Only when there is a reasonable doubt or when the person with primary jurisdiction cannot convince the driver that the accident was preventable should an accident be referred to the review committee.

What happens when the driver is not satisfied with the decision of the accident review committee? In some companies, he or she has no recourse. Other companies, recognizing that such a decision affects employee morale, provide an additional assurance of fair play. Members of the National Safety Council take advantage of the NSC's Accident Review Committee. The recommended practice is to allow the driver to appeal in writing any decision from the company accident review committee within 10 days after being informed of the decision. The driver is asked to state why he or she thinks the accident should have been judged nonpreventable.

To refer an accident to this committee, the company should send six copies of the accident report with all supporting documentation to the National Safety Council with the request that it be referred to the Accident Review Committee for an opinion. Contact the National Safety Council Motor Transportation Department for more information.

The in-house accident review board represents a unique tool for management: it is a decision method outside the framework of the union contract. Most contracts leave accident judgment to the company. Having a preventable accident takes at least a year off the driver's award record. It cannot be worked off like a warning letter. Years later, the driver will have to say, "I've worked 20 years with this company and have a 19-year safe driving record." It will be evident that the driver had a preventable accident. A decision of "preventable" is strong discipline to a proud employee, and it is not subject to the political pressures of a grievance hearing.

CHAPTER 12

Fleet Purchase and Maintenance

This chapter discusses some of the influences the choice of vehicle can have on the safety program. When we talk about the vehicle, we enter the domain of the maintenance department and of those people responsible for the purchase and disposition of equipment.

PURCHASING EQUIPMENT WITH SAFETY IN MIND

When fleet vehicles are purchased, a number of conflicting values usually affect the decision. The purchaser worries about:

- Cost—How much can be purchased with the available dollars? Money must be spent on the right equipment and accessories.

- Availability—How soon can the new equipment be put to use on the job? Any delays can cost the company money.

- Standardization—Usually a fleet is better (and safer) if all vehicles are the same or similar brands. Maintenance is more efficient, drivers know every vehicle, and substitution is easy when a unit breaks down. Stocked parts can be purchased in quantity for additional savings.

- Order size—Generally, a bigger order of the same vehicle reduces the cost per unit. However, some purchasers will bargain the price down between competitors and make minor concessions on the vehicle and equipment for a better price.

- Maintenance convenience—Some vehicles require less work to repair. Specifying maintenance-free batteries, for instance, may save a lot of inspection and servicing time for the shop.

- Operational convenience—The vehicle is bought to do a specific job. The engine, gear ratios, and the like should match the job for greatest efficiency.

- Fuel savings—Vehicles are ordered with special fuel-saving components such as high torque/low RPM engines, temperature-controlled fans, air shields, and radial tires.

- Optional equipment—Devices that automatically shut down, bring engines to an idle, check tire pressure, or warn of overheated cooling systems can help prevent accidents and lower fuel consumption. Onboard computers record road speed, engine idling, vehicle stopped time, and fuel consumption. The data are then transferred to the fleet office computer and analyzed to determine driver and vehicle safety and performance. These data can also document hours of service violations. Data that prove compliance can be a powerful tool in the defense against illegitimate collision claims (Figure 12–1).

- Safety—No fleet purchaser will deliberately buy an unsafe piece of equipment. However, the safety department must define for the purchasing department what is considered safe. Purchasing personnel should agree beforehand that they will consult the safety director early in the purchasing process. Otherwise, this step could be overlooked in the procedure.

The safety director can also prepare general safety specs and ask that they be held in the purchasing department files and referred to before any vehicle purchase. These written specifications should be updated regularly. This step is important because a vehicle, once purchased, will run at least three years and often more. Mistakes made by the purchasing office can live on to become accident-producing nightmares on the job.

Figure 12–1. Data on road speed, engine idling, vehicle stopped time, and fuel consumption can be electronically captured on trip recorders. Courtesy Zepco Sales & Service, Inc., Richardson, TX.

Cooperating with Purchasing

To get cooperation from those who purchase equipment, the safety director should do the following:

- Keep current statistics on accidents or near misses caused by equipment problems and see that the information gets to the fleet purchaser. Maintain good driver communications so that equipment problems are reported.
- Work to build good communications and cooperation with the purchaser.
- Know when fleet purchases will occur, and recommend safety items before the specifications are frozen in bids.
- Ask to accompany the purchasing representative to sales demonstrations, pilot model inspections, and trade shows.
- Learn as much as possible about the maintenance, operational, and financial decisions that dictate the purchase order. Often safety considerations can be presented in a way that supports these other requirements.
- Keep current on government safety regulations affecting the design, manufacture, and maintenance of parts and equipment. Two examples are splash and spray control requirements and air-brake system changes.
- Take charge of training drivers when new engines or vehicles are ordered. Such help will be appreciated and aid in driver acceptance and proper use of the equipment.

Safety-Related Items

Some of the safety-related items to consider when ordering new equipment and retrofitting the existing fleet include the following.

All vehicles.

- Additional or upgraded right-side mirrors
- Heated mirrors for cold climates
- Safely designed vehicle and accessory controls (watch for needless protrusions that could cause injury if the driver is thrown against them in a crash)
- Upgraded comfort features, such as higher-capacity heaters and air conditioners
- Extra interior lights and fog or road lights
- Special wiring for installation of CB or broadcast radios, cellular phones, and other accessories
- Daytime running lamp relay kits or OEM installation
- Backup alarms
- Antilock brakes
- Special seats or six-way power seats

Large vehicles.

- Vision systems to show rear view (Figure 12–2)
- Convex mirrors mounted at front and rear of vehicle (Figure 12–3)
- Radar systems to prevent collisions with pedestrians and other vehicles (Figure 12–4)
- Air-ride seats
- Air-ride suspensions
- Short-ended or breakaway bumper ends that will not jam against a front tire and turn a minor collision into a bad one
- A retarder to reduce brake wear and the likelihood of a runaway in regions with steep grades (may be either engine brake, exhaust brake, electromagnetic, or hydraulic retarder) (Figure 12–5)
- Liberal use of reflective tape and/or light paint on equipment to provide better night visibility and a good daytime image (Figure 12–6)

Large trucks.

- Work lights for hookup or cargo handling
- Better steps and grab rails on cabs and trailers
- Truck semitrailer air and electrical hookup on the road side of the nose, reachable from the ground
- Lifting handles on trailer and converter tongues. Jacks to hold trailer tongues at hookup height
- Mid-trailer turn signals
- Avoid built-in hazards such as cab rear protrusions that may pull trailer air hoses loose on a truck, awkward controls, and weak or unsafe step surfaces such as battery boxes or fuel tanks

Delivery vans and trailers.

- Walkup ramps for use with dollies to minimize lifting, climbing, and falling accidents (Figure 12–7)
- Hydraulic tailgate lifts
- Bulkheads to protect drivers from shifting freight

School buses.

- Strobe-lighted stop arms
- Crossing arm (Figure 12–8)
- Roof-mounted visibility strobe
- Video monitor inside bus for student control
- Roof-mounted escape hatches
- External public-address systems to warn children of danger
- High-back seats

Cars and light trucks.

- Power door locks

Figure 12–2. A rear mounted camera (left) and a dash-mounted monitor (right) give the driver a wide-angle view for backing. A two-way communication system allows voice contact with the spotter. Courtesy Intec Video Systems, Inc.

- Power windows
- Dual airbags

Maintenance equipment.

- Alignment equipment
- Vacuum equipment to capture asbestos during brake service
- Powered exhaust removal system to remove engine exhaust
- Brake balance tester (Figure 12–9)

New Technologies

As developments in consumer electronics cause the prices of complex systems to decrease, more sophisticated equipment will find its way into the transportation business. Developments that look promising include:

- Light-emitting diode brake lamps that are 200 milliseconds faster than incandescent lamps
- Radar systems that make possible:
  Smart cruise control that adjusts following distance
  Alarms that warn when signaling turn into vehicle
- Data loggers similar to airliner black boxes

- Traction control
- Vehicle-mounted scales to measure axle loading

WORKING WITH THE MAINTENANCE DEPARTMENT

The safety and maintenance departments share so many functions that they should work together well. Neither is specifically profit-oriented. Both are constantly striving for zero defects. Both are at the mercy of operating people who can make their work easy or difficult.

Conflicts arise when an overly budget-conscious maintenance worker releases a vehicle that a driver feels is unsafe. Often the driver supervisor ends up in the middle, blamed by both sides for being unreasonable or ineffective.

The solution is simple: if a vehicle is unsafe, don't use it. But applying the solution can be difficult. The shop supervisor is the mechanical expert and should know whether or not a vehicle is safe. But the driver is the one who risks the most and certainly should have the final say. Unfortunately, there are some mechanics who cut corners and some drivers who use breakdowns to draw a salary without having to do the work.

Figure 12–3. A fender-mounted mirror allows the driver to see small children or a student kneeling to pick up a dropped object in front of the bus. Courtesy Lo-Mar Corporation.

The safety director must create a cooperative atmosphere among all the parties. This means ensuring that driver complaints are investigated and repairs are made if necessary. It also means confronting any driver who has frequent and unfounded complaints. It means cooperating to help get "sick but safe" vehicles into a shop to be repaired, and making sure they are safe before they go out again.

The wise safety director will believe the complaints and stories of both drivers and mechanics the first few times. However, they should begin to show doubt when either party seems to have more "bad luck" than other employees.

In general, the maintenance and safety departments are often on the same side, fighting for more money or for an operational change that will allow sufficient shop work to make vehicles safe.

VEHICLE CONDITION REPORTS

Good records must be kept on each vehicle, including a daily statement by the driver on how it performed. This procedure is required for vehicles used in interstate commerce and is recommended for all others. The mechanic can use the driver's record to find out what is wrong with the vehicle, and the driver can check the record later to see what work was done. Nothing improves the trust and cooperation between these workers better than an effective write-up system.

Pre-trip Inspection

To trust a vehicle, the driver must be satisfied that it is fit to go on the street. This means conducting a brief pre-trip inspection. (Forms for truck and bus inspection are shown in Figure 12–10 and 12–11.) Ten minutes is enough time to check the DOT-required components likely to cause safety problems and to log the pre-trip inspection.

Post-trip Inspection

To ensure the safety of the next driver of a vehicle, each driver is required to perform a post-trip inspection. At the end of each workday, each vehicle driven must have a written report covering at least:

Figure 12–4.   The small box below the bumper is one of several electronic motion sensors on this bus. These sensors alert the driver to activity in danger areas around the bus. Courtesy Delco Electronics.

Figure 12–5.   When activated, this electromagnetic retarder in the drive train of a truck slows the vehicle and minimizes the use and overheating of friction brakes on steep grades. Courtesy Telma Retarder, Inc.

- service brakes, including trailer brake connections
- parking (hand) brake
- steering mechanism
- lighting devices and reflectors
- tires
- horn
- windshield wipers
- rear-vision mirrors
- coupling devices
- wheels and rims
- emergency equipment

The forms in Figures 12–10 and 12–11 cover these items and more. They may be used for both the pre- and post-trip inspections, but only the pre-trip needs to be logged. The post-trip report must state that there were no deficiencies or list those that were found. The driver must always sign the report. When deficiencies are detected, the mechanic and the next driver of the vehicle must sign off to indicate they are satisfied with the repairs.

Periodic Inspections

An annual inspection of a vehicle must be conducted by a qualified inspector. The inspection form should show the inspector's name, the motor carrier operating the vehicle, the date of inspection, the vehicle inspected, the components inspected, and their condition. These records must be kept in the vehicle (Figure 12–12). An alternative method is to apply a sticker to the vehicle that indicates compliance and the location of the original report (Figure 12–13). The specific requirements of the inspection and the inspector's credentials should be reviewed to ensure compliance.

EMERGENCY EQUIPMENT

State and federal laws specify the emergency equipment to be carried on trucks and buses. This includes driver safety belts, a fire extinguisher, emergency reflective triangles, spare bulbs and fuses, and on buses, a first-aid kit (Figure 12–14). Vehicles carrying specified hazardous materials must have more or larger extinguishers.

Some operations need to carry a great deal of emergency equipment. Chemical tank trucks normally carry protective clothing, gas masks, cleanup materials, and a breathing apparatus. Drivers have hard hats, face masks, rubber gloves, and rubber boots. Some fleets running in remote areas or in winter carry blankets, survival suits, and emergency rations.

Figure 12–6. Retroreflective material outlines trailers at night, reducing car/truck underride accidents. Courtesy Reflexite Corporation.

UNSAFE OPERATIONAL DECISIONS

The safety department must be alert to operational decisions that affect the driver and the vehicle. Possible pitfalls include unsafe scheduling and routing, unsecured loads, and overloads.

Unsafe Scheduling and Routing

Transportation in the United States is a highly competitive business, more so since deregulation. Competition can force a sales department to make impossible delivery promises, and the problem is then turned over to the operations department. If speeding or running long hours is the only way the company can obtain business, the safety department will be pressured to relax its safety standards.

This point is where the safety program must come of age. The safety director must enlist the strong support of top management and insist that unsafe vehicles, drivers, or schedules will not be tolerated.

Unsecured Loads

Drivers must be sure that their loads and equipment are properly secured to avoid loss of cargo or other items. Debris on the roadway can come from a variety of sources. Consider the following:

- Tanker trailers often have a plastic bucket hooked to one of the various spouts. The bucket is used to collect excess liquid, either food grade or hazardous materials, that may leak out of the spouts during unloading. The bucket is constantly moving as the vehicle travels along the highway. Tanker carriers

Figure 12–7.   This slide-out van access ramp has slots that prevent a build-up of debris or precipitation. Courtesy Magline, Inc.

should determine if they actually need a bucket. If so, the hook must be properly engineered, and the bucket and handle must be able to withstand the swinging action. The driver and maintenance department should include the hooking device and the bucket handle in their inspection.

- Flatbed trailers carry wood blocking material, canvas tarps, chains, binders, cheater bars, and sideboards. Different sizes of boards are strung across the trailer behind the pony wheels and usually secured with a bungee cord. If such equipment must be transported without a container, the company must make sure it is properly stowed.

- Lowboy trailers that are used to transport road-building equipment or construction equipment should be cleaned of mud, dirt, and blocking material before loading and after unloading.

- Trailer chassis used to transport containers receive a lot of abuse during the loading and unloading of the containers. When a driver takes possession of a trailer,

Figure 12–8.   This well-equipped bus has a stop arm, front view mirrors, and a crossing arm to protect the children. Courtesy Specialty Manufacturing Company.

it should be in good condition, with no loose parts that might fall onto the roadway.

- Van trailers carry snow chains, wooden pallets, and spare tires. Pallets that are in need of repair should be checked before they are loaded into the rack under the trailer. Loose pallet boards could fall onto the roadway. Spare tires must be secured in their cages with a chain and lock. The chain should be checked periodically for wear and tear.

- Local pickup and delivery units have hand trucks mounted on the front bumpers or in other locations outside the truck body. The hand trucks must be properly secured and the mounting brackets inspected periodically. This should be part of the pre- and post-trip inspection procedure.

- Dump-trailer loads should be covered to prevent rocks, stones, and dirt from falling onto the roadway. When the trailers are empty, they should be cleaned. Often an empty dump trailer will bounce, causing residual stones and dirt to fall onto the roadway or other vehicles.

- Moving vans have loading/unloading ramps stored underneath the trailer. The devices securing the ramps should be checked periodically and be included in the driver's regular pre-trip inspection.

- Empty car carriers have chains that may come loose and rub along the ground. The chain can eventually break loose and fall onto the roadway or strike another vehicle.

- Tire chocks are often transported on power units. Carriers hauling gasoline use the chock blocks while unloading. These chock blocks should be secured, not just placed, between the fuel tank and frame rail.

Management can take steps to minimize debris-related incidents:

- Evaluate the accident register for debris-related accidents. The problems that have already happened will provide a starting point for corrective action.

- Develop formal written safety rules for stowing, loading, and blocking materials. The pre-trip inspection should include specific checks for these items. If a pre-trip safety lane is used, maintenance personnel should include these items in their visual inspection.

- Require that any equipment carried outside the tractor trailer be approved by management. All drivers and maintenance personnel should be notified of this company policy.

- During orientation, provide training for all new employees on the proper stowing of items secured to the outside of the equipment. Periodic short safety meetings should remind regular drivers of this potentially serious problem. Drivers should also be reminded of the DOT safety regulations that require them to stop to check their cargo and load-securing devices within the first 25 miles of a trip and after every 150 miles or three hours of driving (whichever comes first) during the rest of the trip.

A tragic accident in Milwaukee illustrates the seriousness of this issue. In 1994, a piece of a container trailer's

(Text continues on page 147)

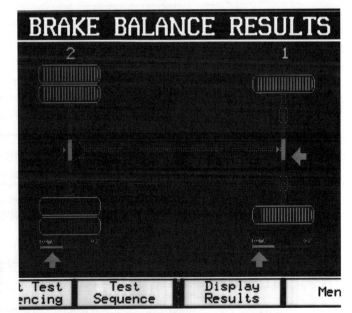

Figure 12–9. Brake efficiency can be tested by this computerized tester. Braking on the mat (left) produces a display in which the number of bars on each tire shows brake imbalances (right). Courtesy Hunter Engineering Company.

DRIVER'S VEHICLE INSPECTION REPORT
AS REQUIRED BY THE D.O.T. FEDERAL MOTOR CARRIER SAFETY REGULATIONS

CARRIER: _____

ADDRESS: _____

DATE: _____ TIME: _____ A.M. _____ P.M.

CHECK ANY DEFECTIVE ITEM AND GIVE DETAILS UNDER "REMARKS"

**TRACTOR/
TRUCK NO.** _____ ODOMETER READING _____

- ☐ Air Compressor
- ☐ Air Lines
- ☐ Battery
- ☐ Body
- ☐ Brake Accessories
- ☐ Brakes, Parking
- ☐ Brakes, Service
- ☐ Clutch
- ☐ Coupling Devices
- ☐ Defroster/Heater
- ☐ Drive Line
- ☐ Engine
- ☐ Exhaust
- ☐ Fifth Wheel
- ☐ Frame and Assembly
- ☐ Front Axle
- ☐ Fuel Tanks
- ☐ Generator

- ☐ Horn
- ☐ Lights
  - Head - Stop
  - Tail - Dash
  - Turn Indicators
- ☐ Mirrors
- ☐ Muffler
- ☐ Oil Pressure
- ☐ Radiator
- ☐ Rear End
- ☐ Reflectors
- ☐ Safety Equipment
  - Fire Extinguisher
  - Reflective Triangles
  - Flags - Flares - Fusees
  - Spare Bulbs & Fuses
  - Spare Seal Beam

- ☐ Suspension System
- ☐ Starter
- ☐ Steering
- ☐ Tachograph
- ☐ Tires
- ☐ Tire Chains
- ☐ Transmission
- ☐ Wheels and Rims
- ☐ Windows
- ☐ Windshield Wipers
- ☐ Other

TRAILER(S) NO. (S). _____

- ☐ Brake Connections
- ☐ Brakes
- ☐ Coupling Devices
- ☐ Coupling (King) Pin
- ☐ Doors

- ☐ Hitch
- ☐ Landing Gear
- ☐ Lights - All
- ☐ Roof
- ☐ Suspension System

- ☐ Tarpaulin
- ☐ Tires
- ☐ Wheels and Rims
- ☐ Other

Remarks: _____
_____
_____
_____
_____
_____
_____
_____

☐ CONDITION OF THE ABOVE VEHICLE IS SATISFACTORY

DRIVER'S SIGNATURE: _____

☐ ABOVE DEFECTS CORRECTED

☐ ABOVE DEFECTS NEED NOT BE CORRECTED FOR SAFE OPERATION OF VEHICLE

MECHANIC'S SIGNATURE: _____ DATE _____

DRIVER'S SIGNATURE: _____ DATE _____

ORIGINAL

Figure 12–10. This sample inspection report form meets DOT regulations. Courtesy J.J. Keller & Associates, Inc.

VEHICLE CONDITION REPORT

USE YOUR SEATBELT

DATE _____

PRINT EXCEPT SIGNATURE, USED PROPERLY THIS CHECKLIST IS PROTECTION

LOCATION (City)　　　STATE　　　ORGANIZATION　　　TRUCK or TRACTOR-TRAILER NUMBERS

DRIVER　　　　　　　　　　　　　DRIVER

INSTRUCTIONS: Drivers will perform necessary inspection. A check (√) indicates satisfactory condition. An "X" indicates unsafe or improper conditions. Items corrected will be circled by management certifier.

INSIDE
☐ Parking Brake (Apply)

START ENGINE

☐ Oil Pressure (Light or Gauge)
☐ Air Pressure or Vacuum (Gauge)
☐ Low Air or Vacuum Warning Device (Air pressure below 40 psi check on pressure build-up. Air pressure above 60 psi deplete air until warning device works). Vacuum below 8 inches Hg. check on build-up. Above 8 inches Hg. deplete vacuum until device works.
☐ Instrument Panel (Telltale lights or buzzers)
☐ Horn
☐ Windshield Wiper and Washer
☐ Heater-Defroster
☐ Mirrors
☐ Steering Wheel (Excess Play)
☐ Apply Trailer Brakes in EMERGENCY
☐ Turn on all lights including 4-way Flasher
☐ Starts Properly

ON COMBINATIONS
☐ Hoses, Connections
☐ Couplings (Fifth Wheel, Tow Bar, Safety Chains, Locking Devices)

EMERGENCY EQUIPMENT
☐ Fire Extinguishers
☐ Flags, Standards, Warning Lights
☐ Fuses
☐ Reflectors
☐ Spare Bulbs
☐ Chains in Season
☐ First Aid Kits

FRONT
☐ Headlights
☐ Clearance Lights
☐ Identification Lights
☐ Turn Signals and 4-way Flasher
☐ Tires and Wheels-Lugs and Serviceability

INSIDE
☐ Release Trailer Emergency Brakes
☐ Apply Service Brake-air loss should not exceed 3 psi per minute on single vehicles, 4 psi per minute on combinations.

SIDE
LEFT　RIGHT
☐　☐ Fuel Tank and Cap
☐　☐ Sidemarker Lights
☐　☐ Reflectors
☐　☐ Tires and Wheels-Lugs and Serviceability
☐　☐ Cargo Tie-downs/or Doors

REAR
☐ Tail Lights
☐ Stop Light
☐ Turn Signals and 4-way Flasher
☐ Clearance Lights
☐ Identification Lights
☐ Reflectors
☐ Tires and Wheels, Lugs and Serviceability
☐ Rear End Protection (Bumper)
☐ Cargo Tie-downs/Doors

MECHANICAL OPERATION
☐ Engine knocks, misses, overheats, etc.
☐ Clutch skips, grabs, other
☐ Transmission noisy, hard shifting, jumps out of gear, other
☐ Axles — noisy, other
☐ Steering loose, shimmy, hard, other
☐ Air, oil, water, leaks
☐ Springs broken, other
☐ Brakes noisy, pulls, soft, other
☐ Speedometer, Tachometer
☐ Tachograph, Speed Control Devices
☐ Other _____

OTHER
YES　NO
☐　☐ Equipment Inspection Enroute
☐　☐ Cargo Securing Devices
☐　☐ _____
☐　☐ _____
☐　☐ _____
☐　☐ _____

START TIME	SPEEDOMETER	END TIME	SPEEDOMETER

REMARKS/OTHER DEFECTS

DRIVER'S SIGNATURE

DEFECTS CORRECTED (Initial)	DEFECT CORRECTION UNNECESSARY (Initial)	CERTIFIED BY	DATE
DEFECTS CORRECTED　☐ Yes　☐ No		DRIVER'S SIGNATURE (If Defects)	DATE

Figure 12–11. Sample driver inspection report for buses, trucks, and tractor-trailers. Courtesy National Private Truck Council, Inc., Alexandria, VA.

USE A PERMANENT IMAGE MARKER OR PENCIL TO WRITE ON THE LABEL
TO COMPLETE THE FORM FOLLOW THE INSTRUCTIONS ON THE BACK OF THE SET

ANNUAL VEHICLE INSPECTION REPORT

DATE _____ _____

INSPECTOR'S NAME (PRINT)

MOTOR CARRIER OPERATOR

THIS INSPECTOR MEETS THE QUALIFICATION
REQUIREMENTS IN SECTION 396.19 ☐ YES ☐ NO

ADDRESS

VEHICLE IDENTIFICATION (CHECK AND COMPLETE ONE)
☐ Lic. Plate No./State   ☐ Fleet Unit Number
☐ Veh. ID No.   ☐ Other _____

CITY, STATE, ZIP CODE

VEHICLE COMPONENTS INSPECTED   mark _X_ Yes, ok, mark _X_ No, not ok; _—_ Does not apply

OKAY		ITEM INSPECTED	OKAY		ITEM INSPECTED
YES	NO		YES	NO	
		1. BRAKE SYSTEM			**7. STEERING MECHANISM**
		a. Service brakes			a. Steering wheel free play
		b. Parking brake system			b. Steering column
		c. Brake drums or rotors			c. Front axle beam and all steering components
		d. Brake hose			other than steering column
		e. Brake tubing			d. Steering gear box
		f. Low pressure warning device			e. Pitman arm
		g. Tractor protection valve			f. Power steering
		h. Air compressor			g. Ball and socket joints
		i. Electric brakes			h. Tie rods and drag links
		j. Hydraulic brakes			i. Nuts
		k. Vacuum systems			j. Steering system
		2. COUPLING DEVICES			**8. SUSPENSION**
		a. Fifth wheels			a. Any U-bolt(s), spring hanger(s), or other axle
		b. Pintle hooks			positioning part(s) cracked, broken, loose or
		c. Drawbar/towbar eye			missing resulting in shifting of an axle from
		d. Drawbar/towbar tongue			its normal position.
		e. Safety devices			b. Spring assembly
		f. Saddle-mounts			c. Torque, radius or tracking components
		3. EXHAUST SYSTEM			**9. FRAME**
		a. Any exhaust system determined to be leaking at a point forward of or directly below the driver/sleeper compartment.			a. Frame members
					b. Tire and wheel clearance
		b. A bus exhaust system leaking or discharging to the atmosphere in violation of standards (1), (2) or (3).			c. Adjustable axle assemblies (Sliding subframes)
		c. No part of the exhaust system of any motor vehicle shall be so located as would be likely to result in burning, charring, or damaging the electrical wiring, the fuel supply, or any combustible part of the motor vehicle.			**10. TIRES**
					a. Tires on any steering axle of a power unit
					b. All other tires
		4. FUEL SYSTEM			**11. WHEELS AND RIMS**
		a. Visible Leak			a. Lock or side ring
		b. Fuel tank filler cap missing			b. Wheels and Rims
		c. Fuel tank securely attached			c. Fasteners
		5. LIGHTING DEVICES			d. Welds
		All lighting devices and reflectors required by Section 393 shall be operable.			**12. WINDSHIELD GLAZING**
					Requirements and exceptions as stated pertaining to any crack, discoloration or vision reducing matter (reference 393.60 for exceptions)
		6. SAFE LOADING			
		a. Part(s) of vehicle or condition of loading such that the spare tire or any part of the load or dunnage can fall onto the roadway.			**13. WINDSHIELD WIPERS**
		b. Protection against shifting cargo.			Any power unit that has an inoperative wiper, or missing or damaged parts that render it ineffective.

CERTIFICATION: This vehicle has passed all the inspection items for the Annual Vehicle Inspection Report in accordance with 49 CFR 396.

©1989 J. J. KELLER & ASSOCIATES, INC.
Neenah WI 54957-0368 ● USA

APPLY TO VEHICLE   237-FS-E3 (Rev. 5/93)

CERTIFICATION: This vehicle has passed all the inspection items for the Annual Vehicle Inspection Report in accordance with 49 CFR 396.

©1989 J. J. KELLER & ASSOCIATES, INC.
Neenah, WI 54957-0368 ● USA

RETAIN IN VEHICLE FILE   237-FS-E3 (Rev. 5/93)

Figure 12–12.   This sample vehicle inspection report meets DOT regulations. It has a self-adhesive transparent protective cover, a self-adhesive label, and a carbon copy to retain in the vehicle file. Courtesy J. J. Keller & Associates, Inc.

```
TO WRITE ON THIS LABEL USE AN INDELIBLE, PERMANENT INK MARKER,
PEN OR PENCIL THAT WILL NOT FADE IN DIRECT SUNLIGHT
```

ANNUAL VEHICLE INSPECTION LABEL NO. **2086647**

COMPLETED: MONTH _____ YEAR _____

A RECORD OF THIS VEHICLE'S ANNUAL VEHICLE INSPECTION REPORT IS
MAINTAINED AT: ☐ MOTOR CARRIER ☐ OTHER ENTITY

_____
COMPANY/NAME

_____
STREET

_____
CITY, STATE, ZIP CODE

_____ | _____
TELEPHONE | MOTOR CARRIER IDENTIFICATION NUMBER

CERTIFICATION: THIS VEHICLE HAS PASSED AN INSPECTION IN ACCORDANCE
WITH 49CFR 396.17 THROUGH 396.23.

VEHICLE IDENTIFICATION: IF THE VEHICLE IS NOT READILY, CLEARLY, AND
PERMANENTLY MARKED, CHECK ONE AND COMPLETE.

☐ FLEET UNIT NUMBER ☐ LICENSE/REGISTRATION NUMBER
☐ VEHICLE IDENTIFICATION NUMBER ☐ OTHER _____

© Copyright 1990 and Published by J. J. KELLER & ASSOCIATES, INC., Neenah, WI 54957-0368   49-SN (Rev. 6/90)

Figure 12–13. This sample self-adhesive sticker can be applied to the vehicle to indicate where the vehicle's annual inspection report is filed. It has a transparent protective cover and meets DOT regulations. Courtesy J.J. Keller & Associates, Inc.

rear I-beam, which holds the stop and turn signal and metal bracket for the mud flap on the chassis, fell onto the roadway. The driver of a passenger van carrying a family of eight was unable to avoid the I-beam, which punctured the van's fuel tank. Sparks ignited the gasoline and six children died as a result of the fire. Their parents survived but were seriously burned.

This incident involved a piece of the truck itself; the same potential exists for any fleet. The only way to prevent this type of incident is to plan, implement, and maintain a formal program of prevention. (This section about roadway debris is adapted from Don Capuano, *The Quill*, 8:2 (Feb. 1995). Indianapolis, IN: Baldwin & Lyons Inc.)

Overloading

Another operational answer to business pressure is to pile more cargo on each vehicle, thus realizing more revenue. But overloaded vehicles wear out more quickly and are difficult to stop. If the company has a lax attitude toward weight laws, drivers are encouraged to cheat on other regulations. Auditing to reveal violations is discussed in the next chapter.

SAFETY CONSIDERATIONS IN OTHER COMPANY VEHICLES

Often a company will have many nonrevenue vehicles on the highway along with its trucks or buses. These cars and service vehicles have accidents too, which can create serious image and liability problems.

Company Cars

Salespeople and executives may have company cars for their business and personal use. These cars should be well-maintained and driven safely. They should be inspected by the safety department at least four times a year. Accident report kits and maintenance schedules should be in each vehicle. Monthly mailings of safety material will keep the drivers aware; the National Safety Council and many insurance companies can provide these.

Cars should be purchased with safety in mind. In most parts of the United States, electrical rear-window defrosters are required. Outside mirrors are vital on the left side and important on the right. Also important are power windows, door locks, antilock brakes, airbags, and other features

Figure 12–14. These folding reflective triangles have a weighted base for stability. They are required for commercial vehicles but are also good safety equipment for noncommercial vehicles. Courtesy Direct Safety Company.

that may be appropriate for the intended service. The configuration of the vehicle should match the job function of the intended user. For example, a sales representative making calls with samples may need a minivan rather than a subcompact car.

Even the passenger injury rate of the vehicle should be considered. It is generally true that passengers in larger cars are more likely to survive a crash than those in subcompacts. The insurance industry compiles statistics on injury rates and makes them available free of charge.

Because the company liability policy is on the line, it is important to keep these drivers out of accidents. Many firms charge the driver some of the accident cost as a fine for preventable accidents. The fine itself makes believers out of many drivers, and having their accidents judged by top executives will bring the rest around. (To save the safety department from political problems, the judgment should be made by an accident review committee. See the National Safety Council's *A Guide to Determine Motor Vehicle Accident Preventibility).*

Finally, there are some people who should not drive at all. Periodic checks with the state Department of Motor Vehicles will show which company employees are being issued citations and being involved in unreported accidents. Motor vehicle records (MVRs) should be run at least annually on all drivers. Discipline may require a great deal of tact and the assistance of the company president. In one case, a salesperson with a poor accident record was invaluable to the company. The solution was to give him his own chauffeur (something even the president did not have).

Service Vehicles

Transportation companies often forget they have small (and sometimes large) trucks on the street to assist the

company shops. The drivers may not be checked for citations, and the vehicles may operate with no compliance review at all.

Sometimes heavy-duty tow trucks, snowplows, and even regular road vehicles are driven by mechanics who do not know how to drive them safely. The basic company rule should be: "Any company vehicle of any size will be driven only by employees licensed to do so, and checked out by a driver supervisor." Drivers of these larger vehicles must have a CDL license.

Driver Supervisors' Vehicles

All the comments regarding company cars apply to supervisors' vehicles as well. In addition, an attempt should be made to provide cars with extra comfort and driving features, so the supervisor will not mind long hours on the road.

Generally these vehicles are station wagons, vans, or midsized cars. They may have features such as cruise control, adjustable seats, nice radios, a spotlight, and heavy-duty suspension. CBs or radio-telephones are often installed. Some fleets install a police speedometer or radar.

These cars need more emergency equipment than most because supervisors respond to accidents and come upon many emergencies during patrol. They should carry a fire extinguisher or two, a large first-aid kit, blankets, assorted fuses, winter and rain gear, a tool kit, flashlights, and perhaps some small spare parts. The accident kit should contain report forms, measuring tape, a camera, marking crayon, hazard pylons, and a small tape recorder. If the company hauls hazardous materials, a cleanup kit with plastic sheets, absorbent material, and a broom may be useful.

Care must be taken that the driver supervisor vehicle is not used to make road calls and haul tires. It must be controlled by the safety department so it will be available for its primary purpose: accident prevention and investigation.

Vehicle Color

Company cars are generally ordered in the color the main user desires. Driver supervisor cars should be a light color for improved visibility. A company sign in a contrasting color gives better visibility in winter months. If there are several cars, a uniform color is impressive and helps in identification.

It is usually best for the supervisor's car to be easily recognized by drivers. A company sign on the car can help identify it as a supervisory vehicle. If the sign is magnetic and removable, the car can be used incognito when desired. The sign should combine the company name with a reference to the vehicle purpose—highway safety. Encouraging supervisors to stop and help stranded motorists when time permits can create a powerful public relations tool.

CHAPTER 13

Scattered Fleet Supervision

Working with widely separated units of a fleet poses special safety problems. In some respects it is similar to administering a safety program for a collection of small fleets, each with separate local management and problems of its own. If a fleet safety program is to be directed effectively from a central location, each fleet unit must be required to operate on a common basis observing standardized procedures and using standard forms, awards, and other program elements established by headquarters.

It often requires considerable work to keep safety programming uniform throughout the company. Communications between headquarters and local fleet management can create many difficulties. These problems probably will be worse in organizations in which transportation is incidental to its basic function. A bakery, utility, insurance company, department store, newspaper, or other enterprise that uses motor vehicles may find it difficult to interest their drivers in safety matters. Yet, companies have gone out of business because they spent more money on accidents then they made in profit on sales.

Profitable operation is safe operation. All segments of an organization must be operated safely, and a good safety record is usually a by-product of good operations throughout the company.

STANDARDIZE POLICY AND ASSIGN RESPONSIBILITY

Standardization of the safety program at all locations of the scattered units of a fleet is the most effective approach to a good safety program. Such a uniform program will actually cost less in terms of management and safety staff time and expenses.

Responsibility for Safety

One of the first steps to standardization is assigning the responsibility for safety: management from top to bottom is fully responsible for safety results. The safety director is an advisor to management: he or she serves in a staff capacity.

Functions of a Home Office Safety Staff

The function of the home office safety staff should be to help both home and field management by (a) providing counsel; (b) participating in the establishment of safety objectives; and (c) analyzing, planning, and organizing the safety program to reach these objectives.

Time spent on the various home office safety activities will vary with conditions, but the percentages are often similar to those shown in Table 13–A, Safety Director's Time Distribution.

In carrying on these activities, items most likely to present a challenge are

- securing the support of the management in a uniform, company-wide accident prevention program,
- securing uniform reporting of accidents,
- determining whether accidents (or accidental damage) are motor fleet accidents or incidents, and then securing acceptance of the decisions about preventability (see the section on Defensive Driving in Chapter 9, Driver Training), and

Table 13–A. Safety Director's Time Distribution

Home Office Activities (40% to 95% of time)	Percent of Time Spent
1. General duties of developing, establishing, and promoting the program, carrying on the necessary correspondence, supervising the reporting, record keeping, and statistics	30 to 50
2. Preparing for and participating in conferences; consulting with officers, management, and committees; developing and guiding the acceptance of the safety program	5 to 20
3. Selecting, training, coaching, and appraising the safety staff	5 to 15
4. Reviewing safety orders, regulations, rules, etc., of regulatory agencies	0 to 5
5. Committee work for trade associations or professional societies—such as National Private Truck Council, National Safety Council, American Society of Safety Engineers, National Fire Protection Association, American Trucking Associations, and National Committee for Motor Fleet Supervisor Training	0 to 5
Field Activities (5% to 60% of time)	
1. Working with company field management on explanation, promotion, and stimulation of safety program, and on inspecting equipment and operating habits	5 to 40
2. Working with official agencies regarding safety orders, rules, regulations, etc.	0 to 10
3. Working with trade associations or professional societies	0 to 10

- establishing a policy for supervisors to counsel employees who violate safe practices or to discipline those who are repeatedly involved in accidental occurrences.

Management Committees

A good way to achieve the goals of the safety program is by establishing an organizational safety committee, discussed in Chapter 7, Employee Safety Program. The committee should include officers (president and vice president) of the company as well as employee representatives (supervisor, drivers, etc.). The committee should review the performance of the company and determine policies, procedures, and features of the safety program. The safety director should counsel and advise this committee.

Such a committee can establish, with authority, the methods of the safety program. The committee will assure that the program is practical, and that it will be fully supported as it is carried out down the line as official company policy.

Always remember that it is management's responsibility to support the safety program and to make policy decisions whether they operate through a management safety committee or not. Firms that operate without such a safety committee forego many benefits.

MAKE THE POLICY KNOWN

One of the first things management should do is to make known and support the company policy on accident prevention.

Safety Policy Statement

Although small (one-location) organizations may be able to function without a formal safety policy statement, larger organizations (especially those operating from scattered locations) are at a disadvantage unless they publish their safety policies.

Basic to such a policy declaration are these statements: (a) that the company intends to comply with all safety laws and ordinances; (b) that the safety of its employees, the public, and its operations is paramount; (c) that safety will take precedence over expediency or short cuts in the operation of the company; and (d) that every attempt will be made to reduce the possibility of accident occurrence.

The policy declaration should be signed by the president. The policy should be given wide publicity throughout the company and should set the pace of operations for both field management and employees.

A safety policy makes it easier to enforce safe practices and conditions, for supervisors to comply with company policy, and for employees to follow safety instruction. Finally, it makes it easier to obtain good preventative maintenance of equipment or to select proper equipment when purchased.

Statement of Specific Rules

The policy statement is by necessity general and more a statement of operating philosophy. The next level of documentation is the statement of the specific rules that employees are expected to follow. If a company does not tell employees specifically what to do in certain circumstances, the employees will understandably make up their own rules. For some types of behavior, that is acceptable. In the area of safety it is not.

If the carrier does not want drivers to use radar detectors, there should be a specific and simply stated rule to that point. If violating that rule warrants termination on the first offense, the rule should be listed with other rules bearing the same level of discipline. The culture of the company; past experiences; labor agreements, if any; and level of management support will need to be considered as the rules are developed by management. Once they are established, communicated to workers, and any publicized grace periods have passed, the rules should be enforced consistently.

Some things might be considered too obvious to need specific mention, but unless a rule is stated, penalties will be difficult to enforce. An example is a statement that all employees are expected to follow the traffic laws when using company cars. Yet observation shows that most drivers do not follow that simple concept. The firm should formally state that the motor vehicle records (MVRs) of all drivers of company vehicles will be checked routinely. The expected level of performance should be part of the rule. With recent court decisions on negligent hiring and negligent entrustment, the fleet manager cannot allow drivers to violate the law and company policy.

Some specifically prohibited driver practices for CDL holders include:

- carrying unauthorized passengers (392.60)
- letting an unauthorized person drive the vehicle (392.61)
- bus driver talking to passengers (392.62)
- pushing or towing a bus with people on board (392.63)
- riding in the back of a closed truck without a ready means of exit (392.64)
- transfer to or from the sleeper without direct access to the cab (392.65)
- driving a vehicle with carbon monoxide in the cab (392.66)
- driving with an open-flame cargo heater on (392.67)

- coasting (392.68)
- driving with two or more people in the sleeper (392.69)
- driving with a radar detector (392.71)

This list would be a good place to start in developing a specific set of company rules. Stating that these practices are prohibited will help convince drivers that the company will not ignore unsafe driving. Enforcing the prohibitions consistently will help sustain future disciplinary action and reinforce the image of responsible corporate behavior in case of civil action.

Company Publications

As a company starts operating in more and more locations, the need for printed procedures, rules, and manuals grows. Field management will be helped by up-to-date publications that outline company policies and practices covering employee selection, training, and supervision. Managers and supervisors need to know methods of investigating and reporting accidents/incidents and detailed outlines covering such important subjects as counseling, retraining, and discipline.

All the codes, standards, and instructions issued by the main office are ultimately designed to help the company make a profit by ensuring safe, cost-effective operation. As a result, manuals must clearly show overall policy and standard methods of procedure, but they should not be so needlessly detailed as to discourage employees from reading them.

MAKE THE POLICY CLEAR

The benefits of a clearly articulated policy will be reflected in improved performance as new employees are more carefully selected, effectively trained, adequately appraised as to their job performance, and well supervised. Accidents that do occur will be more thoroughly investigated to get the facts, so all can learn how to prevent future accidents. The safety director should check to see that procedures are complied with, but it is up to management to enforce them.

Safety Audit

One of the tasks of a safety director at both headquarters and any other company location is to sample or audit local programs, practices, and procedures. The purpose of such an audit is to (a) check understanding of and compliance with the company's established, published policies and practices and (b) make sure safety inspections are adequate. By checking actual field practices, the safety director will be able to help field management do a better job. Often, uncovering weak points can help supervisors improve their understanding of company policies and practices. The safety director should develop a checklist for evaluating the safety program and for checking conditions or practices during field visits.

Compliance Audit

The *Federal Motor Carrier Safety Regulations* state clearly that no carrier can require or permit a driver to violate the out-of-service provisions. This puts the burden on the carrier to know what its drivers are doing. The carrier must also know what the dispatcher is telling the driver to do. With the number of sources of information available today, if a carrier does not supervise its drivers and take responsibility for their actions, someone else will do it. The "someone else" will be a federal Office of Motor Carriers compliance officer, state enforcement official, or plaintiff's attorney investigating a client's claim against the carrier.

Obviously, it is in the carrier's best interests to make sure the rules are being followed. The American Trucking Associations offers the *Hours of Service and Driver's Logs Manual* for training drivers and the employees who will audit their logs.

The log is just one of the many items a comprehensive audit must consider. For drivers required to keep a log, the rules are simple. A driver cannot be allowed to drive:

- more than 10 hours following eight consecutive hours off duty,
- after being on duty 15 hours, or
- after being on duty more than 60 hours in any 7 consecutive days.

In addition, a motor carrier operating vehicles every day of the week cannot allow any driver to drive after more than 70 hours on duty in any eight consecutive days.

The rules are very simple. But whole books are written on how to keep records in compliance with the law.

The various pieces of the audit puzzle work together to ensure compliance. Selection of the appropriate auditor is the first and possibly the most important step in implementing an audit program. The auditor should be respected for fairness, honesty, and objectivity throughout the organization to be audited. The auditor should not have an adversarial attitude toward the company.

Effective auditors view the deficiencies found as opportunities for system improvements, not a new notch in their belt. They are persistent and firm but not offensive. They never get into a contest of wills with either drivers or management about anything regarding their audit. Instead, they leave and return when local management can deal with its shortcomings more objectively. Effective auditing is not an easy task.

Before the audit begins, the auditor must make sure the policies of the unit being audited are in compliance. If the policies are out of date or not compatible with legal or corporate requirements, proceeding with the audit will not make much sense. Once the review is complete, the auditor should meet with the highest-level manager at the site to be audited. The auditor should explain what is going to be done, along with a proposed time for the wrap-up meeting at the end of the audit.

The audit begins with a fleet manager submitting the list of drivers. If previous audits revealed problems with some of the drivers on the list, they should be included in the audit to check for effective corrective action. Two other groups of drivers should be selected: several recent employees and several with about two years experience on the job. The new drivers' qualification files should be checked for accuracy. The longer-term drivers' files should document periodic events such as medical examinations, MVR checks, license renewal, and management review of the files.

Even if the hours-of-service log appears to be in compliance, further checking is appropriate. The auditor can cross-check the log by using a variety of other documents. The hours driven should match the mileage between locations claimed. The driver's receipts from toll roads, fuel purchases, repairs, and overnight accommodations should support the log claims, which should also be checked against the dispatcher's records. Trip recorders, if used, also provide irrefutable evidence for claims.

Computer programs can check the compliance of handwritten logs. The data are keyed into a personal computer, and the software does the calculations.

The auditor should also verify the accuracy of maintenance records. A driver's inspection report should exist for each day of use. If a problem was found, the mechanic and the next driver should both have signed off their acceptance. If the mechanic takes equipment out of service, neither the dispatcher's records nor any other documents should show that equipment in use during that period.

When the audit is complete, the auditor should share the findings with the top staff personnel. The report should be fair and, above all, accurate. If an error is pointed out, the auditor must acknowledge it and immediately modify the audit notes. The auditor should send a formal report to the unit staff as soon as possible, making it clear that a written plan for corrective action is expected in response. The next audit should begin with a review of previous audit discrepancies to check for effective corrective action.

If a fleet is not conducting audits of this type, costs can soar. DOT compliance personnel are certainly checking, and plaintiffs' attorneys will check if the opportunity arises. If a fleet has records of audits and of effective corrective action, both the compliance audits and the court

proceedings will hold fewer surprises and be less costly. Compliance must be measured to be controlled.

If a fleet is not under DOT regulation, the audit will be different. The items checked will be determined by company policy and possibly insurer mandate or recommendation. In either case, the audit will reveal what is happening with the fleet.

Whether the focus is DOT, OSHA, company safety policy, or another purpose, the safety audit approach is identical except for the agenda items to be checked.

DOCUMENT PROGRAM EFFECTIVENESS

For a program to be effective, it must be documented through good record-keeping, reported accurately and uniformly, and followed up regularly by visits to scattered fleet units.

Home Office Records

The home office should keep the official company accident statistical counterpart records. However, the various locations of the company should also keep local counterpart records of accidental occurrences. This policy is often required by law or regulations such as the *Federal Motor Carrier Safety Regulations* or OSHA and workers' compensation laws. Even when central records are not required, they are desirable to:

- check company accident trends,
- determine which departments or areas need attention,
- discover what basic types and causes of accidents are most prevalent,
- identify employees who have earned safe driver awards,
- learn what safety program features are needed, and
- calculate how much accidents cost the company.

Local statistics will indicate the local accident story, but the whole picture will be available only through central reports.

Home office records are necessary because employees transfer from one location to another or from one department to another. Without central records, it would be extremely difficult for management to keep track of changes and to record entries.

Statistical Reports

Home office central accident records can be used to compile monthly, quarterly, and annual reports. Issuing such reports keeps the various branch managers informed of their relative safety performance. Such comparison helps improve local accident control by encouraging interest in accident prevention and building a spirit of friendly competition among the various units of the company.

Special reports, summaries, and analyses of accident experience by type, basic cause, and other factors should be prepared for management. These are discussed in detail in Chapters 4, Motor Fleet Accident Data, and 6, Employee Injury Record Keeping and Analysis.

In general, periodic reports should cover:

- injuries to employees at work
- injuries to employees off the job
- injuries to the public (the people who come onto company property or are involved in accidents that involve a company vehicle)
- product liability situations
- motor vehicle accidents
- fires
- loss and damage to cargo or persons
- theft
- vandalism
- other details

The report should include the cost of these factors during the reporting interval. As mentioned in Chapters 4 and 6, statistics on motor vehicle accidents should be based on ANSI standard D15.1, *The Method of Recording and Measuring Motor Vehicle Fleet Accident Experience and Passenger Accident Experience,* which is now out-of-date but still used as a reference.

The reports covering motor vehicle accidents should be broken down by operation units and should include at least the following:

- number of fleet accidents
- mileage operated by vehicles (breakdown by types if more than one)
- frequency rates for each category
- number and percent of fleet accidents judged preventable

Statistics on employee injuries should be compiled in accordance with OSHA reporting criteria. Management should make special studies of motor vehicle accidents to guide the direction of the accident prevention program. Items that they should carefully analyze include:

- types of accidents
- basic causes
- geographic locations (spot maps are useful)
- types of vehicles involved (owned by or operated for the company)
- drivers involved
- hour of day and day of week of occurrences

- other factors deemed significant by repeated occurrence

The category "drivers involved" should reveal employees who are accident repeaters. Supervisors should catalog any significant factors about drivers who have accidents the most often.

Uniformity of Reporting

Accident reporting must be uniform for a scattered fleet's safety program to be effective. Establishing uniformity may be a time-consuming and difficult undertaking, but it is essential. Any difficulty will probably be due to the program's not being fully understood or accepted by various company units.

Field management may have a tendency to cover up or minimize accidents or poor safety performance in order to look good or to avoid embarrassment. Sometimes a branch manager will try to protect an employee rather than to report all accident facts and conditions accurately.

Whatever the reason, lack of uniformity in reporting accidents hampers the accident prevention program and erodes morale and effective supervision.

Fortunately, guidelines exist that can help a safety director impose uniformity. The National Safety Council, through its Safe Driver Award rules, has established a workable method to determine the preventability of accidents. When all units in a company understand and practice these guidelines, uniform reporting of accident statistics will result.

The Council provides an accident review committee service to decide questionable or borderline cases. Individual cases can be submitted to the Council for a decision.

Most companies have written procedures governing how and by whom accidents will be classified as to reportability and preventability. These procedures vary from company to company, but most require that the first decision be made at the local office. When necessary, a local committee—usually composed of the employee's supervisor, the supervisor of the garage or maintenance unit, and two coworkers—can review borderline cases or protested decisions. The local decision is then submitted to the home office for a final review. Any decision based on inadequate or biased information should be returned to the local manager for correction if it contradicts company policy. (See Chapter 11, Accident Review Committees, for details.)

Headquarters Follow-up

Periodically, headquarters safety staff should personally check the terminals or branch locations of scattered fleet units. Evidence of poor accident reporting and investigation is a strong clue that an audit is needed.

Poor safety performance often goes hand in hand with poor local management. When headquarters staff uncover poor management in a unit, they usually try to discover what caused the local breakdown. The safety director can participate in these audits as well to evaluate the safety performance of such units.

Accidents are among the early warning signs that indicate local management may be ineffective. Other evidence includes unusual coverage or shortages, unusually high damage claims, expensive road failures, increased theft, and declining morale.

CHARACTERISTICS
OF THE SCATTERED FLEET

Although running the units of a scattered fleet resembles in many respects operating a small fleet, each local unit benefits from (a) the specialized headquarters staff and (b) well-established company guidelines. Thus, the accident record of local units should be better than the average of several small fleets.

Headquarters safety staff can best aid the units of their scattered fleets by (a) preplanning schedules for training consultation, driver meetings, and introduction of new systems and equipment; (b) systematizing procedures; (c) preparing standard forms; and (d) establishing interfleet contests using comparative records.

When headquarters staff visit the units, they should use their time wisely. They should plan well in advance. They can have forms and instructions sent ahead to allow local supervisors to prepare and to review any instructions and new information. This is the time to conduct supervisory safety-training sessions.

A smoothly functioning line of communication between headquarters and the local units helps to create and maintain a strong safety effort. A definite program of visits and follow-ups should be developed; deviations from this schedule can undermine an otherwise well-planned accident control program.

Calling on local units requires the highest degree of diplomacy and tact from headquarters staff, especially safety personnel. Safety managers or directors must remember that they are there to advise management. Theirs is a staff function; they must not assume any line of authority. The safety director should report defects and unsafe practices to line management, which is responsible for correcting them. At the same time, the safety director must make it clear that company standards will be upheld and that the organization will not accept substandard safety performance from any unit.

Job
Safety
Analysis

anagement must institute an ongoing program of safety activities to uncover hazards that may have been overlooked in the layout of a terminal or maintenance facility or in the design of machinery, equipment, and processes. Some hazards may have developed after operations were begun. One of the most important of these ongoing activities is to conduct job safety analyses (JSA).

CONDUCTING A JOB SAFETY ANALYSIS

Companies can conduct job safety analyses at any point in their operations. Jobs analyzed may be new tasks or tasks that have been performed for many years. The JSA provides a way to conduct a systematic, logical analysis of all work steps and of all hazards that could cause injury or death to workers.

Definition

Companies use a job safety analysis to:

- identify hazards or potential accidents associated with each step of the job

- develop a solution for each hazard that will either eliminate or control the exposure

Once a company knows the hazards of a job, it can develop the proper solutions. Some solutions may be physical changes that control the hazard, such as placing a guard over exposed moving machine parts. Others may be job procedures that eliminate or minimize the hazard, for example, instituting safe methods of loading cargo in and out of cars, vans, trucks, buses, or other vehicles.

Steps in Job Safety Analysis

Although some job steps may have no hazards associated with them, other steps may have one or more hazards each. Some hazards are work or environmental conditions; some are actions by workers and managers. All are potential causes of accidents.

A job safety analysis can be written in the manner shown in Figure 14–1. In the left-hand column, the basic steps of the job are listed in the order in which they occur. The middle column describes the hazards or potential accidents associated with each job step. The right-hand column lists the safe procedures that should be followed to safeguard against identified hazards and to prevent potential accidents. For convenience, both the job safety analysis and the written description are referred to as a JSA. An outline for making a job safety analysis follows:

I. Prioritize and select the job to be analyzed based on its relative risk according to the following factors:
   A. Frequency of accidents
   B. Number of disabling injuries
   C. Severity potential
   D. Newly established jobs
   E. Existing jobs with procedure modifications
II. Selection and preparation of the person who will demonstrate the procedure
   A. Select a cooperative, competent person
   B. Explain the purpose of the demonstration
III. List the steps in the procedure in the first column of the JSA form, using active verbs
IV. Check the accuracy of the steps with the person who performs the job
V. Identify the hazards and list them in the second column of the JSA form
   A. Observe the job demonstration for potential accident causes (strain, sprain, slip, fall, etc.)
   B. Observe the demonstration for environmental hazards (vapors, gases, heat, noise, etc.)
VI. Develop solutions by discussing controls and changes with operators
   A. Job change
   B. Step change
   C. Environmental change
   D. Repair or service change
   E. Check modifications

Prioritize and select the job. A job is a sequence of separate steps or activities that together accomplish a work goal. However, jobs that are too broadly defined in terms of what work is accomplished (transporting material, building a plant, mining iron ore) are not suitable for a JSA. Suitable jobs for analysis include assignments that a line supervisor may make, such as operating a vehicle, washing a vehicle, or piling boxes at a terminal. These tasks are neither too broad nor too narrow.

Even though jobs may fit the description just given, they should not be selected at random for analysis. Management should choose first the most hazardous ones and those with the worst accident experience. This approach will yield the quickest possible return from a JSA program.

When selecting jobs to be analyzed and establishing the order of analysis, supervisors of a division should be guided by the following factors:

- Frequency of accidents. A job that has repeatedly produced accidents is a prime candidate for a JSA. The more accidents associated with a job, the higher its priority for a JSA.

- Number of disabling injuries. Every job that has disabling injuries associated with it should be given a JSA. The injuries indicate that past preventive actions were not successful.

National Safety Council	JOB TITLE (and number if applicable):		DATE: 6/21/9-	☒ NEW ☐ REVISED
JOB SAFETY ANALYSIS *INSTRUCTIONS ON REVERSE SIDE*	Jumping a Battery PAGE _1_ OF _2_ JSA NO.			
	TITLE OF PERSON WHO DOES JOB: Mechanic	SUPERVISOR: Joe Singer	ANALYSIS BY: Pete Moore	
COMPANY/ORGANIZATION: Acme Trucking Co.	PLANT/LOCATION: Garage	DEPARTMENT: Maintenance	REVIEWED BY: Don Hub	
REQUIRED AND/OR RECOMMENDED PERSONAL PROTECTIVE EQUIPMENT: Protective eyewear, gloves			APPROVED BY: Pat Zale	

SEQUENCE OF BASIC JOB STEPS	POTENTIAL HAZARDS	RECOMMENDED ACTION OR PROCEDURE
1. Place the two vehicles in position so that the cables reach from battery to battery.	1. a) Grounding, if two vehicles make contact. b) Vehicles may roll.	1. a) Park vehicles so that they will not make contact. b) Turn off ignition; shift both vehicles into neutral or park; set parking brake.
2. Make certain both batteries are of the same voltage, and both vehicles are similarly grounded.	2. Battery may be permanently damaged or may explode.	2. Check battery for indication of voltage. Conventional batteries (non-maintenance free) have one filler vent cap for each two-volt cell. Check whether the negative or positive terminals are grounded to the vehicle body. If both vehicles are positive ground, follow the standard procedure except using reverse polarity.
3. Check to see that the dead battery has adequate electrolyte (water and acid mixture) and is not frozen.	3. Battery may be permanently damaged or may explode.	3. If battery has vent caps, remove them to check for frozen electrolyte; add water if low. Maintenance-free batteries can be tilted or carefully shaken to see if the electrolyte is frozen, making certain not to ground out the nongrounded terminal.
4. Put a cloth over each battery. Uncap a vented battery.	4. Escaping gases from a charging battery are explosive.	4. Cover each battery with a cloth. Keep open flames, cigarettes, and sparks away from the batteries.
5. Identify the positive battery terminals.	5. Connecting the batteries in a crossed polarity can permanently damage or explode the batteries.	5. The positive terminal on a battery can be identified by the color code red, or +, P, or POS on the battery case, post, or clamp.

Figure 14–1a. This Job Safety Analysis shows the safe way to jump a battery.

- Severity potential. Some jobs may have no history of accidents but may have the potential to inflict severe injury.
- New jobs or tasks. New jobs created by changes in equipment or in processes obviously have no history of accidents, but their accident potential may not be fully appreciated. A JSA of every new job should be made as soon as the job has been created. Analysis should not be delayed until accidents or near misses occur.
- Modified existing jobs. Existing jobs whose procedures have been modified can present special safety problems. These changes could create hazards where none existed before. A JSA should be made to determine any new accident potential.

Select and prepare the demonstrator. The worker selected should be experienced, skilled, cooperative, and willing to share ideas. Such a person will be easy to work with on an analysis.

If the employee selected has never participated in a JSA, the supervisor should thoroughly explain the purpose of the analysis and provide a copy of a completed JSA. Demonstrators must be reassured that their safety performance is not being evaluated. They should understand (a) that the purpose is to study the job, not the person doing it, and (b) that they were selected to be demonstrators because of their experience and skills.

List the job steps on the JSA form. Before the supervisor begins searching for hazards, he or she should break down the job into its basic steps. The steps should describe what is being done at each stage in the job and should be listed in proper sequence. Details should be omitted for the purpose of this analysis.

Supervisors generally commit two common errors in breaking a job down. One error is to make the breakdown too detailed. The result is a long list of job steps, many of them unnecessary or repetitive. The other error is to make the job breakdown too general, which means important basic steps are not recorded.

As the supervisor watches the work being performed, he or she should ask, "What is the first basic step of the

	JOB TITLE (and number if applicable): Jumping a Battery PAGE _2_ OF _2_ JSA NO.		DATE: 6/21/9-	☒ NEW ☐ REVISED

National Safety Council

JOB SAFETY ANALYSIS
INSTRUCTIONS ON REVERSE SIDE

TITLE OF PERSON WHO DOES JOB: Mechanic	SUPERVISOR: Joe Singer	ANALYSIS BY: Pete Moore

COMPANY/ORGANIZATION: Acme Trucking Co.	PLANT/LOCATION: Garage	DEPARTMENT: Maintenance	REVIEWED BY: Don Hub

REQUIRED AND/OR RECOMMENDED PERSONAL PROTECTIVE EQUIPMENT: Protective eyewear, gloves	APPROVED BY: Pat Zale

SEQUENCE OF BASIC JOB STEPS	POTENTIAL HAZARDS	RECOMMENDED ACTION OR PROCEDURE
6. Attach one battery jumper cable between the two positive terminals.	6. One vehicle may be positively grounded instead of negatively grounded.	6. A positive ground system can be identified by the cable leading from the positive terminal of the battery to the vehicle body. In positive-grounded, connect the negative terminals of the batteries instead of the positive terminals.
7. Attach one end of the other battery jumper cable to the negative terminal of the booster battery and the other end of the cable to the engine block of the vehicle to be started.	7. a) Final connection may cause potentially dangerous sparks. b) One vehicle may be positively grounded.	7. a) The final connection to the engine block should be at least a foot from the battery and to a clean, unpainted metallic surface. If final connection draws large sparks, you may have polarity wrong. Go back to Step 5.
8. Try to start the vehicle needing the jump.	8. a) Batteries may explode. b) Booster battery may begin to run down.	8. a) Stand clear of batteries while attempting to start vehicle. b) Start the booster battery vehicle to maintain a battery charge.
9. After the vehicle with the discharge battery has started, remove battery jumper cables.	9. a) Sparks may be produced in breaking the jumper circuit. b) Injuries from the vehicle's fan belt may occur.	9. a) Disconnect the last cable connection made to the engine block first, then the other end of this cable; next, remove the other cable connection to the battery that was jumped. b) Keep cables and tools from making contact with or falling into moving parts.

Figure 14–1b.   This Job Safety Analysis shows the safe way to jump a battery.

job; what starts the job? What is the next basic step?" and so on. Key points in breaking a job down into successive basic steps are:

1. Select the right person to demonstrate the job.
2. Explain the purpose of the analysis.
3. Observe the job steps.
4. Record each step in the breakdown.
5. Check the breakdown with the person who is observed.

The supervisor should number the job steps consecutively in the first column of the JSA work sheet. Each step should describe what is done, not how it is to be done. The wording for each step should begin with a verb or an "action" word, like "remove," "open," "weld," "lift." The description of each job step is completed by naming the item to which the action applies, for example, "remove extinguisher," "open valve," "weld seam," "lift box out of trunk."

Check the steps for accuracy. After the supervisor has completed the list of steps, the JSA should be reviewed by the demonstrator. The supervisor should get agreement on what is done (not how it is done) and on the order in which the steps are taken. When the listing has been completed, the supervisor should thank the demonstrator for his or her cooperation.

Identify the hazards and list on the JSA form. Each step is then analyzed for hazards and potential accidents. The purpose is to identify *all* hazards in order to make each step, and eventually the entire job, safe and more efficient.

The supervisor should look for specific types of potential accidents. For each basic step in the job breakdown, ask the following questions:

• Can employees strike against, be struck by, or otherwise be injured by making contact with an object?
• Can they be caught in, on, or between objects?

- Can they slip or trip? Can they fall on the same level or from one level to another?

- Can they strain themselves by pushing, pulling, or lifting?

- Does the environment present a hazardous exposure (toxic gases, vapors, mists, fumes, dusts, heat, radiation, and so on)?

Observation plus knowledge of the job should give supervisors the answers to these questions. A job should be observed as often as necessary until all hazards and potential accidents have been identified.

While observing each step, the supervisor should record the hazards that might result in accidents. Only two items of information are required: the type of accident and the agent involved. For example, to record that an employee might be injured on the legs or feet by dropping a fire extinguisher, the supervisor should simply write "might be struck by extinguisher."

Each hazard or potential accident should be recorded on a separate line in the center column on the JSA work sheet. A hazard or potential accident pertaining to a particular job step should be kept parallel with that step. If a job step entails several hazards or potential accidents, they should be identified by the letters "(a)," "(b)," "(c)," and so on.

After the hazards and the potential accidents have been recorded, the supervisor should have the demonstrator check the list. The employee's experience with the job may suggest ideas that did not occur to the supervisor.

The supervisor should also check with others who have had experience with the job. By alternately observing the job and discussing its dangers with experienced people, the supervisor will soon develop a reliable list of hazards and potential accidents.

Develop solutions. The final step in the job safety analysis is to develop controls and changes to eliminate the hazards or to prevent the potential accidents. Discuss solutions with the operators. The principal solutions are as follows:

1. Find an entirely different way to do the job.

2. Change the conditions that create the hazards. If possible, engineer out or design out the hazard.

3. Revise the job procedure if changing the conditions does not eliminate all the hazards.

4. Reduce the frequency of the job by correcting the conditions that make it necessary.

Occasionally, it is possible to find or devise an entirely different way to do the job that will eliminate the hazards. Management should determine the ways in which the work goal of a job can be accomplished, and then analyze the procedures to see if any one method is entirely safe. When

such a study is being made, work-saving tools and equipment should be considered.

If a different and safe way to do the job cannot be found, then management should ask the following question regarding each hazard and each potential accident: "What change in physical conditions, such as a change in tools, materials, equipment, or location, will eliminate the hazard or prevent the accident?"

When a physical change to make the job safe is in order, supervisors should study it carefully to determine what other benefits, such as increased production or savings in time or labor, will also result from the change. These other benefits should be pointed out when the proposed change is presented to higher management—they will make good selling points.

In some cases, the hazards cannot be eliminated either by finding another work method or by changing the physical conditions. The next solution is to investigate changing job procedures.

For each hazard and each potential accident recorded on the JSA work sheet, supervisors should ask this question: "What should the employee do—or not do—to eliminate this particular hazard or prevent this particular potential accident?" Where appropriate, supervisors should also ask: "How should this action be done?" In most cases, supervisors will be able to answer these questions from their own experience.

However, the answers must be specific and concrete if a new recommended safe procedure is to be worthwhile. Such general instructions as "Be alert," "Use caution," or "Be careful" are useless. Answers should state precisely what workers are to do and how they should do it.

"Make certain the wrench does not slip and cause loss of balance." is a poor recommendation for a safety procedure. This statement does not tell workers how to prevent the wrench from slipping. In contrast, a good safety recommendation provides specific, detailed instructions: "Set the wrench securely. Test the grip of the wrench by exerting a slight pressure. Brace yourself against something immovable, or take a solid stance with feet wide apart before exerting full pressure, to prevent loss of balance if the wrench slips."

Often a repair or service job has to be done at frequent intervals. For such repetitive jobs, this question should be asked: "What can be done to eliminate the cause of the condition that makes excessive repairs or service necessary?" If the cause cannot be eliminated, then the question "Can anything be done to minimize the effects of the condition?" should be asked.

For example, machine parts on some equipment may wear out rapidly and require frequent replacement. A study of the problem may reveal that if excessive vibration is eliminated or reduced substantially, machine parts will last longer and need to be replaced less often. This action reduces the number of times the machine needs to be repaired or serviced, thus controlling the hazard.

However, reducing the frequency of a job contributes to safety only because it limits a worker's exposure to potential injury. Supervisors should still make every effort to eliminate hazards and prevent potential accidents through changing physical conditions, revising job procedures, or both.

The supervisor should check or test proposed changes by observing the job under the new conditions and by discussing the changes with employees who perform the work. Their ideas about the hazards and proposed solutions can be invaluable. Workers can judge the practicality of proposed changes and perhaps suggest improvements.

Such discussions, however, are more than simply a way to check the accuracy and value of a JSA. They also serve to promote awareness of job hazards and safe procedures among employees.

BENEFITS AND USES OF JOB SAFETY ANALYSIS

The major benefits of a job safety analysis generally come after it has been completed. Nonetheless, there are real benefits to be gained from doing the analysis itself.

While conducting a JSA, supervisors learn more about the jobs they supervise. When employees are encouraged to participate in JSAs, their safety attitudes improve and their knowledge of job safety increases. As a JSA is developed, safer and better job procedures and safer working conditions are developed.

But these benefits represent only a portion of those gained from the JSA program. The principal benefits come when the supervisor uses the JSA in the following work areas:

- providing individual training to employees
- making employee safety contacts
- instructing the new person on the job
- preparing for planned safety observations
- giving prejob instructions on irregular job tasks
- reviewing job procedures after accidents or near-accidents
- studying jobs for possible improvement in procedures

When a JSA is distributed, the supervisor's first responsibility is to explain its contents to employees and, if necessary, to give them further individual training in safe work practices. The entire JSA must be reviewed with people who perform the job so they will know how to work without accidents.

The JSA also can furnish valuable material for planned safety contacts. All basic job steps included in the JSA should be used for this purpose. Those steps that present major hazards should be emphasized and reviewed again and again in safety contacts.

New workers on the job must be trained to recognize the hazards associated with each job step and to take the necessary precautions. There is no better guide for this training than a well-prepared JSA.

Occasionally, the supervisor should observe people as they perform jobs for which JSAs have been developed. The purpose of these observations is to determine whether the workers are doing the jobs in accordance with the safe job procedures. The supervisor should prepare for this task by reviewing the JSA in question to keep the new procedures firmly in mind.

Many jobs, such as certain repair or service jobs, are done infrequently or on an irregular basis. The people who do this work will benefit from prejob instruction so they can avoid important hazards and take the necessary precautions. Using the appropriate JSA, the supervisor should give this instruction when assigning workers a particular maintenance or repair job.

Whenever an accident or near-accident occurs on a job covered by a job safety analysis, the supervisor should review the JSA to determine whether it needs to be revised. If the JSA is updated, the supervisor should explain the changes to all employees concerned with the job and instruct them in any new procedures.

If employees fail to follow the JSA procedures and an accident or near-accident results, the supervisor should discuss the JSA with all the employees who do the job. The supervisor should make it clear that the incident would not have occurred had the JSA procedures been followed.

All supervisors are concerned with improving job methods to increase safety, reduce costs, and increase production. The job safety analysis is an excellent starting point for questioning the established way of doing a job. Study of a JSA may well suggest further improvements of job methods or lead to other safety measures. Steps for preparing a job safety analysis are available in audiovisual programs and manuals from the National Safety Council.

CHAPTER

15

Off-the-Job Safety Programs

A fleet safety program director's knowledge, experience, and credibility can be a positive influence in the private lives of others. Although the number and type of work-related accidents are serious, off-the-job (OTJ) accidents, injuries, and deaths are an even greater problem.

- Statistics show that employees are safer on the job than they are on the highway, on the street, or in the home.
- According to the records of a large manufacturing corporation, its employees had 18 times as many OTJ injuries as on-the-job injuries. Fatalities were 35 times more likely to occur off the job.
- On the average, employees suffer about 91 OTJ accidental deaths and approximately 14,200 OTJ disabling injuries every day in the United States.

BENEFITS OF AN OTJ SAFETY PROGRAM

A community safety program to reduce OTJ traffic accidents benefits everyone: the community, the company, and the safety director.

Community Benefits

In the mid-1990s, it was estimated that motor vehicle accidents killed over 40,000 per year—more people than all other accident causes combined. With figures this high, nearly everyone's life has been touched by a traffic accident that disabled or killed a family member or friend. Any community's residents would welcome leadership in instituting a safety program to reduce OTJ accidents.

Company Benefits

A key reason for a company to become involved in OTJ safety is to conserve employee power. Although companies now have a legal responsibility to prevent injuries on the job, they have a moral responsibility to try to prevent injuries away from the job. All injuries are a waste of a valuable resource: people. Injuries and fatalities happen to people who call on customers, make a product, service equipment, keep the books, and do every other job involved in running a business.

Employers bear a large part of OTJ accident costs. Some cost is paid directly in the form of wages to absent workers and hiring and training of replacement workers. Some of the cost is hidden. For example, if skilled drivers, technicians, or salespersons are injured and not replaced immediately, their absence may result in late deliveries, lost production, lost sales, and lost customers.

OTJ injury, illness, and death are as emotionally and financially costly to employees and their families as injury, illness, and death from on-the-job accidents. Moreover, the impact of OTJ incidents on employers' profits can be considerable. To offset even a $150 accident involving only minor emergency medical treatment, an organization must produce at least that much in profits. If a company makes a 10-cent profit on every dollar, it has to sell $1,500 worth of goods or services just to cover that accident expense.

In 1993, OTJ accidents cost the nation at least $124.5 billion. Approximately one-third of this cost is paid by employers. This figure includes all or part of the premiums for hospitalization, medical, accidental death, and wage continuation insurance.

Some of the costs are hidden even deeper. As accidents in a community increase, so do insurance costs, taxes, and welfare contributions. Probably no company is fully aware of all the expenses that result from OTJ accidents and their impact on operations and profits. Enough experience has been accumulated, however, to develop a simplified plan for estimating such costs (discussed later in this chapter).

These facts indicate the seriousness of OTJ accidents and the need to do more to reduce them. An OTJ safety program is one effective solution. It can reduce OTJ accidents in much the same way traditional safety programs reduce occupational accidents.

If your company is too small, or otherwise unable to promote an OTJ safety program, a community safety program may be the solution. Individuals or groups interested in starting a project should contact the Council for community safety resource materials and kits.

Safety Director Benefits

Involvement in an OTJ safety program increases the safety director's visibility both within the company and within the community. By contributing valuable knowledge and time to the welfare of others, the safety director can also advance his or her own professional development and career track.

Safety directors can enhance their public image as a safety expert in the following ways.

Recognize the director's influence over others. Other people respect the safety director and are influenced by what the person says and does. Because of the director's position, he or she can actually improve the way people behave behind the wheel.

Consciously exercise the role. The director should present the image of a person who is more than casually interested in better driving—who is, in fact, vitally concerned about promoting better driving both on and off the job.

Speak about traffic safety. The director should accept opportunities to speak at community, company, or industry functions. Public speaking skills can be improved by taking a class at a local college or joining a speaking club. For further information, write Toastmaster International, 23182 Arroyovista, Rancho Santa Margarita, CA 92688.

Traffic safety can be a frequent subject of private conversations. Speak up to express positive attitudes and to correct misconceptions about traffic rules and driving techniques. Show that you regard traffic safety as a serious matter that deserves the informed support and cooperation of every individual.

The safety director's objective in speaking about traffic safety, both publicly and privately, is to encourage but not push people's attitudes in the right direction.

Know the safety field. To be a positive influence, the safety director must know the facts. One of the easiest ways to increase one's knowledge of the field is through reading. In addition to the books listed in the bibliography, a basic fact source is the driver's handbook issued by the state driver licensing bureau.

Be a good driver. The example the safety director sets as a driver says more about his or her attitude toward traffic safety than anything else. The director should practice good driving principles, learning each basic driving maneuver and performing it correctly every time.

Support other traffic safety efforts. If high school or adult education courses or driver improvement training are available in the safety director's area, helping with such courses will repay the individual's time and effort with effective influence on other drivers. Helping with the National Safety Council's Defensive Driving Course can aid both the public and fleet drivers.

As the safety director becomes more familiar with traffic safety, he or she will find more and more groups and agencies devoted to making driving safer. Among these are the local safety council, the safety committees of churches and service clubs, and high school groups like Students Against Driving Drunk. Each views the problem from a different angle. They can learn a lot from the safety director and the director can learn from them.

Take part in trade association safety activities. Most associations have committees or divisions working on safety matters. The Council of Safety Supervisors of the American Trucking Associations is an excellent example, since it is national but consists of local councils within each state trucking association.

The Motor Transportation Division of the National Safety Council has four sections (commercial vehicle, fleet administrator, transit, and school bus), which meet nationally. The National Private Truck Council's safety and driver training programs offer excellent opportunities for professional growth. The National Association of Fleet Administrators (NAFA) deals with issues facing managers of fleets consisting of cars and light trucks. The National School Transportation Association promotes school bus safety.

These groups study, work, and learn to improve their abilities and to educate others in the field of fleet safety. By investing time and effort, safety directors can gain knowledge and stature in their field and can influence the laws that govern their company's operations.

Join a professional safety organization. Anyone working full-time as a safety professional should join a professional association such as the American Society of Safety Engineers (see Appendix E, Bibliography and Additional Resources, for the address). Here, safety professionals will meet leaders in the tremendously broad field of general safety. They will have an almost endless stream of resources in fellow experts at their disposal. They will also have the chance to build the field of motor fleet safety into an area of greater interest in these groups, which recognize it as a branch of safety engineering.

Seek professional certification in safety. After gaining experience in the safety profession, the next logical step for the safety director is to seek professional certification. Attaining the required experience and preparing for examinations, will help a safety director grow professionally. Certification means recognition for one's professional accomplishments. An organization that offers certification is the Board of Certified Safety Professionals (see Appendix E, Bibliography and Additional Resources).

SELLING THE PROGRAM TO MANAGEMENT

As a safety director's professional stature increases through self-education and participation in group activities, his or her suggestions will become more highly respected by company management.

The first step is to sell management on the idea that a safety program is good business. This will be somewhat harder for an OTJ program than an on-the-job program, because management may not see the connection at first between the two. To enlist management support, prepare a written proposal for a working OTJ safety program and present it, in person, to the appropriate manager. The proposal should include:

- Published data showing the high cost of OTJ accidents to companies and the benefits to the firm of reducing them. Examples can be found throughout this chapter.

- An estimate of present OTJ accident costs and projected cost savings. A simplified plan for estimating such costs is shown later in this chapter.

- A description of how the OTJ safety program will work in the safety director's fleet. The director should gear the program to the fleet's needs, and hold to a realistic budget. Explain (a) how accidents will be reported, (b) how much time and money the program will take, (c) how the program will be introduced (list specific activities and costs), and (d) how its effectiveness will be measured. Plans for setting up an actual program are described later in this chapter.

- Information on how the OTJ program's increase in safety awareness can improve on-the-job safety records.

- An explanation of how an OTJ safety program can be integrated with current on-the-job safety activities without involving heavy expenditures of money or time.

- Plans for measuring and evaluating the program's effectiveness (following the guidelines given later in this chapter).

To estimate present OTJ accident costs, the safety director must calculate direct and indirect costs of disabling and nondisabling injuries. To project savings, base the program's budget on a percentage of the company's return on investment.

Direct costs. Direct costs are wages and benefits paid to injured drivers and other employees while they are recuperating off the job. These costs include disability insurance payments, employees' medical and hospital costs, and medical and hospital costs for retirees and employees' families. Firms insured by an outside carrier should determine cost based on the premiums they paid on the portion of their health and accident policies that cover accident experience. Organizations that are self-insured should base cost estimates on the amount of claims paid for OTJ injuries plus the costs of administering their program.

Indirect costs. Indirect costs can involve considerable expense. The estimated indirect costs of disabling injuries equal the direct costs, or the value of wage losses even if wages are not paid for all lost time. Indirect nondisabling costs are about two-thirds of the indirect disabling costs. These are conservative estimates. Indirect costs can range from one to 10 times the direct costs, depending on the type of industry or organization involved. These costs may include:

- Human resources costs of hiring replacements.

- Wage costs of supervisors for time spent training replacement drivers and other employees.

- Wage costs due to lower output of replacement drivers or employees during break-in period.

- Costs of vehicles, products, materials, tools, and other items damaged by replacement workers during break-in period.

- Wage costs of time lost by other employees who needed the injured employee's input.

- Wage costs due to absence of injured employee.

- Wage costs due to decreased output of injured employee after return to work.

- Wage costs of other employees who are slowed down because the injured employee was slow or absent or needed their help.

- Damage to vehicles and spoilage of products or materials due to less efficient work because of the injury.

The following example shows how to estimate these costs. Company X carries full accident and health insurance, as well as disability insurance, on all of its 1,000 employees. (For purposes of this example, family coverage is excluded.) According to company X's insurance carrier, 20%, or $150,000, of the annual premium for both group insurance policies went to pay for employee OTJ injuries. Estimate the direct and indirect costs as follows:

Direct cost (insurance benefits paid for OTJ injuries)	$150,000
Indirect disabling injury cost (calculated in 1:1 ratio to direct cost)	150,000
Indirect nondisabling injury cost (calculated as $2/3$ of indirect disabling injury cost)	100,000
Total annual estimated direct and indirect OTJ employee injury cost	$400,000
Cost per employee (1,000 employees)	$ 400

These costs vary among companies depending on the insurance plans in force, scope of coverage, and plan provisions. For example, one company's disability insurance plan may require a waiting period before paying. Thus, the disability costs will be less than for a plan that pays disability from the first day of an absence due to an OTJ accident.

Projected savings. Set a target number and date for the reduction of OTJ accidents. This will tell management the direction and goals of the program. The reduction in accidents can be translated into a goal for dollar savings.

The program budget can be based on a percentage of the company's return on investment projected for a two-year period or less. For example, suppose an organization's OTJ injury cost is $250,000. The safety director might project that with a budget of $7,500, the company could save $37,500 (15% of the total OTJ injury cost). The estimated net return would be $30,000, or 400%

If management can expect a reasonable return on investment, they are more likely to back the program. Point out that OTJ accidents are so costly that any reduction in accident rates will bring substantial savings to the organization.

An OTJ safety program can be integrated easily with an on-the-job program. Much of it requires no increased expenditure, only broader, more inclusive thinking regarding the concept of safety and responsibility for safety. People should think safety all the time, not just at work. Thus, an OTJ program can be viewed as a natural extension of the existing safety program.

DESIGNING THE PROGRAM

Once the program has been accepted by management, the safety director will be closely involved in designing and implementing the OTJ safety program.

Scope of the Program

OTJ safety programs are similar in many respects to on-the-job safety programs. Management backing and an operating budget are just two requirements in common. The program tools used in OTJ safety are, for the most part, the same ones used in safety awareness training on the job. They include safety talks, in-house publications, films, videos, displays, posters, reference booklets, contests, defensive driving courses, and safety fairs.

Generally, the purpose of an OTJ safety program is to train individuals in safe practices and to create safety awareness. The program must depend on education and motivation to communicate its message. Once employees leave the garage, office, plant, or job site, they are away from any direct supervision.

There are three major reasons why people commit unsafe practices, whether off or on the job:

- Lack of knowledge
- Inattention or distraction
- Intentional violation of safe practices

Lack of knowledge can be overcome by providing OTJ safety education and training. The latter two problems are more difficult. An example of inattention or distraction is a person who is preoccupied and drives through a red light. An example of intentional violation of safe practices is a driver who decides not to wear a seat belt. When the problem is not a lack of knowledge, more creative countermeasures are needed, such as OTJ safety awareness and motivational activities.

Influencing Attitudes

Individuals cannot be forced to behave safely. Until a person recognizes that the safe approach is the best one, any motivational efforts will be futile. The only practical approach to OTJ safety programs is to educate, motivate, and sell, thus influencing the attitudes of employees and their families. The safety director should emphasize that almost any activity can be performed safely with the correct procedures and equipment. It sounds simple, but keep in mind the following:

- Don't preach or try to coerce. The facts should speak for themselves.
- Be positive. Avoid negative phrases like "Don't do that." Stress the benefits for the individual employee.
- Don't scold or patronize; that approach alienates others.

When employees and their families begin to be aware of unsafe conditions and activities in their daily lives, the OTJ safety program will have accomplished a major objective.

Guidelines for Success

Based on reports from companies that have conducted successful OTJ safety campaigns, the National Safety Council has identified six factors essential to an effective program:

- Participation must be vocal, visible, and continuous at all levels, from management to first-line supervisors to hourly employees. Convey management's concern for employees. Give employees a stake in the program by involving them in its development. Use employee-management safety committees to develop OTJ safety programs.
- Results are always better when the safety message gets into the home. The family can be a powerful influence in changing workers' attitudes. Consider the role many children play in making sure their parents recycle. The materials that are sent to the home should be attractive, well organized, and informative to capture readers' attention. A letter from the fleet manager or other management official always gets attention.
- The interest of cooperating drivers and others should appear as spontaneous as possible. Play down the notion of a systematic campaign, which will make the safety message seem more of a management than worker concern.
- Use management authority when appropriate, but go easy. Most of the activity should be conducted by the drivers and other employees.
- Order all safety materials well in advance and have them on hand before beginning the campaign. Make sure all participants know their parts and will carry out their duties as scheduled. Timing is important.
- Keep individual safety campaigns going at a good pace, but terminate them at definite, predetermined dates. Don't overdo it!

Implementing the OTJ Safety Campaign

The basic steps in implementing an OTJ safety campaign are as follows:

1. Determine how much ground to cover in the campaign. This depends on the extent of the OTJ safety problems.
2. Itemize campaign objectives and establish a timetable for accomplishing them.
3. Estimate cost/benefit factors. Be realistic and include labor, planning time, meeting time, work interruptions, and other inputs.
4. Obtain management commitment.
5. Organize the campaign strategy.
6. Order and receive materials.
7. Prepare employee publications.
8. Organize and train campaign supervisors.
9. Announce the campaign to employees.
10. Start the campaign.
11. Set up ways to track the campaign's success and measure the results.
12. Plan for the future.

Communicating the Plan

How does an organization communicate the OTJ program once it is implemented? There are four basic methods available to promote OTJ safety to drivers and their families.

- **Personal.** Communications that reach employees through private and social channels.
- **Public.** Media-centered communications directed toward more general populations.
- **Peer/supervisor.** Communications conducted at work.
- **Corporate.** Formal communications that reflect the corporate philosophy, policy, and other guidelines.

By using all these means of communication, the company will provide a variety of stimulating messages to gain the audience's attention and commitment. The formats for such messages may include the following program tools:

- **In-house publications.** This form of publicity is convenient, inexpensive, and effective. It reaches all employees from top management to drivers and their families.
- **Reference booklet or magazine.** A reference booklet has distinct advantages. It is permanent and can serve as a directory for answering specific safety questions. The National Safety Council's *Family Safety and Health* magazine reaches more people than any other OTJ safety publication. It has a proven record of motivating its readers to take safety and health precautions.

- **Safety calendars.** A safety calendar conveys safety information in a timely manner. The National Safety Council publishes a popular one.
- **Posters.** Workers may see a poster at a quick glance, but remember its message (which should be simple) for a long time. A poster can summarize major safety messages to reinforce more detailed how-to information. The National Safety Council publishes "POP" posters that can be placed in garage areas, on the dashboard, or right at the "point of problem" (Chapter 7, Employee Safety Program).
- **Contests.** One of the most successful ways to help people retain information and/or safe behavior is through some type of contest in which the winner receives something of value. Two widely used contest ideas that involve drivers' families are writing essays and making posters.
- **Films, videos, and slide shows.** Although a visual message communicates better than a spoken message, a combined visual and spoken message is better yet. This means of communication can provide detailed information and memorable graphics.
- **Safety fair/company picnic/family night.** Social events offer excellent opportunities to reach employees and their families.
- **Youth activities.** Sponsorship of activities like bicycle rallies can result in strong positive community sentiment.
- **Recreational motor vehicle programs.** These company-sponsored clinics are usually popular with employees. Skilled instructors teach workers and their families how to safely operate and inspect their own motorcycles, bicycles, and other leisure-time vehicles.
- **Vacation/holiday programs.** Vacation time is an opportunity to offer safe driving tips and promotional literature for travel on the road. Special cautions teach drivers to avoid common safety problems, especially driving while fatigued and driving too fast for conditions.
- **Safety talks.** Safety talks can cover both occupational and OTJ safety concerns at the same time.

Developing Program Topic Ideas

Generally, individuals are more receptive to program content that fits their normal routines. Figure 15–1 lists major OTJ safety program topics.

By offering drivers and other employees the chance to purchase safety equipment at wholesale prices, the company also reinforces the safety message. For instance, before summer arrives, offer first-aid kits and car restraints for children. Set up a payroll deduction system to help make the purchase of these items more affordable. All of the items sold should meet applicable quality control and safety standards.

OTJ TRAFFIC SAFETY PROGRAM TOPICS BY SEASON		
SPRING	**FALL**	**YEAR-ROUND**

New signs, signals, pavement markings
Motorcycles
Recreational vehicles
Vehicle maintenance
Vacation safety
	Back to school–
	   young pedestrians
	Winter car maintenance–
	   battery, snow tires,
	   chains,
	   defroster check
		Railroad grade crossings
		Defensive driving
		Occupant protection–
		   safety belts,
		   child restraints
		Alcohol and other drug abuse
		Two-wheelers–
		   bicycles,
		   mopeds,
		   minibikes
		Roadside hazards

SUMMER	**WINTER**	

Trailer towing
Hot-weather vehicle maintenance–
   cooling system,
   tires
	How to "jump start" a car
	Winter driving techniques–
	   how to avoid getting stuck,
	   how to handle a skid, etc.
	Snowmobiles	

Figure 15–1. These off-the-job safety program topics all have a motor vehicle theme.

Timing

Timing is important to the success of any program. Set an appropriate interval between the initial announcement and each featured safety topic. Changing topics too frequently will not meet the goal of saturating the audience, but leaving too much time between topic changes can result in a loss of interest. The minimum time suggested is one month for each topic or six months for the entire campaign. The best approach is to make OTJ safety a permanent part of the company's relationship with its employees. The problem never ends so why should the prevention effort?

LAUNCHING AND MAINTAINING THE PROGRAM

Before a new safety program is announced, several months of program activities should already have been developed and be ready for use.

The different program phases can be covered several times in a year—when the overall OTJ safety program begins and at the start of each campaign within the program. Keep in mind that employee support and participation can be gained only if workers know about the program.

Advance publicity helps ensure driver support by communicating the program's objectives, plans, and activities. Also, an informal, personalized letter from senior management sent to each employee's home will emphasize the organization's concern for the safety of the drivers and their families. An introductory meeting for drivers can be followed by a meeting to which family members are invited.

The organization's in-house publication also can announce the various program topics, which can be reinforced by company bulletin boards, posters, and displays. As always, a well-organized contest will promote employee involvement and generate enthusiasm.

Once an OTJ safety program has begun, continuing program responsibilities include the following:

- Assess previous and ongoing OTJ safety program activities.
- Maintain the wholehearted support and involvement of management, employees, and their families.
- Survey outside organizations to learn what programs worked and how well.
- Make changes as needed to revitalize individual programs.
- Encourage continuous program ideas and feedback, possibly through a joint employee-management or OTJ committee and an employee suggestion box.
- Report the program's status to management periodically.
- Monitor, record, and publicize the organization's progress in reducing OTJ fatalities, injuries, and illnesses. Let the drivers and their families know what a good job they're doing.

RECORDING AND CLASSIFYING DATA

The safety director and safety staff should collect and analyze data about off-the-job accidents and injuries, just as they do for those on the job. This information will reveal how well the safety program is working and where efforts should be intensified. The OTJ accident reporting procedures can be added to the absence and sickness reporting system the fleet uses to operate the payroll.

Reporting OTJ Accidents and Injuries

In any OTJ safety program, accidents should be analyzed to find the most frequent causes of injury. The accident-reporting procedure should list the nature and primary causes of injuries. This is best done with uniform reports made through a predetermined channel. Reports should include:

- Name of employee involved in the accident
- Date and time of day the accident took place
- Brief description (for example, "painting second-story window frame when ladder slipped")
- Nature of injury (such as "broken right forearm, sprained back")
- Estimated number of calendar days employee was disabled (when disability extends into more than one quarter of the year, days in each quarter should be counted, but the accident should be counted only in the quarter when it happened)

The reporting system can either be based on voluntary employee cooperation or delegated to first-line supervisors to initiate the reports. Although the voluntary approach cannot give the complete picture of an accident, it does provide sufficient data to develop an effective prevention program. In addition, a sincerely conducted voluntary reporting program increases worker interest and cooperation in OTJ safety.

A required reporting system will generate a considerable body of information in about six months. This will enable management to plan an effective program to combat specific off-the-job accidents revealed by the data.

With either system, the safety director and staff must respect employees' privacy by keeping their names out of press releases, announcements, and other published materials unless workers give specific permission. An accident can cause embarrassment to the parties involved; the same code of privacy and confidentiality that medical records deserve applies here.

While waiting for statistics to accumulate on specific accident information, concentrate on the major off-the-job accidents: slips, trips, falls, and auto accidents.

Measures of OTJ Injury Experience

Organizations should use a uniform method for determining OTJ injury experience, but current methods of gathering, recording, and measuring employee OTJ injury information vary substantially from one organization to another. Comparing injury data from one organization to another is only possible when organizations treat their injury data uniformly. The same holds true for nationwide OTJ injury rate data.

When compiling OTJ injury data, companies are urged to follow the practices recommended in ANSI Z16.3–1989,

Recording and Measuring Employee Off-the-Job Injury Experience (a revision is in process). Some of the basic concepts used in this standard are given here. These define the minimum information that should be collected.

- **Employee.** Any person who is on the direct payroll of the employer as a full-time employee. This excludes part-time employees and temporary persons who are paid by an outside agency. Part-time employees are excluded only because of the complications their inclusion introduces into the record keeping. Companies wanting to include part-time employees are encouraged to do so.

- **Injury.** Any harm or damage to the body, or bodily systems, resulting from intentional or unintentional violence, poisoning, or other external cause.

- **Off-the-job (OTJ) injury.** Any injury that does not arise out of or in the course of any employment, that prevents an employee from working (see "injuries with lost workdays" and "deaths" below) and that is not included as a work injury under the OSHAct, OSHA regulations and Bureau of Labor Statistics record-keeping guidelines.

- **Injuries with lost workdays.** Any OTJ injury that results in the inability of an employee, on any scheduled work shift, to perform effectively throughout one or more full shifts the essential functions of a regularly established job that is open and available to him or her in the establishment where he/she is employed.

- **Death.** Any OTJ injury that ultimately results in death regardless of the time between the occurrence of the injury and death.

Injuries with lost workdays and deaths are the cases used to calculate incidence rates and other measures of OTJ safety. The definition of OTJ injury includes such cases as the following:

- suicide or attempted suicide,
- purposely inflicted injury,
- legal intervention,
- disasters such as earthquakes, tornadoes, or conflagrations, or
- civil disturbance;
  and excludes such cases as:
- illness,
- legal execution,
- moonlighting, and
- heart attack or stroke.

The ANSI Z16.3–1989 standard gives more information on the classification of special cases.

The ANSI Z16.3–1989 standard defines the OTJ injury incidence rate in terms of a 200,000-hour unit of exposure so as to be directly comparable to the OTJ lost-workday cases incidence rate most employers already compute for employee work-injury experience. For example, if your organization's OTJ injury incidence rate were 5.0 for employees and your OSHA lost-workday case incidence rate were 1.0, that would indicate that your organization was having five times more OTJ injuries than job-related injuries (per 200.000-hour unit of exposure). The formula is as follows:

$$\text{OTJ injury incidence rate} = \frac{\text{No. of OTJ injuries} \times 200,000}{312 \times \text{average no. employees} \times \text{no. of months}}$$

The 312 figure in the formula assumes that an employee works eight hours a day, five days a week. Excluding eight hours for sleeping, this leaves eight hours a day or 40 hours a workweek of OTJ exposure time. In addition, the employee has two days of 16 hours' nonwork exposure each weekend, making a total of 72 (40 + 16 + 16) multiplied by 4⅓ weeks a month totals 312 hours of nonwork exposure each month. Since overtime is considered to be offset by holidays, vacations, and other absences, no special allowance is provided for it.

Optional Broader Coverage

The data collected on employees can be supplemented with injury information on other classes of people less directly related to the organization than full-time employees, including the following:

• **Employee's family.** Spouse or dependents of an employee who live at home with the employee and/or are covered under the employee's accident and health insurance plan.

• **Retiree.** Retired employee of employer who is covered under the employer's accident and health insurance plan.

• **Part-time employee.** An employee who works less than 35 hours per week.

Injury information on these people can be useful in planning OTJ programs, but injury incidence rates are normally computed for employee exposures only. If spouse, dependent, and retiree OTJ injury experiences are also being recorded, it would be difficult to calculate OTJ rates for them because their OTJ exposures vary tremendously. Usually, raw numbers and costs are reported and categorized separately from employee OTJ injury experience.

Evaluating Results

Although it is difficult to measure how many accidents an OTJ safety program actually prevents, bottom-line results should include a reduction in overall OTJ injury rates and OTJ injury costs.

For instance, an overall reduction in motorcycle injuries following a special campaign to promote motorcycle safety would suggest a possible cause-and-effect relationship. However, other variables may also have affected the reduction in injuries. Perhaps little rain fell during the spring and summer, reducing hazardous driving conditions. In the absence of exposure information and controlled studies, one can only assume the safety campaign was effective.

Employees' attitudes about themselves, their families, and their workplace also affect the results of an OTJ safety program. If an organization has both an occupational and an OTJ safety program, the two should be coordinated for maximum impact.

Conducting Audits

Periodically, the OTJ safety program should be audited to measure the quantity and quality of an organization's efforts to prevent OTJ accidents. An audit may include the following questions:

• Is there appropriate OTJ accident information on employees and their families?

• What is the OTJ performance record in this area?

• What is the quality of OTJ safety meetings with employees?

• Are the OTJ safety meetings monitored or audited by management?

• Are speakers' performances critiqued?

• What type of OTJ material is being distributed to employees and their families?

• Are families of employees being reminded of OTJ safety through print media, community meetings, television, radio, films, videos, slide shows, or a combination of these?

• Have readership and viewer surveys been done to determine the quality and use of these OTJ materials?

• Are there reports from employees on lives saved and serious accidents prevented?

The safety director should monitor and record an organization's OTJ injury experience (Figure 15–2) and modify the program as necessary. Management should be kept informed of the program's progress.

SUCCESSFUL OTJ SAFETY PROGRAMS

Many companies around the country have influenced their employees' lives for the better through their OTJ safety programs. The National Safety Council's *Off the Job Safety*

EMPLOYEE OTJ INJURY REPORT FORM

DIV. _____   LOCATION _____   MONTH _____   YEAR _____

Total No. of Off-Job Injuries This Month: _____
Year-To-Date _____

Transportation	1 No. Cases	2 No. Fatal-ities	3 Days Lost	4 Days Old Cases	5 Tot. Cal. Days Lost This Month
Motor Vehicle:					
Auto. Truck					
a) Collision					
b) Repair work					
c) Pedestrian					
d) Miscellaneous					
Bus Streetcar					
Bicycle					
Motorcycle, Moped					
Railroad					
Aircraft					
Watercraft					
Other					
TOTAL					

Total Calendar Days Lost This Month: _____
Year-To-Date _____

Home	1 No. Cases	2 No. Fatal-ities	3 Days Lost	4 Days Old Cases	5 Tot. Cal. Days Lost This Month
Fall, Slip					
Fire, Explosion					
Firearm					
Animals, Insects					
Exposure: Heat, Cold					
Lifting					
Pushing, Pulling					
Struck By Object					
Struck Against Object					
Toxic Material					
Electricity					
Machinery, Tools					
Sharp Object					
Other					
TOTAL					

Total No. of Fatalities This Month: _____
Year-To-Date _____

Public	1 No. Cases	2 No. Fatal-ities	3 Days Lost	4 Days Old Cases	5 Tot. Cal. Days Lost This Month
Fall, Slip					
Fire, Explosion					
Firearm					
Animals, Insects					
Exposure: Heat, Cold					
Lifting					
Pushing, Pulling					
Struck by Object					
Struck Against Object					
Toxic Material					
Fight, Assault					
Sports					
Recreation					
Other					
TOTAL					

Col. 1.   **Number Cases.** Include all off-the-job **Injuries** occurring this month when one or more working days are lost.
Col. 2.   **Number Fatalities.** Include all fatalities occurring this month.
Col. 3.   **Days Lost.** Total calendar days lost on injuries occuring this month.
Col. 4.   **Days Old Cases.** Records **additional days** lost this month due to injuries previously reported.
Col. 5.   Total calendar days lost this month (Cols. 3 + 4).
            Total Number of Off-Job Injuries This Month (Cols. 1 + 2—Include Fatalities).
Fatal Injuries: Give brief description of accident below. If death results from injury reported previously, refer to month and classification of original reporting.

Remarks: _____

_____   _____
Report Prepared By   **Date**

Figure 15–2.   This employee off-the-job injury report form will help the safety director monitor and record OTJ injury experience.

Program lists many resources that can be used to build an effective program. Examples of programs that made a difference follow.

Seat-Belt Campaign

When the safety task force at Kodak in Rochester, New York, set out to encourage the use of safety restraints, it distributed brochures, stickers, posters, and greeting cards with the slogan "common sense for safety." Response to the safety restraint campaign was both enthusiastic and effective, as shown in before-and-after surveys of seat-belt use conducted by Kodak's safety task force.

One month before the campaign started, the number of people who arrived at work with their seat belts fastened was counted. The plant parking lot held 4,000 vehicles and provided a sampling of Kodak Park's total employee population of 30,000 (at the time), according to Kodak's statistics. The first survey established a benchmark. The percentage of drivers wearing seat belts was close to the national average.

The second survey, taken two months after the program began, showed belt usage had increased by 2.6%.

The real proof of success for Kodak came on the third survey, five months later, when 3.1% more of the drivers observed were wearing their seat belts. This was an increase of 5.7% over the precampaign survey.

OTJ Injuries Reduced by 47%

Armco, Inc., a diversified metals fabricator, had a compelling reason for starting its OTJ safety program—management discovered that eight times as many of its people were being hurt off the job as at work. Armco put some of its on-the-job safety know-how to work in preventing accidents and injuries off the job with a program called "Safety for the Family."

Armco's OTJ statistical evidence is striking. Recent reports showed the total number of OTJ injuries recorded dropped from 16 to just one in four years. The total number of OTJ injuries to Armco employees went down 47% in five years. Days lost from work because of OTJ injuries dropped 36%. Finally, the OTJ injury frequency rate was reduced by 23%.

Although Armco statistics point to success at preventing OTJ accidents, Armco management admits that it is impossible to determine exactly how or why people change their behavior. Regardless, the bottom line is that Armco employees are having fewer accidents off the job.

Hazards Corrected

A cement company conducted a home fire-safety campaign over a period of several weeks. It used departmental meetings, bulletin board notices, and posters.

Although it was impossible to estimate how many home fires, if any, were prevented by the company's effort, feedback from employees indicated the material was well received and motivated them to correct a number of hazards in their homes.

No Serious Accidents

A mining company located in a small community used its in-house publication, the local news media, posters, and reference booklets to prevent injuries to employees and their families over the vacation period.

Was the campaign a success? The company believes it was. Not one employee was injured or involved in a serious accident during the vacation period. The year before, when there was no extensive campaign, there were 23 serious accidents—two of them fatal.

OTJ and community safety programs do work, and their importance cannot be overemphasized. Integrating an OTJ safety program with the fleet safety program can increase the cost-effectiveness of a company's operation. The safe way is usually the most efficient way.

APPENDIX

A

Getting Publicity from Safe Driver Awards

DEVELOPING A NEWS RELEASE

ADVERTISING POSSIBILITIES

Many times company publications and local newspapers, radio, and TV will carry a story based on presentation of Safe Driver Awards (also of Safe Worker Awards, see Chapter 7, Employee Safety Program). But to carry a story, they must know in advance that these awards are going to be presented.

The news media are alert to the public's interest in the street and highway accident problem. Hardly a family in the United States has been left unaffected: each year over 40,000 persons are killed and more than 2.2 million persons are injured in motor vehicle accidents. Moreover, virtually everyone either operates or rides in a motor vehicle and should therefore be interested in safe driving.

Pictures and personality sketches of the drivers being recognized at the award presentation or a story about the accident prevention program are certain to attract reader interest and result in goodwill for your company as well as promote interest in better driving. The award presentation itself can build goodwill. Community knowledge that your company has many award-winning safe drivers can result in sales being directed your way.

DEVELOPING A NEWS RELEASE

Advance planning counts. Plan the program and set the date at least a month ahead for daily and weekly media, three months for monthly magazines and newsletters. This permits the story to be printed about the same time the award is made. Some media will cover the presentation itself. Your company publication will probably do both.

The amount of publicity will usually be in proportion to the importance you place upon the awards, the number of awards, and the length of time between awards. You can't make a big event over one or two awards given each month, but you can over 15 or 20 awards given once a year. Company officers can be present—city and state officials can be invited. Some firms invite a representative of the local safety organization.

Each edition of a newspaper or a magazine needs fresh news. Community papers and regional editions of larger papers feature local people, companies, and events. Editors know this increases readership.

However, since the space is limited and the competition for coverage is strong, there is no assurance that every editor contacted will give space to the story. Chances for media coverage are greatly increased when the information is sent well in advance of the event and is presented in a concise, clear, and interesting manner. A widely accepted method is to mail a news release with photo, if available, and some background information on the company to the attention of the community affairs editor (Figure A–1).

When preparing a news release, remember that editors are trained to ask six questions about all stories—who? what? why? when? where? and how? So tell them who is getting the awards and who will be there to give them, why this event is important to the editor and to the readers, what the award means, when the event will take place, where it will be held, and how the editors can get more details if they want them.

Give them the facts. Let them determine the relative importance. Of course, try to present the facts in such a way that they will interest the editor. The editor usually tries to find some angle, some approach to handling the story that will appeal to the readers and be different from the stories other news media carry. Work with the editor, if requested.

The news release will not only contain details of the ceremonies, but also tell about the award winners themselves. Some editors may send a photographer. Others may ask you to get photographs for them. Usually, you'll want to take your own pictures in addition to photographs for the editor.

The maximum number of people in a photograph is usually three to four. Photos should have some action—even a nice smile gives some variety to the "present plaque—give handshake" routine.

When photos are needed to accompany an advance news release, a company official and the award recipients can be photographed before the event, in a simulated ceremony. The following example illustrates a simple method of preparing a news release.

Fast Delivery Service, a company operating a fleet of 50 delivery trucks, has just received Safe Driver awards from the National Safety Council. Fifteen of its drivers have operated their vehicles for at least a year without a preventable accident. The safety director lists the following facts to help the local newspaper editors prepare the story.

Who? Fast Delivery Service, Evansville, Indiana.

What? Presentation of National Safety Council Safe Driver awards. National recognition for safe driving to 15 of 55 drivers.

List the winners as follows:

4 years

3 years

2 years

1 year

Why? Awards are given in recognition of 15 drivers having driven a total of 100,000 miles, four times the distance around the earth, during the past year without having a preventable accident.

When? The awards are to be presented by the company president, Craig Wilson, to the qualifying drivers on

Thursday, June 15, at 7:00 P.M. A list of the guests expected to be present follows; it gives their names and titles and their companies' names and addresses.

Where? The awards are to be presented at a dinner meeting at the Johnson Inn.

Other highlights. (List other outstanding figures or facts pertaining to the fleet as a whole, the drivers as a group, or their safety program.)

Statements. (Give quotations from the president's presentation speech, the National Safety Council statement, and guest speakers' speeches.)

The safety director then writes the story in a news release format (Figure A–1 on page 178). The news release should be printed on company stationery with the words "NEWS RELEASE" in bold lettering near the top of the page. It is important that the name and phone number of the safety director, or other contact person, be given in the release.

ADVERTISING POSSIBILITIES

Many companies, especially operators of passenger-carrying vehicles, stress safety in their advertising. Newspaper display advertising can be purchased to announce awards and to play up fleet safety records. Be sure to keep clear the distinction between advertising and publicity—you pay for advertising. Publicity is free, and it is entirely up to the editor how much space you are going to get, if any. Although the editorial departments of the news media are friendly to advertisers, the editor must judge news on its merits.

Company Name   For Your Information:
Address   Name and Title
Phone Number   Phone Number
                                                                  For release by June 15

NEWS RELEASE

Four times around the earth, 100,000 miles, driven this year without a preventable accident.

June 15, 19–. That's the record 15 drivers for the Fast Delivery Service set during the past year on the streets of Evansville and its suburbs. In recognition of their accomplishments, the drivers were presented with National Safety Council Safe Driver awards. The presentations were made at a dinner held tonight at the Johnson Inn that was attended by all drivers in the Fast Delivery Service fleet.

27,000 Safe Miles

Those drivers honored: John Smith, 1608 Maple Avenue, 1st year award; Vicki Brown, 458 E. Second Street, 2nd year award; and Harold Klien, 103 Fifth Avenue, 3rd year award.

Smith had the best safety record, operating his truck 27,000 safe miles during the past year.

Klien compiled his safety record despite volunteering to drive under almost impossible conditions during the recent floods near Evansville. He transported drinking water around the clock to needy families, often with part of his truck submerged in the flood waters.

Green Praises Drivers

In the winter, the drivers provide a real public service by keeping the roads open, clearing their routes with a huge, specially built snow plow-equipped tractor.

Traffic Captain Henry Green, speaking briefly at the dinner, gave tribute to the winners' fine records. He said, "You have proved safe driving is a good investment. I hope your example will be followed by every driver in the city. It goes to show what caution and good sense behind the wheel can do."

Green pointed out that five persons had met death in our city in automobile accidents since New Year's Day. "Every one of these accidents could have been prevented had the drivers shown the courtesy and care exercised by you award winners," he asserted.

Accidents Down by 30 Percent

Craig Wilson, President of the Fast Delivery Service, cited official figures from the National Safety Council in his presentation talk and noted that the overall company safety program had reduced the fleet's accident rate by more than 30 percent in the past year. He thanked the award winners and also voiced his appreciation to the entire group of drivers and other employees for their cooperation.

MEMBERS OF THE MEDIA. Photos of the award winners, biographical sketches of them, and a company brochure are enclosed. For further information or to arrange personal interviews, please contact: Name of safety director and phone number.

Figure A–1.   This news release presents the facts in a clear and interesting manner; it would have a good chance of obtaining media coverage of the safety awards ceremony.

Safety Meetings for Commercial Drivers

Safety meetings for drivers are an important part of any balanced motor fleet program. Management's reasons for holding safety meetings should be to arouse and maintain interest in accident and injury prevention, develop attitudes sympathetic to the safety program, and educate and train drivers and supervisory personnel in all facets of safe vehicle and equipment operation.

Group safety meetings can further the efficiency of all operations. They can cause a common bond of interest and a closer feeling of identity between co-workers that results in stronger company loyalties.

OBJECTIVES OF SAFETY MEETINGS

There are numerous ways of classifying safety meetings, but the simplest and most direct groupings are (a) motivational meetings, (b) recognition of accomplishments in accident prevention, and (c) group instruction and training.

Motivational Meetings

The purpose behind motivational meetings is to spark interest and encourage participation in the safety program. Current safety problems should be mentioned, along with management's proposals on how to minimize or eliminate the risks to drivers, employees, and company property. The supervisory personnel in charge of ongoing accident and injury prevention projects should give progress reports, stressing positive results, and ask for continuing and increased support of their efforts.

Management could mention any operating cost savings that have been realized because of a successful safety program. This should definitely be done when the cost reductions have caused additional benefits to be given to the drivers, such as greater job security, higher wages, or a better employee benefit package.

The mood of the motivational meeting should be positive and encouraging; any favorable effect or by-product of the safety program would be an appropriate topic for discussion. Because safe driving is also courteous driving, an effective safety program will probably give management the opportunity to talk about an elevated company image within the community and local media coverage of safety award ceremonies.

Recognition Meetings

These meetings are called as the occasion demands. This may be at the close of a contest, for presentation of bonuses or awards, or at any time for the express purpose of recognizing good records. The theme closely parallels that of the motivational gathering. The talks are positive and there is little opportunity for training. When practical,

it is desirable to hold a ceremony of this kind in conjunction with a meal function as this helps to give it the significance of an important event. These recognition meetings can be scheduled at times convenient for family and friends to attend. How to get maximum publicity from these awards meetings is discussed in Appendix A, Getting Publicity from Safe Driver Awards.

Group Instruction and Training Meetings

Drivers must understand the operating policies of the company and all the factors that enter into the safe and efficient handling of the business. They should be instructed in the elements of safe, courteous, and efficient driving and be informed about accidents that have occurred and how they could have been prevented. Group instruction and training affords the most practical medium for accident and injury prevention education and is indispensable to an effective safety program. (See Chapter 9, Driver Training, for more information.)

FACTORS TO CONSIDER

Scheduling

The first step in planning the program should be to arrange a schedule of meetings extending over a designated period such as six or 12 months. This schedule should be considered as a course of safety education with each meeting planned to cover a desired objective. Safety meetings are far too important to call on short notice without (a) careful consideration of the field to be covered, (b) intelligent selection of the discussion subjects, and (c) time required to cover the subjects. The topics and outline for each meeting can be put into a booklet sent out at the beginning of the year and furnished to each location where meetings are required.

Specialized meetings. Most meetings can be planned to be of interest to all drivers. In large fleets, however, where the operations include several distinct types of driving, it may be advantageous to schedule separate meetings for different groups. Even when this practice is followed, it is advisable to hold several meetings during the year for all personnel. The program for these gatherings can be planned accordingly. Employees should not be required to attend meetings where the instruction and training is irrelevant to their particular work.

Small meetings. The size and nature of the fleet will determine arrangement of meeting schedules. Operations in scattered locations or including more than one shift may necessitate smaller groups. Regardless of how small the meetings may be, they should be scheduled and planned in advance. Even in fleets of no more than three to five vehicles, drivers and the owner or manager should meet to discuss safety. In small meetings, group discussion should be emphasized.

Short meetings. Many of the firms that do not hold regular meetings of an hour or more conduct brief meetings lasting 10 to 15 minutes. The general practice is to hold these meetings at least once a week; in some instances, they are made a part of each workday.

Early morning meetings are far superior. The employees are receptive and receive the safety message at a time when it will do the most good—just before they set out for the day's work. Some fleets have been successful in holding safety breakfasts. Meetings at the end of the day are not successful because drivers are tired and anxious to get home and by the next morning the safety message is forgotten.

It is not necessary to accomplish actual training or to enter into detailed discussion at short meetings. Their purpose is inspection or issuance of warnings about current, daily hazards. Usually, one subject is treated at each meeting. Some firms using this plan prepare special bulletins that are read to the group and then posted on the bulletin board for future reference. Such bulletins can be used to caution drivers about seasonal hazards.

Full-length meetings. Extensive educational meetings require more time. However, full-length meetings should not exceed one hour (except dinner meetings and other special events). A one-hour (or less) program each month is preferable to longer sessions every two or three months.

During the full-length meeting, instruction should be given to improve driving techniques. This training should be supplemented by a thorough analysis of the accident experience as well as a discussion of recent accidents. Continuous training is necessary for both new and old drivers.

Generally, it is not advisable to attempt to cover more than two subjects at any one meeting, even if it is a long one.

Meeting Times

Conditions peculiar to each fleet govern the hour at which meetings are held. In many operations, it is practically impossible to hold meetings during working hours because not all drivers can be present at the same time. Dinner meetings are held during nonworking hours.

Meetings should be scheduled at regular intervals, such as the second Tuesday of every month. Select a time when most employees are able to attend. In most operations, the second week of the month is good because summaries of the accident experience for the preceding month will have been prepared and can be discussed at the meeting.

Some fleets do not schedule full-length meetings during the summer months but substitute early morning sessions so the routine will not be disrupted. Many fleets have more accidents from November through February, and find it beneficial to schedule full-length meetings beginning in the fall.

Meeting Places

The meeting place should be free from noise or other distractions. Short 10- or 15-minute meetings may be held in the garage, if suitable facilities are available. But longer sessions require a room with adequate heat, light, and acoustics. Some transportation companies use a mobile trainer as a classroom. This can be either a large travel trailer or a truck semitrailer. The unit is equipped with heat, air conditioning, light-proof windows, audiovisual equipment, and chalkboards. It might have mockups of mechanical systems. Usually it can be conveniently parked and plugged into a building's electrical supply. Such a training unit can be easily shuttled between terminals.

Teaching rooms are described in the section on where to teach in Chapter 9, Driver Training.

Subjects to Cover

Although the major emphasis should be placed on instruction and training, motivation should also be an objective. The proportion of time allocated to each phase is determined by the fleet's accident experience and employees' interest and morale. Some of the more important subjects to cover are listed below (of course, those related to the most serious problems of the particular operation should receive attention first):

- thorough explanation of operating and public relations policies of the firm
- instruction in driving practices, courtesy, and safety in general
- traffic rules and regulations with explanation of the purpose, intent, and language of the regulations
- mechanics of the vehicle, its care, and maintenance, with demonstrations conducted by expert mechanics or specialists
- explanation of the physical problems involved in driving, such as reaction time, stopping distance, skidding, passing distance, centrifugal force, and force of impact
- thorough coverage of past accidents, common situations, unusual accidents, seasonal hazards, what to do in case of an accident, how to report an accident, analysis of the frequency and severity of major types of accidents, driver discussion of accident causes and prevention, costs, trends, prevalent types, and accident repeaters
- first aid and general health, importance and value of regular physical examinations, discussion of fatigue,

and explanation of company policy regarding these subjects

- loading and unloading, how to lift, proper storage of cargo, and handling of passengers
- necessity for and proper use of special equipment such as emergency warning equipment, flags, chains, standards, foglights, spotlights, tarpaulins, ropes, tailgates, the fifth wheel, air brake equipment and connections, and lighting equipment and connections
- special safety topics, such as hazardous materials handling, and treatment of passenger problems
- open forum with questions to be asked and answered

A full discussion of what to teach is given in Chapter 9, Driver Training.

PLANNING THE PROGRAM

Each program should be planned sufficiently ahead of time to assure its success. Variety and unique methods are needed to maintain interest and assure attendance; drivers must look forward to each meeting. Strive to make the program interesting, entertaining, and educational. Do not become discouraged if the first meetings fall short of this goal. Continued poor attendance by employees calls for a review of planning and handling techniques.

The chairperson should prepare a training plan (or it may be done for all locations by a central safety department). The plan shows the key discussion points on the right side of the sheet, with the trainer's actions on the left (such as "write accident rate on chalkboard"). The plan should include a list of materials needed for the meeting (see sample plan in Figure B–1).

Types of Speakers

Specialists and instructors. The selection of the specialists who will be instructing is very important. They should be able to talk authoritatively, instill confidence, and convince listeners of the benefits of safety. Unqualified speakers or teachers cause employees to lose confidence and interest. Outside speakers add variety but should not be used for a major share of the program. Persons not familiar with the details peculiar to each fleet may make conflicting statements if required to cover too broad a subject. A company's policies and procedures manual should be furnished to all employees engaged in a supervisory capacity. It will guide those who act as instructors in presenting recommended practices correctly and uniformly.

Company officials. The fleet safety director or other persons responsible for safety should preside over the meeting. In addition, at least one official of the firm

should participate in every meeting. This is of utmost importance in demonstrating management's interest and support. If possible, this assignment should be rotated throughout the year among different executives. By scheduling subjects in advance, impromptu talks can be discouraged. A well-directed 10-minute talk by the management representative is usually sufficient. Courtesy, company plans for the future, employees' welfare, plant deliveries, progress, and financial condition are suggested subjects.

Insurance company representatives. The insurance company representative can help by taking part in the meeting program. It must be remembered, however, that he or she services other fleets and cannot be expected to know every detail of operation peculiar to each fleet.

Training Aids and Quizzes

Training aids and quizzes are discussed in Chapter 9, Driver Training.

Door Prizes

Many fleets introduce some sort of door prize to stimulate attendance. The expense involved is small and the results exceptionally good. One plan is for the employees who attend to place their names in a box at the beginning of the meeting. At the close of the meeting, the winning card is drawn from the box. One fleet uses a $10 bill as a prize at every meeting. Other prizes that may be used are parts of uniforms, safety shoes, tools, goggles, pen and pencil sets, gloves, and household and personal items. This plan reduces tardiness because the cards must be deposited before the meeting begins.

As a refinement, a card carrying a safety message can be given out at one meeting and collected at the next for a drawing. Drivers with accidents that month would not be eligible. If everyone goes accident-free, the door prize might be increased.

Program Arrangement

The character of the program and the sequence in which the various parts should be presented depends, of course, on the type of meeting. An essential requisite of every safety meeting is stimulating interest. There must be no lag in the discussions, no lull in the proceedings, and no tiresome or aimless digressions from the subjects.

The following features are typical for a motivational program where good records are recognized:

- dinner (often with music)
- entertainment (if desired)
- introduction of visitors (by chairperson)

SAMPLE TRAINING SESSION PLAN

Meeting date: October 15th
Topic: Forklift Safety
Meeting times: 0630, 0730, 0830 (30-minute meeting)
Location: Terminal Conference Room
Group: Dock and Local Drivers

Materials needed:
15 copies of company forklift rules for each session (total 45)
List of forklift injuries this year
NSC poster showing forklift accident

Chalkboard	Eraser
Chalk	3 Sign-in sheets

What to Do	What to Say

PUT *14* ON BLACKBOARD.
HAND OUT SIGN-IN SHEET.
	1. Open meeting:
	  a. Greetings
	  b. Introduce Terminal Manager—brief remarks by him

WRITE *FORKLIFT INJURIES* AFTER *14*.	2. There have been 14 forklift injuries in the company this year compared to 9 a year ago.
	3. (Read description of forklift injuries. Don't allow comment yet.)
WRITE *3* ON BOARD.	4. Three of the injuries were here. (Discuss result of John Brown case.)

HOLD UP POSTER.
WRITE POINTS ON BOARD.
	5. How can you keep this from happening to you?
	  a. Pre-trip your lift before using it.
	  b. Look where you are driving.
	  c. Hold your speed down.
	  d. Keep forks down when empty.
	  e. Never enter trailer unless wheels are blocked.
	  f. Don't run forklift into a bobtail unless supervisor approves.
	  g. Use horn or pause at blind aisles.
	  h. Fuel lifts only in Bay 2 and put gas can back in proper place.
	  i. No horseplay.
	  j. Be extra careful to watch for other workers when moving in a trailer.
	  k. No riding on forks or loads.
	  l. No pulling with chains to mast.
	  m. Never raise forks above six feet.
	  n. Watch mast height in trailer.

HAND OUT FORKLIFT RULES.	6. Here is your copy of the posted company forklift rules. Sign the attached slip and turn it in as you leave. Keep the rules and refer to them.
COLLECT SIGN-IN LIST.	7. There will be a brief test on these rules next meeting.
WRITE *NOVEMBER 12TH* ON BOARD.	8. Thanks for attending. The next safety meeting is November 12th.

AFTER THE MEETING, PREPARE MEETING REPORT FORM 23 AND SUBMIT IT TO THE SAFETY DEPARTMENT.

Figure B–1. Sample training session plan.

- welcoming address and preliminary remarks
- principal speaker
- presentation of awards (by the company's president or manager)
- closing remarks (by chairperson)

The typical features of a group instruction and training meeting include:

- roll call (or pass sign-in sheet)
- introduction of visitors (by chairperson)
- preliminary remarks with emphasis on high-frequency accidents—the topic of this meeting (by the safety director)
- films or other visual aids on the subject
- discussion led by safety director, followed by an open forum
- summary and conclusion (by chairperson)

A buffet lunch is appropriate to this type of meeting. Some organizations feel that if the lunch precedes the meeting, the employees are in a more receptive mood for the meeting. Others find value in the good fellowship and discussion that result from mingling while food is served at the close of the meeting.

CONDUCTING THE MEETING

Many meetings fail because seemingly insignificant matters are not taken care of beforehand. An ample number of chairs, for example, should be placed in an orderly arrangement before the meeting begins. The room must be kept at a comfortable temperature and be well ventilated. A hat and coatrack or closet should be available. Drinking water should be furnished for speakers. If films or slides are used, be sure windows have shades or curtains and a screen of adequate size is provided. Spare projector light bulbs should be available, as well as necessary extension cords. The following points should receive special attention when conducting a meeting.

Chairperson. The person responsible for the safety program, the drivers' immediate supervisor, or some selected representative of management should preside.

Criticism. Because criticism can evoke resentment rather than willing cooperation, it has no place in a group meeting. Individuals should not be corrected or reprimanded during group gatherings. Discipline should be handled by private conference at other times. Of course, the correction of individual faults is covered indirectly during general discussions of bad practices.

Formality. The meeting should be conducted in an orderly manner with sufficient formality to lend the program dignity and respect, but not make it stiff and boring. It should be started, carried through, and adjourned according to schedule. Humor should not be injected where it will detract from emphasis on serious points.

Personal touch. Collection of invitation cards at the door by an official of the firm affords an opportunity for a personal handshake or greeting and tends to stimulate attendance. It also serves to express management's interest and to add credibility to the proceedings.

Attendance. A record should be kept of all those in attendance at each meeting. One safety director sends a personal note to the home of each absent driver, saying that he or she was missed at the meeting and hoping that he or she will be present at the next one.

NOTIFICATION OF MEETING AND PUBLICITY

Announce the meeting well in advance, giving details such as time, place, and the nature of the program. Notices are more impressive when signed by the safety director or another official. They should be posted on all bulletin boards and published in employee publications. Some firms inform drivers of meetings by letter. Others issue invitation cards or tickets. Those are collected at the meeting and often must be signed by the person attending.

Of course, attendance at meetings held during working hours can be mandatory; this is the rule in many companies. The expenditures involved usually return big dividends to the companies because the biggest weakness of voluntary safety meetings is that those who need the message most are the least likely to show up.

Develop interest in the meeting by building it up through publicity channels. Report regularly in company publications interesting developments in connection with each meeting. Keep employees informed of the purpose of each meeting and the subjects that will be discussed.

APPENDIX
C

Skill Drills
and
Test Courses

Skill drills and test courses are used to train new drivers as well as to test the skills of trained drivers. The experience will help new drivers seeking their commercial drivers license (CDL).

This course is based on the National Truck Driving Championship of the American Trucking Associations, Inc., 2200 Mill Road, Alexandria, VA 22314. Copies of the book, *The National Truck Driving Championship*, may be ordered from its Department of Safety.

The National Truck Driving Championship, formerly called the Roadeo, is designed to determine through a series of challenging competitive events the contestant's driving skills and knowledge of safety, courtesy, efficiency, and first aid. In addition to being a testing and training device, the competition serves as a community goodwill project and promotes better employee relations.

To be eligible to take the entrance tests, a contestant must have had at least one year's service as a professional truck driver and a minimum of one year of accident-free driving. Preliminary tests consist of a written examination on the trucking industry, safe driving rules, first aid, and firefighting. The contestant is then given a personal interview to judge attitude, general appearance, and self-expression.

Following the interview, an equipment defects test is administered to grade the contestant's ability to properly conduct a pretrip inspection of the vehicle. Lastly, the contestant competes in the field test course, which is a series of driving problems simulating everyday operating conditions.

A general layout of a test course is shown in Figure C–1. Dimensions can be adjusted to fit the size and type of vehicle that is being driven.

TYPICAL FIELD TEST COURSE

(Dimensions shown indicate placement of problem to accommodate largest class of vehicles. Refer to individual problem diagrams for dimensions of each problem)

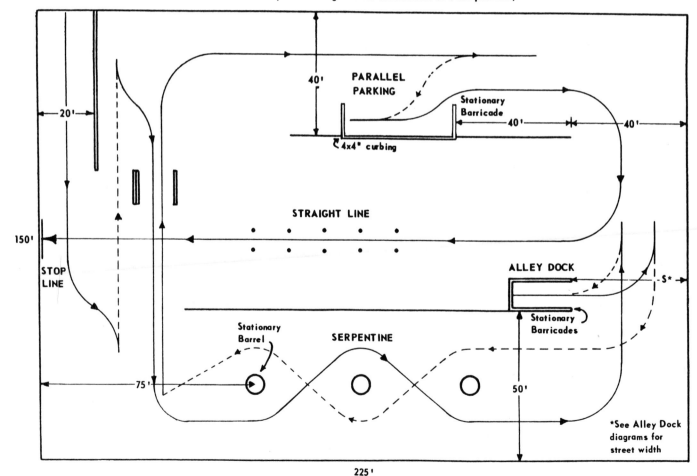

Figure C–1. General design of the field test course used for the National Truck Driving Championship. Reprinted with permission from the copyright holder, the American Trucking Associations, Inc.

Some of these skill tests in a typical competition are described below. They can be changed to suit the training situation, and additional problems may be added. The test course includes the following maneuvers:

- **Parallel parking.** The object of this test is to determine the driver's ability to park parallel to a simulated curb as in making a curbside street delivery, or in moving the unit off to the side of the road.

- **Alley dock.** This test determines the driver's ability to back the vehicle into a narrow space, to back through a restricted area without hitting either side, and to stop close to, but not touching, the dock.

- **Offset alley.** Here, the driver is judged on ability to make a right turn in a continuous movement through a confined space and to properly control the speed while avoiding touching the two pairs of barricades.

- **Forward serpentine.** The driver is tested on ability to maneuver the vehicle in and out of tight places in forward movement. The test is designed to simulate conditions that might be encountered when disabled or wrecked vehicles partially block a highway, when negotiating detours, when moving in heavy traffic, and when unusual situations require expert skill and control of the vehicle. In the skill drill, the driver must drive around drums or barrels arranged somewhat like a slalom run for skiers.

- **Backward serpentine.** This test is similar to the above, except that vehicle movement is backward. It is designed to test the driver's ability to back the vehicle into narrow places.

- **Straight line.** This test challenges the ability of the driver to accurately judge the position of the right wheels of the vehicle and to steer the vehicle in a straight line. It simulates conditions in which the driver must keep as far to the right as possible on narrow streets and highways when meeting oncoming traffic. It helps the driver to gage distances on the right-hand side of the pavement to avoid running off onto a highway shoulder, which can cause loss of control, tire abuse, and "dusting" of the following traffic.

- **Stop line.** Here the driver's ability to judge the position of the front bumper with respect to a fixed line is challenged. This problem simulates the conditions encountered in stopping at a marked crosswalk, or a situation in which it is advantageous for the driver to pull as far forward as possible in close quarters without hitting a stationary object or vehicle.

Drivers successfully negotiating the test courses are sometimes awarded certificates or trophies as proof of their expert driving abilities.

Watching a truck driving championship can be exciting for company employees and the general public. Companies planning these events should send a press release to their local media to receive advance publicity and press coverage (see Appendix A, Getting Publicity from Safe Driver Awards).

APPENDIX
D

Work-Related Motor Vehicle Injuries

TYPES OF MOTOR VEHICLE ACCIDENTS

CALCULATING FREQUENCY RATE

SOURCE OF DATA

According to Guy Toscano, economist for the Office of Safety, Health, and Working Conditions, Bureau of Labor Statistics (BLS), there were 1,232 work-related fatal highway incidents in 1993. This is by far the leading cause of occupational fatalities (20% of the total). Beginning in 1992, the BLS started using a new approach to gathering statistics on these injuries called the Census of Fatal Occupational Injuries. This new methodology has increased the accuracy of the data so that there can be more effective targeting in injury prevention efforts.

The results summarized here are based on the data published by the BLS for 1993. The fatal injuries addressed here will be only those of the driver or employee passenger.

TYPES OF MOTOR VEHICLE ACCIDENTS

The following tabulation shows the various types of work-related fatal highway incidents:

	Number	Percent
Total highway fatalities	**1,232**	**100**
Collision between vehicles	652	53
Moving in same direction	99	8
Head-on	244	20
At intersection	120	10
Moving and standing vehicle	52	4
Collision with stationary object	188	15
Noncollision	333	27
Jackknifed, overturned	235	19
Ran off highway	57	5
Other or unspecified	59	5

Half of the 1,232 workers killed in highway motor vehicle incidents were driving or riding in a truck—usually a tractor-trailer rig, or to a lesser extent, a pickup truck. Highway fatalities typically occur during daylight hours, between 9 A.M. and 4 P.M. Another 20% of occupational fatalities involve nonhighway transportation incidents in mines, logging operations, fisheries, agriculture, and aircraft. In composite, transportation equipment accounted for 40% of all occupational fatalities.

CALCULATING FREQUENCY RATE

To put the number of fatalities in perspective, it is necessary to consider the exposure. A frequency rate is determined as follows:

$$\frac{N \times 100,000}{W} \qquad (1)$$

where N = number of fatal work injuries and W = employees.

Using this formula, it is seen that the average worker dies of occupational injuries at the rate of 5 per 100,000 workers. Truck drivers die at more than five times that rate, 26 per 100,000 workers. Taxi cab drivers have nearly double the death rate of truckers, but it must be pointed out that homicide is the most likely cause. Statistics can be very useful but care must be used to assure that the right corrective action is implemented for the right reasons. Even when considering the ride for hire business, the cab driver is most likely to be robbed and killed by the customer while the limousine driver is more likely to be killed by a noncustomer. The root cause of the problem needs to be determined before effective countermeasures can be implemented.

SOURCE OF DATA

The development of the BLS Census of Fatal Occupational Injuries was a result of recommendations in 1987 by the National Academy of Sciences and other safety and health organizations. It was emphasized that there was a need to obtain detailed characteristics on fatal workplace injuries on a timely basis to develop and implement effective safety measures. The recommendations included using multiple data sources such as death certificates and workers' compensation reports to identify and profile fatal work injuries for all workers, including the self-employed. The data sources ultimately used include:

Source Document	Fatalities	
	Number	**Percent**
Total	**6,271**	**100**
Death certificates	4,409	78
State workers' compensation reports	2,244	36
Coroner, medical examiner, and autopsy	3,195	51
OSHA reports	1,840	29
News media	2,332	37
Follow-up questionnaires	1,310	21
State motor vehicle reports	332	5
Other federal reports	283	5
Other reports	3,775	61

This new technique has identified work-related fatalities that previously went unreported. This improved accuracy allows a more focused attack on the sources of fatal injury.

Bibliography and Additional Resources

BOOKS, MANUALS, AND STANDARDS

PERIODICALS AND NEWSLETTERS

AGENCIES, ORGANIZATIONS, AND SOCIETIES

CONTESTS AND AWARDS

EDUCATION PROGRAMS IN FLEET MANAGEMENT

No single book or reference source can provide all the information that someone involved in motor fleet safety requires, especially in an individual's area of specialization where more in-depth information is needed. Therefore, the following bibliography has been carefully selected to provide a balanced resource.

Because available information in this field is expanding rapidly, agencies, organizations, and societies that promulgate regulations and publish standards, as well as those that collect and share their specialized knowledge, are listed and described.

BOOKS, MANUALS, AND STANDARDS

American National Standards Institute, 1430 Broadway, New York, NY 10018.
   Loading Dock Levelers and Dockboards, ANSI/ASME MH14.1–1987.
   Method of Recording Basic Facts Relating to Nature and Occurrence of Work Injuries, ANSI Z16.2–1962 (R1969). (Update pending.)
   Method of Recording and Measuring the Off-the-Job Disabling Accidental Injury Experience of Employees, ANSI Z16.3–1989.
   Motor Vehicle Traffic Accidents, Manual on Classification of, ANSI D16.1–1989.
   Recordkeeping for Occupational Injuries and Illnesses, Uniform, ANSI Z16.4–1977. (Update pending.)
   Powered Industrial Trucks, ANSI/NFPA 505–1995.
   Powered Industrial Trucks—Low Lift and High Lift Trucks, Safety Standard for, ANSI/ASME B56.1–1993.
   Recording and Measuring Motor Vehicle Fleet Accident Experience and Passenger Accident Experience, Method for, ANSI D15.1–1976. (Withdrawn but still in use for National Fleet Safety Contest Rules.)
American Society of Safety Engineers, 1800 East Oakton, Des Plaines, IL 60018.
   Dictionary of Terms Used in the Safety Profession.
   Photographic Techniques for Accident Investigation.
   Profitable Risk Control.
American Trucking Associations, Inc., 2200 Mill Road, Alexandria, VA 22314.
   ATA Hazardous Materials Tariff, 1983.
   Bulletin Advisory Service (3 vols.), 1983.
   Effective Truck Terminal Planning and Operations, 1980.
   Fundamentals of Transporting Hazardous Materials, 1982.
   Fundamentals of Transporting Hazardous Waste, 1980.
   National Truck Driving Championship, 1986.

Association of American Railroads. Washington, DC.
   Rules Governing the Loading, Blocking and Bracing of Freight in Closed Trailers and Containers for TOFC/COFC Service, 1992.
   Products in Closed Trailers and Containers for TOFC/COFC Service, 1990.
Baker, J.S. *Traffic Accident Investigation Manual*. Evanston, IL: Northwestern University Traffic Institute, 1986.
Best's Safety Directory, 34th edition. Oldwick: A.M. Best Company.
Fricke, L.B. *Traffic Accident Reconstruction*. Evanston, IL: Northwestern University Traffic Institute, 1990.
Kirk-Othmer Encyclopedia of Chemical Technology, 4th edition. New York: Wiley Interscience, 1991.
National Committee for Motor Fleet Supervisor Training and Certification, *Motor Fleet Safety Supervision, Principles and Practices*, 4th edition. Alexandria, VA: National Committee for Motor Fleet Supervisor Training, 1987.
National Fire Protection Association, Batterymarch Park, Quincy, MA 02269.
   Flammable and Combustible Liquids Code, NFPA 30.
   Fire Prevention Code, NFPA 1.
   Fire Protection Handbook, 17th ed., 1991.
   Hazardous Chemical Data, NFPA 49.
   Life Safety Code Handbook, 1994.
   National Electrical Code Handbook, 1993.
National Private Truck Council. *Driver Trainer Manual*. Washington, DC: National Private Truck Council, 1981.
National Safety Council, 1121 Spring Lake Drive, Itasca, IL 60143–3201.
   Accident Facts. (Published annually).
   Accident Investigation, 2d edition.
   Accident Prevention Manual for Business & Industry, current edition, *Administration & Programs* volume. *Engineering & Technology* volume.
   Car Phone Safety, Users Guide.
   Chemical Hazard Fact Finder.
   Dock Plates and Gangplanks, Occupational Safety & Health Data Sheet 12304–0318.
   Fleet Accident Rates. (Published annually.)
   14 Elements of a Successful Safety & Health Program.
   Fundamentals of Industrial Hygiene, current edition.
   A Guide to Determine Motor Vehicle Accident Preventability.
   Occupational Health and Safety, 2d edition.
   Million Mile Club.
   National Fleet Safety Contest.
   National Standards for School Buses and Operations.
   Off-the-Job Safety Program Manual.
   Professional Way—Defensive Driving.
   Safe Driver Award Program.
   Small Business Safety and Health Manual.
   Supervisors' Safety Manual, current edition.
Peterson, Dan. *Techniques of Safety Managements*, 2d ed. New York: Aloray, 1989.

Sax, N. Irving, and Benjamin Feiner. *Dangerous Properties of Industrial Materials,* 8th edition. New York: Van Nostrand-Reinhold Publishing Co., 1993.

U.S. Department of Labor, 200 Constitution Avenue NW, Washington, DC 20210.
   Occupational Safety and Health Standards. (CD-ROM or DOL Electronic Bulletin Board, 202/219–4784.)
   OSHA Compliance Operations Manual.
   OSHA Recordkeeping Requirements.
   OSHA Job Hazard Analysis.

U.S. Department of Transportation, 400 Seventh Street SW, Washington, DC 20590.
   Federal Motor Carrier Safety Regulations.
   Hazardous Materials Emergency Response Guidebook.

U.S. Government Printing Office, North Capitol and H Streets NW, Washington, DC 20402.
   Code of Federal Regulations:
      Title 29—"Labor"
      Title 40—"Protection of the Environment"
      Title 49—"Transportation"

PERIODICALS AND NEWSLETTERS

Commerce Clearing House. Employment Safety and Health Guide. Chicago: Commerce Clearing House, updated weekly.

National Safety Council, 1121 Spring Lake Drive, Itasca IL 60143–3201.
   Driver Letter. Bimonthly.
   Family Safety and Health. Bimonthly.
   Fleet Safety Newsletter—Motor Transportation.
      Bi-monthly.
   Safety and Health. Monthly.
   OSHA Up-To-Date. Monthly.
   Today's Supervisor. Monthly.
   Traffic Safety. Bimonthly.
   Safe Driver. Monthly.

AGENCIES, ORGANIZATIONS, AND SOCIETIES

American Public Transit Association

1201 New York Avenue, NW
Washington, DC 20005

The American Public Transit Association's purpose is to represent the operators of and suppliers to public transit: to provide a medium for exchange of experiences, discussion and comparative study of industry affairs; to research and investigate methods to improve public transit; to provide assistance in dealing with special issues; and to collect, compile, and make available data and information relative to public transit. Established 1882.

American Society of Safety Engineers (ASSE)

1800 East Oakton Street
Des Plaines, IL 60018

The American Society of Safety Engineers is the only organization of individual safety professionals dedicated to the advancement of the safety profession and to the fostering of the well-being and professional development of its members.

American Society of Mechanical Engineers (ASME)

345 East 47th Street
New York, NY 10017

This society, a professional mechanical engineers' organization, encourages research, prepares papers and publications, sponsors meetings for the dissemination of information, and develops standards and codes under the supervision of its policy board.

American Trucking Associations, Inc. (ATA)

2200 Mill Road
Alexandria, VA 22314

The American Trucking Associations, Inc., offers guidance to the state trucking associations and their councils of safety supervisors. They publish and distribute timely information to the motor fleet industry and are responsible for rules and procedures used in state and national truck driving championships.

Board of Certified Safety Professionals (BCSP)

208 Burwash
Savoy, IL 61874

The BCSP provides professional certification for safety practitioners. Candidates who meet the education and experience criteria and pass the series of two, one-day examinations are awarded the Certified Safety Professional (CSP) designation. Through the Joint Committee of the BCSP and the American Board of Industrial Hygiene, certification is also offered at the occupational safety health technician and technologist level.

Department of Transportation (DOT)

400 Seventh Street SW
Washington, DC 20590

The Department of Transportation establishes the nation's overall transportation policy. Under its umbrella, there are nine administrations, (including the Office of Motor Carriers) whose jurisdiction includes highway planning, development, and construction; urban mass transit; railroads; aviation; and the safety of waterways, ports, highways, and oil and gas pipelines.

National Association of Fleet Administrators (NAFA)

120 Wood Avenue South
Iselin, NJ 08830

The National Association of Fleet Administrators is an organization committed to helping expand the educational and professional horizons of the motor fleet industry. Its members are managers of fleets of cars and light trucks in both the public and private sectors.

National Committee for Fleet Supervisor Training and Certification (NCFSTC)

2200 Mill Road
Alexandria, VA 22314

The membership of the National Committee for Motor Fleet Supervisor Training and Certification has for many years contributed immeasurably to the education of motor fleet supervisory management personnel.

National Highway Traffic Safety Administration

U.S. Department of Transportation
400 7th Street, SW
Washington, DC 20590

National Institute for Occupational Safety and Health (NIOSH)

4676 Columbia Parkway
Cincinnati, OH 45226

The National Institute for Occupational Safety and Health (NIOSH) was established within the Department of Health and Human Services under the provisions of the OSHAct. NIOSH is the principal federal agency engaged in research, education, and training related to occupational safety and health.

National Private Truck Council (NPTC)

66 Canal Center Plaza, Suite 600
Alexandria, VA 22314

The NPTC is the only independent organization representing exclusively the interests of private truck operators.

National School Transportation Association (NSTA)

P.O. Box 2639
Springfield, VA 22152

The National School Transportation Association is the national organization representing school bus contractors before Congress and federal regulatory agencies. NSTA works with parents, students, schools, and other interested parties in promoting school bus safety.

Northwestern University Traffic Institute

405 Church Street
Evanston, IL 60204

The Traffic Institute was established at Northwestern University in 1936 for the purpose of expanding the scope of university-level education and training in traffic

safety. Since that time the Institute has broadened its original objective to include training and consulting in police operations and management, accident investigation, transportation engineering, and driver education. The traffic safety community is also served through the Institute's research programs, publications, and on-site technical assistance.

Occupational Safety and Health Administration (OSHA)

200 Constitution Avenue NW
Washington, DC 20210

The Occupational Safety and Health Administration (OSHA) came into existence officially on April 28, 1971, the date the Williams-Steiger Occupational Safety and Health Act became effective. This agency was created in the Department of Labor to discharge the Department's responsibilities under the Act.

CONTESTS AND AWARDS

The Golden Shoe Club

2001 Walton Road
P.O. Box 36
St. Louis, MO 63166

Awards are made to employees who have avoided serious injury because they were wearing safety shoes.

Million Mile Club

National Safety Council
1121 Spring Lake Drive
Itasca, IL 60143–3201

Membership in the Million Mile Club is exclusive. Enrollment is open only to professional drivers who have achieved 1,000,000 miles (or 25,000 hours) of accident-free driving. Applications are accepted only from those firms that are members of the National Safety Council, Division of State and Local Safety Organizations, American Trucking Associations, Inc., or cosponsoring organizations of the National Fleet Safety Contest.

National Fleet Safety Contest

National Safety Council
1121 Spring Lake Drive
Itasca, IL 60143–3201

An exciting nationwide competition, the National Fleet Safety Contest gives recognition to motor vehicle fleets with outstanding safety records. Fleets compete with other fleets of comparable size and operations. Only Council members (with fleet operations), government agencies, and military units are eligible to participate.

Safe Driver Award Program
National Safety Council
1121 Spring Lake Drive
Itasca, IL 60143–3201

The Safe Driver Award Program is the recognized trademark of professional drivers who have proven their skill in avoiding traffic accidents. The more than six million drivers who have earned this award since 1930 have made it the preeminent award for professional safe driving performance.

Wise Owl Club
National Safety Council
1121 Spring Lake Drive
Itasca, IL 60143–3201

Founded in 1947, this is the oldest of all such clubs. Membership is restricted to industrial employees and students who have saved their eyesight by wearing eye protection.

EDUCATION PROGRAMS IN FLEET MANAGEMENT

U.S. Dept. of Education
Washington, DC 20902

Office of the Assistant Secretary for
Vocational and Adult Education
202–205–5451
Augusta S. Kappner, Assistant Secretary

Division of Vocational–Technical Education
202–205–9441
Winifred I. Warnar, Director

Alabama
Trade, Industrial, and Technology Education
50 North Ripley Street
Montgomery, AL 36130
205–242–9112
Bruce A. Baker, Technology Education Specialist

Alaska
State Department of Education
801 West 10th, Suite 200
Juneau, AK 99801
Barbara Thompson, Administrator Adult and Vocational Education

Arizona
Division of Vocational Technological Education
1535 West Jefferson Street
Phoenix, AZ 85007
602–542–4361

David A. Muenibauer, Associate Superintendent and State Director, Voacational–Technological

Arkansas
Vocational and Technical Education, Division of Education
2 Capitol Mall
Luther S. Hardin Building
Little Rock, AR 72201–10883
Don Hartan, Associate Director for Vocational–Technical Schools

California
Department of Education
721 Capitol Mall, 4th Floor
Sacramento, CA 95814
916–445–6726
Chris Almeida, Program Administrator, Industrial and Technical Education

California
California Community College
1107 9th Street
Sacramento, CA 95814
916–455–0486
William M. Anderson, Dean of Vocational Education

California
Coastal Regional Office
1800 Harrison Street, Rm 970
Oakland, CA 94612
415–464–0955
Richard Dehl, Industrial and Technical Education, Technical Care

Colorado
State Department of Education
1391 North Speer, 6th Floor
Denver, CO 80204
303–620–4000
Jerry Atkinson, Technical, and T & I, Program Manager

Connecticut
State Department of Education
Division of Education Programs and Services
Vocational–Technical School System
25 Industrial Park Road
Middletown, CT 06457
203–638–4000
Juan Lopez, Superintendent

Delaware
Department of Public Instruction
The Townsend Building
P. O. Box 1402

Dover, DE 19903
Clark Green, Education Associate, IA and TE

District of Columbia
State Office of Vocational and Adult Education
Penn Center Administrative Unit
1709 3rd Sreet, Ne Room 204
Washington, DC 20002
202–576–6308
Dr. Cynthia M. Bell, State Director, Vocational & Adult
Education

Florida
Division of Applied Technology & Adult Education
1114 Florida Education Center
Tallahassee, FL 32399–0400
904–488–8961
Pat Hall, Bureau Chief, Vocational Programs and Services

Georgia
Instructional Services, Vocational Education
1752 Twin Towers East
Atlanta, GA 30334–5040
404–657–8300
Division of Vocational Education
Earl Williams, T & I Education Coordinator

Hawaii
Office of Instructional Services
Occupational Development
2530 10th Avenue, A22
Honolulu, HI 96816
808–733–9120
Kenneth Furubawa, T & I Education

Illinois
Department of Adult, Vocational and Technical Education
100 North First Street
Springfield, IL 62777
217–782–4870
Ron Engstrom, Principal Consultant, Industrial/Occupational

Iowa
Grimes State Office Building
Des Moines, IA 50319–0146
515–281–8260
Roger Foelake, Chief, Bureau of Technical and Vocational
Education

Kansas
State Education Building
120 East Tenth Street
Topeka, KS 66612
913–296–3951
Tom Moore, Director, Technical Education

Kentucky
Department of Technical Education
500 Metro Street Capital Plaza Tower
Frankfort, TN 40601
502–564–4286
John Marks, Industrial Technology Consultant,
Vica State Advisor

Louisiana
Vocational Education
P. O. Box 94064
Baton Rouge, LA 70804–9064
504–342–3524
Gerald Saucier, Supervisor, T & I Programs

Maine
Division of Adult & Community Education
State House Station #23
Augusta, ME 04333–0023
207–287–5854
Chris Lyons, Director, Division of Applied Technology

Maryland
Division of Career Technology and Adult Learning
200 West Baltimore Street
Baltimore, MD 21201
301–333–2075
Katherine M. Oliver, Assistant State Superintendent

Massachusetts
Division of Occupational Education
1385 Hancock Street
Quincy, MA 02169
617–770–7350
David F. Cronin, Associate Commissioner

Michigan
Office of Career and Technical Education
P. O. Box 30009
Lansing, MI 48909–7509
517–373–3373
Robert Taylor, Consultant, T & I Education

Minnesota
State Council on Vocational–Technical Education
314 McColl Building
366 Jackson Street
St. Paul, MN 55101
612–296–4202
Brenda M. Dillon, Executive Director

Mississippi
Office of Vocational and Technical Education
P.O. Box 771
Jackson, MS 39205

601–359–3088
Therrell Myers, Associate State Superintendent

Missouri
Department of Elementary and Secondary Education
Jefferson City, MO 65102
314–751–2660
Frank Drake, Assistant Commissioner and Adult
Education
Fred Linhant, Director, Vocational Planning
and Evaluation

Montana
Department of Vocational Educational Services
Office of Public Instruction
106 State Capitol
Helena, MT 59620
406–444–4452
Jeff Wulf, T & I and TE Specialist, Vica Advisor

Nebraska
Division of Education Services
301 Centennial Mall South
P.O. Box 94987
Lincoln, NE 68509
402–471–2432
Tim Obermier, Director, Industrial Technology

Nevada
Department of Education, Occupational and Continuing
Education
400 West King Street
Capitol Complex
Carson City, NV 89710
702–687–3144
Mike Raponi, Consultant, Trade T & I Education

New Hampshire
Bureau of Career Technology and Transition
State Office Part South
101 Pleasant Street
Concord, NH 03301
603–271–3880
Ed W. Taylor, Consultant, T & I Education

New Jersey
New Jersey State Department of Education
Division of Vocational Education
225 West State Street CN 500
Trenton, NJ 08620–0050
609–292–6340
Thomas A. Henry, Director of Adult and Occupational
Education
State Director of Vocational Education

New Mexico
Education Building
Santa Fe, NM 87501–2786
505–827–6670
Tom Tujillo, Assistant Superintendent, Vocational–
Technical & Adult Education

New York
Office of Workforce Preparation and Continuing Education
Workforce Preparation Teach 1
Cultural Education Center, Room 5045
NYS Education Department
University of the State of New York
Albany, NY 12230
518–474–4889
Robert Poczik, Team Leader

North Carolina
Department of Public Instruction
301 North Wilmington Street
Raleigh, NC 27601–2825
919–715–1626
June S. Atkinson, Director, Division of Vocational–
Technical Education Services

North Dakota
600 East Boulevard Avenue, State Capitol, 15th Floor
Bismark, ND 58505–0610
701–224–3180
Rueben T. Guenthner, Director and Executive Officer,
Vocational–Technical

Ohio
Division of Vocational and Adult Education
Ohio Departments Building
65 South Front Street
Columbus, OH 43215–4183
614–466–3430
Richard Dieffenderfer, Consultant

Oklahoma
Oklahoma Department of Vocational–Technical Education
1500 West Seventh Avenue
Stillwater, OK 74074–4362
405–377–2000
Roy Perters, Jr., State Director, Vocational–Technical
Education

Oregon
Office of Professional Technical Education
255 Capitol, NE
Salem, OR 97310
503–378–3584
J. D. Hoye, Associate Superintendent

Pennsylvania
333 Market Street
Harrisburg, PA 17126–0333
Ferman B. Moody, Director, Bureau of Vocational–
Technical Education

Puerto Rico
Department of Education
P.O. Box 759
Hato Rey, PR 00919
809–763–5355
Nicolas De Jesus Pla, Director of Vocational IE
Program

Rhode Island
Vocational–Technical Education
Roger Williams Building
22 Hayes Street
Providence, RI 02908
401–277–2691
Frank M. Santoro, Director

South Carolina
Department of Education
Board of Technical and Comprehensive Education
111 Executive Center Drive
Columbia, SC 29212
803–737–0320
Michael McCall, Executive Director

South Dakota
Office of Adult, Vocational and Technical
Education
700 Governors Drive
Pierre, SD 57501–2291
605–773–4736
George D. Rockhold, State Supervisor, Technical
Education & Data Collection

Tennessee
Division of Vocational–Technical Education
710 James Robertson Parkway
Gateway Plaza, 4th Floor
Nashville, TN 37243–0383
615–532–2800
Ed Alexander, State Consultant, T & I Education

Texas
1701 North Congress Avenue
Austin, TX 78701
512–463–9311
Ann Pennington, Director, T & I Education

Utah
State Office of Education
250 East 500 South

Salt Lake City, UT 84111
801–538–7840
Ralph A. Anderson, Specialist, T & I Education

Vermont
Career & Lifelong Learning, Department of Education
120 State Street
Montpelier, VT 05620–2501
802–828–3101
Gerard Asselin, Manager, Career & Lifelong Learning

Virgin Islands
Department of Education, No. 44–46
Kongens Gade
Charlotte Arnalie
St. Thomas, VI 00802
Anna L. Lewis, State Director, Vocational, Technical
& Adult Education

Virginia
Department of Education
P.O. Box 2120
Richmond, VA 23216–2120
804–225–2870
Roy Carter, Specialist T & I Education

Washington
State Board for Community and Technical Colleges
319 Seventh Avenue
Olympia, WA 98504–2495
206–753–3672
Raymond L. Harry, Vocational Education Program
Coordinator

West Virginia
State Office Building #6
18900 Kahawba Boulevard East
Charleston, WV
304–348–2346
Adam J. Sponaugle, Assistant Superintendent, Technical
and Adult Education

Wisconsin
Wisconsin Technical College System
310 Proce Place
P.O. Box 7874
Madison, WI 53707
608–266–1207
Dwight A. York, State Director

Wyoming
Department of Eductation
Hathaway Building, 2nd Floor
2300 Capitol Avenue

Cheyenne, WY 82002–0050
307–777–7413
Lois Motronen, Consultant, Equal Opportunities
for Vocational Education

Canada

Alberta
Devonian Building, 11160 Jasper Avenue
Edmonton, Canada T5K 0L2
403–427–2984
Keith Wagner, Deputy Director Curriculum

British Columbia
Ministry of Education
620 Superior Street, 5th Floor
Victoria, British Columbia V8V 2M4
604–356–2317
Velma Hoslin, Coordinator, Partnership in Education

Manitoba
Manitoba Education and Training
W240–1970 Ness Avenue
Winnipeg, Manitoba R3J 0Y9

New Brunswick
416 York Street
P.O. Box 6000
Francophone, New Brunswick E38 5H1
506–453–8201
Bernard Paulin, Assistant Minister, Educational
Services

Newfoundland
Department of Education
P.O. Box 8700
St. Johns, Newfoundland AJ8 4J6
709–729–3026
Frank Marsh, Advance Studies

Northwest Territories
5102 50th Avenue
Yellowknife, Northwest Territories X1A 3S8

403–920–6306
Mark Cleveland, President, Arctic College #1

Nova Scotia
Department of Education
P.O. Box 578
Halifax, Nova Scotia B3J 2S9
Robert Moody, Deputy Minister

Ontario
Ministry of Education
Mowat Block, Queens Park
Toronto, Ontario M7A 1L2
416–325–2542
Graham Carr, Education Officer, Curriclm Policy
Development Branch

Prince Edward Island
Department of Education
P.O. Box 2000
Charlottetown, Prince Edward Island C1A 7N8
902–368–4676
Gordon S. Bernard, Vocational Education Coordinator

Quebec
Minstere de l'Education
Direction Gendrals de la Formation Professalonnetic
1035 Rue de la Chevrotiere 8c Etage,
Quebec, Canada G1R 5A5
418–643–1562
Claude Page, Director General

Saskatchewan
Education, Training, and Employment
2220 College Avenue
Regina, Saskatchewan S4P 3V7
306–787–6030
John Biss, Director, Institutional Liason Unit

Yukon Territory
Eductation
P.O. Box 2703
Whitehorse, Yukon Territory Y1A 2C6
John Gryba, Senior Industrial Training Consultant

Index